Looking for lyrics with Tyson

A Thousand Threads

A Memoir

Neneh Cherry

SCRIBNER
New York London Toronto Sydney New Delhi

Scribner
An Imprint of Simon & Schuster, LLC
1230 Avenue of the Americas
New York, NY 10020

First Scribner hardcover edition October 2024

SCRIBNER and design are trademarks of Simon & Schuster, LLC

Simon & Schuster: Celebrating 100 Years of Publishing in 2024

For information about special discounts for bulk purchases, please contact Simon & Schuster Special Sales at 1-866-506-1949 or business@simonandschuster.com.

The Simon & Schuster Speakers Bureau can bring authors to your live event. For more information or to book an event, contact the Simon & Schuster Speakers Bureau at 1-866-248-3049 or visit our website at www.simonspeakers.com.

Manufactured in the United States of America

10 9 8 7 6 5 4 3 2 1

Library of Congress Cataloging-in-Publication Data is available.

ISBN 978-1-9821-6104-0
ISBN 978-1-9821-6109-5 (ebook)

This long song is for my family, from our inner sanctum to the edges of its extended threads, and to the memory of my brother David Cherry, who went in search of his next riff (1958–2022).

I want to live the rest of my life, however long or short, with as much sweetness as I can decently manage, loving all the people I love, and doing as much as I can of the work I still have to do. I am going to write fire until it comes out of my ears, my eyes, my noseholes—everywhere. Until it's every breath I breathe. I'm going to go out like a fucking meteor!

Audre Lorde

CONTENTS

A THOUSAND THREADS

PROLOGUE

I am standing in my kitchen. John Coltrane's *A Love Supreme* is playing. I've been listening to these songs since before I can remember. The melodies are in my blood. The fight and the freedom of the music is in me. I let it soothe me, speak to me in a language I understand. A rebellion is happening in the sound. I feel it. I hear it. *Change had to come. Have faith, soldiers.*

I had three parents—I guess that's what we call a gift. Moki, Don, Ahmadu: givers of life. My parents were rebels, all three bound in a history so long and painful it hurts. I've always been a rebel. My children and grandchildren have it, too. Those same creative channels I was brought up in have carried me all the way here. What they made is how we lived, how *I've* lived as I forged my own life. The music tells me that here is now.

Africa opens up under a sky shadowed by Swedish pine trees dressed in silks. Now, west London thrums on.

Last night I soaked a bowl of pinto beans. Today I wash them until the water runs clear, just as my mother taught me. Boil them hard for ten minutes, remove the froth. A sweet smell circulates through the house and, for a second, I'm climbing the stairs of a Lower East Side tenement building, a memory of boiling beans and hair grease like another song in another life.

I cut a head of garlic, drop the two halves into the pot, a whole Scotch bonnet pepper, a chopped onion, and handful of thyme on its stem. Memory, familiarity, doing things that we know; this rhythm of life I return to again and again. I understand how to do this, and it brings security in a world spinning out of my control. I need to create these small gifts, offerings to life, for my sanity and for the people I love. I tip a can of coconut milk into the pot, stir and trust those pintos to do what they do. The beans want to be left alone, just a stir every now and then, with a wooden spoon that belonged to my grandmother, one of its corners worn away from a lifetime in the turn of her hand.

I live for love and music. These elements make life bigger, deeper, richer—but I know I cannot do it all on my own. I have always been a collaborator. To trust and to love is a strong survival instinct. I will not betray the trust of those I love, who helped me become who I am today. But, with grace and respect, I also want to express some of the things that have happened. They are part of the journey.

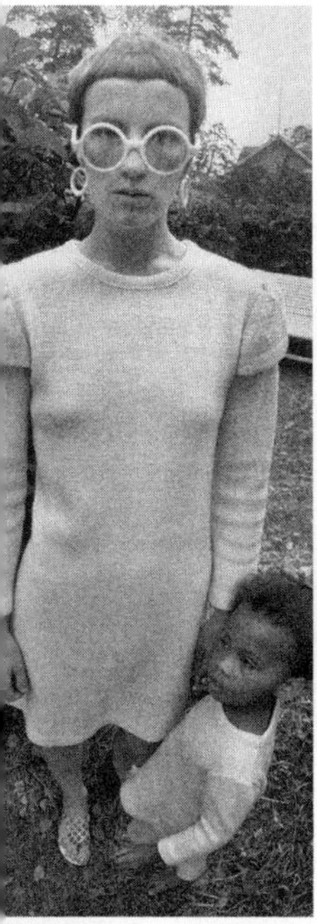

PART ONE

My mother, Moki, and me, circa 1966 • The only photo I have of my mother and father together • Moki, Don and me, and my doll Anita, in Gamla Stan, Stockholm • Outside a café in Paris • Family time • A lazy Sunday afternoon • When Eagle-Eye left his seat to join Don on stage • I loved being in New York

MY MOTHER AND HER PEOPLE

One day, many moons ago in Norrland, or "northland"—a large province in the very far north of Sweden—my great-grandmother Ida found a needle in a haystack. The family lived in a tiny hamlet called Bjurå in Norrbotten, the northernmost county of this northern province, just below the Arctic Circle. To the east lies the border with Finland; to the west is Swedish Lapland. Norrland stays black and white in the persistent winter darkness; in the summer months, it's flooded by endless sunshine. This pitiless environment gives its people a resilience and freedom of spirit. Even today, this remote northland feels quite separate from the rest of the country. There is a natural magic in the landscape. So few people live there, but it is home to many millions of trees. It is a place of legends. The forest whispers, deep and dark and knowing. Its hushed tones weave enchantment into the stories of my ancestors.

Ida's house is quiet with the hush of her five small sleeping children, my grandmother Marianne among them. It is time to go check on her cows and settle them in safely for the night. Ida walks across the yard to the summer barn. Inside are the six cows that are her livelihood. More than that, they are like beloved members of the family. The winter barn has a fireplace burning bright to keep them warm through the freezing nights. Now, though, in the summer barn, Ida needs to draw the dark heavy curtains to shield her resting herd not only from mosquitoes but also the relentless midnight sun.

She steps inside and softly pulls closed the curtains, casting a blue shade across the backs of the sleepy beasts. The swallows, nesting in the dark of the eaves, are also at rest. Every year, they leave behind the sweltering West African heat, an intuition telling them that it is time to fly north. Straight up from Sierra Leone to Norrland, the swallows fly more than 5,000 miles. The birds navigate the skies, sometimes covering 200 miles a day, never once touching the ground until, at last, they arrive with the light and promise of summer to nest in Ida's barn. I imagine them swooping low over her head in celebration and reunion, worms dangling from beaks.

Ida spreads some fresh hay on the barn floor, then slips out through the curtains and closes the door behind her. When she looks down at her pinafore, she sees that the needle she always keeps pinned there is gone.

Dread rushes through her. In the farmyard, flooded in the bright night sun, you could hear a pin drop, yet she had not heard her needle fall. Did she lose it when she bent over to pick up hay? She is in despair at the thought of what might happen to any one of her cows who finds it with their soft mouth. Hurriedly she retraces her steps, and long into the night that is an endless day she searches the barn. How many hours did she spend looking? Nobody knows. But in the end, and as the story goes, Ida found her needle in the haystack.

I like to imagine Ida with the warm breath of the resting cows on her face, carefully picking through the hay with meticulous determination, each strand like the filament of a life, or a death, as all around the forest whispers loudly.

•

My mother, Monika Marianne Karlsson, known as Moki, was born on February 8, 1943, in Koler, Norrbotten. Her father, Werner, my *morfar*, was one of nine children. He grew up on a farm at the opposite end of the country, in Finja, in the Gräsabygget, literally the "grasslands," near Hässleholm, Skåne, the southernmost county in Sweden.

At sixteen, Morfar left home. After a spell as a farm labourer and then in the merchant navy, he took a qualification to work as a stationmaster on the railways. At twenty-five he was posted to Norrland, where he met and fell in love with my *mormor*, Marianne, Ida's daughter. A year later, when she was just nineteen, they married.

My grandparents moved often as my grandfather took up posts in different parts of the country. In Koler, the first place that Moki lived in was a beautiful black station house with a red ochre trim. The plates rattled in their old oak dresser when the long cargo trains rumbled by. At night in bed, she would pretend she was in a sleeper car.

When she was barely two, her mother gave Moki her first pair of scissors, made of steel, small and very sharp. Marianne showed her how to hold them to a sheet of paper so that she wouldn't cut her fingers. By the heat of the wood-burning stove, the smell of the birch-bark kindling on fire, porridge and cinnamon in the air, Moki would sit shredding paper in the kitchen. It was like magic, seeing the paper separate, slicing a beautiful line: instant love. Next, she was handed a mail-order catalogue from which she cut out tiny household objects such as pots and pans, beds and chairs. She began to craft miniature domestic worlds.

In another time, in another kitchen with Mormor Marianne, I did the same thing. By then my grandparents were living in Rinkaby, Skåne, not far from Morfar Werner's family, in what had also been a station house. The former waiting room was now a post office, run by my grandmother. I spent a lot of time in this red-brick house with the train tracks at the back. Mormor would settle me down with an old mail-order catalogue and some scissors and then go to work behind the post office counter on the other side of the wall. I was happy, lost in my own world, cutting out whole households, putting tiny paper kettles and toys, cups and tables, inside an empty box to make a home.

When Moki was four, she taught herself to read by cutting out letters and words from newspapers and gluing them next to the household objects from the catalogues. She never lost her fascination with and passion for words. Later in life she would sometimes spend all day in bed reading, eating peanut butter from a jar, with me and my little brother, Eagle-Eye, content beside her.

It was Moki's aunt Gertrud who introduced her to the world of fabrics, threads, and sewing machines. Gertrud worked as a dressmaker and would order the Paris fashion magazines to copy the latest modes, and she also created her own designs. In her parlour, Moki could delve into baskets full of fabric scraps from which she would make dolls and wonderful creatures.

Just before Moki turned five, my grandfather's work brought the family south to Södervidinge, on the west coast of Skåne. Again, they lived upstairs in a station house. It was the happiest era of Moki's childhood. Her mother would tell her not to leave their yard, but as soon as she could Moki would escape and go exploring in the village, knocking on people's doors and asking to visit. She discovered three old sisters in an old house, singing quietly and making exquisite gloves from the softest kidskin for the aristocracy; the blacksmith hammering horseshoes and the blacksmith's wife who gave her coffee, forbidden at home and which she loved; a man who made sundials and astronomical clocks; a chicken farm where two women from Japan sorted the newly hatched chicks. She went around the houses asking for old magazines, which she brought home and cut up with her scissors. Then she returned and sold her collages to the villagers. One time, someone came to the house and told my grandfather that they had bought "such a lovely collage" from Moki. He went berserk. The idea that people might think they needed the money made him angrier than Moki had ever seen him. Much later she said it was probably the anxiety from this experience that made it hard for her to engage with selling her work.

In 1950, when she was seven, Disney's *Cinderella* was released. Watching the famous scene where, as Cinderella sleeps, the birds and the mice get busy with scissors, tape measure, and needle and thread to fix up her mother's old dress, transforming it with pink ribbons and bows so that she might, after all, go to the ball, Moki was transfixed. She knew this was what she wanted to do. A dream began to form.

After the magical discovery of reading, Moki found school a disappointment. She was more interested in snails and butterflies than in humans. She spent most of her days after class on her own, outdoors in the forest. Dressed in dungarees, she would go out riding on her bike, a shoebox attached to the pannier rack to collect insects. For a while she had a pet hedgehog called Totte.

In 1962, when she was nineteen, Moki moved to Stockholm to attend classes in cutting, patternmaking, and drapery. The haute couturier Rune Ullhammar had offered her a design apprenticeship, but when she got into Beckmans Designhögskola, an alternative art and design college in Stockholm, she moved on.

Young, talented, and passionate, Moki was having the time of her life. In the early sixties, Stockholm was a hub of cultural innovation. She and her artist friends made things happen. She went to see all the musical greats, the young kings, masters of jazz, mostly at the city's Golden Circle, a club that hosted experimental players including Ornette Coleman, Cecil Taylor, and, later, Don Cherry's group. There she hung out with people like Albert Ayler, a young horn player who, Don said, sometimes played so deep that he spat blood. Moki and Albert became friends, and he often came to her studio to practise while she worked. People gravitated to Moki's apartment for vibes and for music. Mostly, though, they came for her.

I love hearing her friends talk about her: fun, creative, central. She had a great record collection, and she always looked fabulous. She cut her hair very short. She did it one night herself. She made a short leather skirt the colour of red wine, with a matching short top that buttoned at the back. Moki was cool, so people wanted to be around her. She had her own little circle.

Then she met my father, Ahmadu Jah.

MY TWO FATHERS

Moki and Ahmadu found each other at a student party, a week after his arrival in Stockholm, in autumn 1962. She had just started at Beckmans College. He was in his early twenties, on a scholarship to complete his engineering studies at KTH Royal Institute of Technology. As she told it, he was magnificent, beautiful, elegant in a Savile Row suit that she would later discover had been bought for him by a wealthy London lady friend. The plan was that when he finished his postgraduate degree, he would return to an independent Sierra Leone and use his knowledge to make things better back home. They say you should never tell God your plans. Before long, Moki and Ahmadu were living together in an apartment in the centre of the city, on Birger Jarlsgatan.

Ahmadu and six other young men had boarded a liner in Freetown two years previously. They were the first students from Sierra Leone to go to university overseas on scholarships; my father was probably the only Muslim. They made the front page of the Freetown newspaper—young, beautiful pioneers in fine new suits and hats, photographed on the gangway of the ship. They had no idea how the cold would bite, how hard and unforgiving the Western world could be.

Our ancestors were nomads of the Fulani tribe. My great-great-grandfather Cherno Abass had walked south through the bush with his two wives and ten cows from Senegal to Sierra Leone. They paused at Labé in the north of Guinea, and finally they reached a village settlement called Gbinti. Here they stopped. They sold some of the cows and built a hut out of mud and grass. Some of it still stands. And now, all these years later, we are scattered across the world, but Gbinti is still our Jah family headquarters.

Ahmadu's mother—and my namesake, Haja Neneh—married her first husband, my grandfather Cherno Abass Sere Jah, in her teens. She was one of two wives. She bore him four children, all sons, my father, Ahmadu, among them. When Ahmadu was two years old, his father died young and suddenly from fever. The tradition was that if the brother-in-law next in line wanted to inherit the wives of his dead older brother, he could. Haja Neneh was young, beautiful, and had borne four strong sons. Her husband's brother wanted her. All at once my father had a whole new set of siblings. One of them, his stepbrother (turns out he was my grandmother's youngest brother, i.e., his uncle) Lamin Sadiki, was like a father to him.

When Ahmadu was six, Haja Neneh sent him to live with his uncle outside a big town called Port Loko, so that he could attend a local school. Every morning the call to prayer would pull him out of his dreams—that, and the squawking chickens running loose in every yard. His little bare feet on the dirt track, walking to class in the growing light, the bunion on his right foot just starting to push through the bone on the side near his big toe. (I have one, too, in the very same place.) My father did well at junior school and won a boarding scholarship to the Prince of Wales School in Freetown. Sierra Leone in the late forties was still a British colony, and this prestigious school catered primarily to the children of the white expat British governing class, those of the Sierra Leonean Krios (Creoles), often the country's upper-middle class, and the kids of the wealthy Lebanese. Ahmadu always told me that he was the first Muslim student to attend his school, and the other kids bullied him relentlessly. But Ahmadu was smart. He graduated with outstanding grades, after which Haja Neneh put him forward for the scholarship to study in the West.

Those scholarship boys left home as the chosen ones, but they arrived on the east coast of America as second-class citizens. The labels "Black" and "African" stripped them of all their grace and beauty and made them barely human. The United States of America? Rosa Parks had not yet boarded that bus. It was brutal. While some of his fellow Sierra Leoneans stayed, Ahmadu did not want to settle there. Instead, he sailed to London to study civil engineering. He rented a room in a boarding house run by a respectable English widow. "My African boy has very good manners," she would say if anyone asked. She was nice enough, he said. At some point on this journey, Ahmadu discovered jazz. He spent most of his spare time in record stores or hanging out at the various clubs in the West End. Dancing and listening, he found expression through the music.

When Ahmadu arrived in Stockholm, he brought with him all this extraordinary African music, new sounds and levels that Moki had not heard before. He also showed her how to make the food of his childhood: peanut stew, pepper soup, and fufu (stews were Ahmadu's speciality). I picture them at home, Ahmadu's furniture draped in fabrics, the tables covered with wooden bowls and calabash instruments from home, the steam and the warmth of the kitchen, something fragrantly spicy bubbling on the stove, the music on the record player.

Before long, my mother was pregnant with me. When she told Ahmadu the news, he was initially unsure. He suggested that the child—me—should be sent to Sierra Leone for his mother to bring up. Ahmadu's response shocked Moki. It had never entered her head that they would not raise this child together. She spent the weekend in bed with me inside her. She was craving the sweet, sticky flesh, so she bought a whole box of oranges and then lay in bed, reading and peeling the fruit, eating them one after the other, throwing the peel on the floor. And then, on the Monday, she knew what she was going to do. She was going to keep me and bring me up. That weekend, we had our first conversation.

In November 1963, when she was five months pregnant with me, Moki was on her way home from a jazz club when she saw my father in the street with another woman. She knew of others, too. Ahmadu found it impossible to be monogamous. (As the family tree attests, his branch is heavy!) And while it cut Moki to the core, she was never bitter about his infidelities. She knew who he was, this breathtakingly beautiful young man who sent the women in Stockholm crazy. She was able to focus on the love they shared, which was bigger than the hurt. She said that they never had a single fight.

•

I was born in Stockholm on March 10, 1964. Whenever Moki talked about my birth, it came with its own soundtrack. I like how romantic it is.

"You were born at midday exactly," she would tell me. "The church bells were ringing over Södermalm as you exited me and entered the world."

She would speak of me sitting, with a little support, straight back, steady and strong on her lap at the table, just one month old. Firm flesh, chubby but solid. She always said that the children in our family have perfectly round heads. I loved hearing her tell the story, with a single-minded devotion to what she saw as my perfection. I love that it was me she was talking about—what she saw and felt when she held me.

Though they never met, my grandmothers, Mormor Marianne and Haja Neneh, were connected the moment I was born. My new blood made them family. A vast landmass between them, their cultures so far apart they might as well have been on different planets, yet they were bound in the sisterhood of women. The motions in which they loved and held their children, stroked a feverish forehead, hummed at the stir of a pot, cussed at the men when they interfered with their daily rhythm, were the same. More than 5,000 miles apart and still connected.

When Moki arrived home from the hospital with me, she found blond hairpins in the bed. Three months later, she told my father they were done, and she packed up his stuff. She did not back down. She stayed in the apartment; Ahmadu moved out. She knew he was not able to change. The time they shared had been magical and, despite everything, they had never fallen out of love, but still she chose to end it. I did not see Ahmadu again until I was nine.

•

Moki met Don Cherry on January 17, 1963, a year before I was born. He was on tour with the Sonny Rollins Quartet. It was the first time that Don had travelled beyond North America, and half of Stockholm's inhabitants, it seemed, had flocked to the concert house to listen to Sonny Rollins, Don Cherry, Henry Grimes, and Billy Higgins. That night in January, Moki and Ahmadu had joined the excited crowd. Moki later wrote: "There was a fire in the subway below the building. Smoke was seeping through the floor, but no one moved. When Don Cherry's sound appeared, it reminded me of the magic I had found by myself in nature while growing up."

After the concert, Moki went with some friends down the street to the smaller Golden Circle, where Johnny Griffin's group was playing. Sonny Rollins's band was already there, sitting in with them. At one point, Moki and Don noticed each other. "I saw this woman wearing bamboo glasses, short hair, and amazing clothes," Don would say about the moment he first saw Moki. He came over and spoke with her. Moki wrote, "We stood in the floor-to-ceiling window on the second storey looking out at the snowy street, talking about love on some other elevated plane—music. I was nineteen. My motto was: to help make a more beautiful world."

Ten months later, in November 1963, when Moki was pregnant with me, she went with Ahmadu to see Don performing at the Golden Circle with Archie Shepp and the New York Contemporary Five. She was tired afterwards, but Ahmadu didn't want to go home, so Moki took a taxi with a friend. That was the night she saw him in the street with another woman. She asked the driver to turn around and headed back into the club. Don was there. That was their beginning.

When they parted that night, Don told Moki that he would return to see her. And he did. In October 1964, Don was back in Stockholm, on tour with Albert Ayler. By then I was six months old, and Ahmadu and Moki had broken up. After the tour ended, Don travelled to Africa, visiting the Rif Mountains in Morocco, where he met with the Master Musicians of Joujouka. On his return to Europe in December, he went once more to Stockholm, just to see Moki and me. It was then that they decided, in Moki's words, "to find a way to share our lives together."

Don was a very special, unusual man. With his lean, graceful frame, he was beautiful. As a father, musician, collaborator, and teacher, he had a gift for inspiring others to see their own untapped potential. He was a leader and a lifelong learner.

Don was born into a musical family in Oklahoma City in 1936. When he was four, like so many other "Okies," his family moved to Los Angeles. There Don's father, Ulysses, ran the bar at the Plantation Club, a leading jazz venue in Watts, where local musicians of the LA bebop scene played with visiting stars like Billy Eckstine and Erskine Hawkins.

When Don was fourteen, his mother, Daisy, bought him his first trumpet. Although Ulysses did not approve—he did not want his son getting mixed up with musicians, fearful that he would fall prey to "the dope thing"—the trumpet took over Don's life. He skipped classes to roller-skate to a neighbouring school, where he snuck into the lessons of the legendary music teacher Samuel Browne. Mr. Browne encouraged his brass-band students to play music by Dizzy Gillespie and Stan Kenton. It was exciting, until Don's actual school cottoned on to his "playing hooky" and he was sent to an all-boys disciplinary school. There he met and started to play with the drummer Billy Higgins.

Don and Billy would roller-skate far out of the Watts neighbourhood to the other side of the city to catch the music coming from basement jazz clubs, manoeuvring clumsily on their skates to peer down through the window slats, straining their eyes to catch a glimpse of the players, and their ears to hear them talk and warm up.

By 1954, and still in high school, Don had earned a union card and was playing professionally. Often, he would compete in talent shows around the neighbourhood with people like Johnny "Guitar" Watson. Don said that Johnny, slicker than the rest, always won. With Billy, George Newman, and Pee Wee Williams, they formed a group called the Jazz Messiahs, playing bebop and jazz in clubs around town. Together they played R&B clubs, going as far north as Vancouver. That's when the drugs came in. Ulysses's worst fears for his son were not unfounded. By seventeen, like many other jazz musicians in his circle, Don was addicted to heroin.

During that time, through his schoolfriend Jayne Cortez, Don became friendly with the young Ornette Coleman. Jayney, as they called her, grew up in the same neighbourhood as Don and his sister Barbara in Watts (and later married Ornette). She was the hippest woman in the hood and introduced them all to the newest sounds. No doubt she felt that Ornette and Don needed to connect. Her instinct was right. It was a sweltering hot LA afternoon on the day they first met, but Ornette was dressed in a wool coat and two-tone shoes, his hair worn long. Don said that he looked like the "Black Jesus Christ."

That meeting was to change the course of jazz history: Ornette asked Don and Billy to join his group, along with the bassist Charlie Haden, becoming the Ornette Coleman Quartet. Together they threw out the rule books to create a whole new type of free jazz. They moved to New York to record with Atlantic Records and, in November 1959, secured a residency at the Five Spot Cafe. Everybody who was anybody came to hear them: Leonard Bernstein, Charles Mingus, Thelonious Monk. The quartet's innovations blew the minds of many, who hailed them as the "New Thing," but some people just didn't get it. The "free" in free jazz did not mean that their playing had no structure. In fact, they rehearsed Ornette's compositions all day long until they could play each piece back to front—literally—so that when it was time to stretch out, they were free to push beyond the limitations of traditional musical structures.

In the beginning, Don and Ornette performed to limited audiences and received little acknowledgement for their groundbreaking work. Kindred spirits, they understood each other—they were both reaching for freedom, in ideas and politics. It was the music—bold, inquisitive, uncompromising—that spoke for them. Don and Ornette found that they could spread their wings and fly high, through pain, hope, rage, and beauty. It was an absolute necessity, a lifeline. The way in to a way out.

America was a hostile environment that held no respect and offered no dignity for young Black men and women. Don and Ornette blew all that anger into their music, making something unique and powerful. Rebels turning musical structure on its head, they made a world that could change things. It changed them, allowing them to see clearly, inviting them to live in a different realm. And as they flew, they spread that potential, passing it on to all who heard their sound. Music is about so much more when it is about *everything*—about the fight, about being men, being human. I look at the 1961 Ornette Coleman Quartet *This Is Our Music* album cover now—all four men in suits, Don in shades—and I am floored, full of pride and admiration.

When Don played with all those gifted musicians, he would reach for the outer limits. But then he would put down his trumpet and step back into a place that, for a Black man, could be so harsh, so unforgiving, so cruelly unfair. Everyday life was one of financial hardship, racial discrimination, and often abuse.

In contrast to Don's life as a musician in America, in Europe in the fifties and sixties, he and many of his contemporaries enjoyed a positively rapturous reception. In Sweden, this strange clean place, full of people who were mesmerised by their music, they were treated like kings, or, at least, rock stars. Indeed, in November 1962, when the John Coltrane Quartet arrived at Arlanda Airport in Stockholm, they rolled out the red carpet. Little wonder, then, that Europe became a place where a lot of artists came, stayed, and made new lives.

•

By 1965, Don, Moki, and I were living in Gamla Stan, literally Stockholm's old town: *gamla*, meaning "old," and *stan*, a contraction of *staden*, meaning "town." Today this small island with its museums, palaces, and gabled town houses is a popular tourist destination, but in the sixties the buildings were crumbling and many had been divided and subdivided into tiny apartments. Our building was at number 9 Baggensgatan, a dark cobbled alley, by the corner down to the square with *St. Göran och Draken*, the statue of St. George and the Dragon.

On the ground floor was a hairdresser's shop where, apparently, the young Greta Garbo had been a regular client. We lived on the second floor in a small flat with double doors and high ceilings. There wasn't even a bath or a shower, but the rent was cheap. Off the hall to the left was an old non-flush latrine. We had a tiny kitchen with a two-ring gas stove and a sink with a cold tap. No running hot water. Once a week or so, we would have a bath—a big red plastic tub for Moki and Don, and a smaller tub for me and, later, my brother Eagle-Eye. Moki would heat up the water on the stove and she and Don would take turns in the big tub. Don sitting in that red tub, me sitting in the little tub next to him, playing with his arm, the feel of his soft soapy skin.

When Moki's new term at college started in January 1965, I was always with her, mostly sleeping soundly in my basket under her desk. Don went to Paris for the first time. There he met Karl Berger, a pianist and vibraphonist from Germany; Argentinian saxophonist Gato Barbieri; French bassist François Jenny-Clark; and Italian drummer Aldo Romano. They formed a group called Togetherness, successively known as the Don Cherry Quintet, the Complete Communion Band, and the International Quintet.

In March, Don returned to Stockholm for my first birthday. He needed a piano, so the day before he arrived, Moki ran into a second-hand piano store owned by two elderly men. She made her way around the shop, sitting at every single one, placing her fingers on the keys, gently producing sound. She stopped at a light grey one, then went back around the room to try each of them again before returning to it. The sound it made had roused something deep inside: a feeling of rightness filled her heart.

"This is the one," she said. She told the wizened old piano dealers that she could put down an initial payment of 50 kronor and asked if they could arrange delivery for the following morning.

"All right. For you, yes—because you picked well," came the reply. Don would later tell an interviewer that, although Moki was not a pianist, she had somehow chosen the most wonderful piano in the shop. It had, he said, "a golden throat to it," and on it he wrote some of his most important compositions. Some years afterwards Moki painted the piano's carvings in her steady hand, embellishing it in glorious bright reds, pinks, yellows, and blues, giving it its own identity. On that piano, Don's son David discovered music, and my brother Eagle-Eye's little fingers wrote his first tune. Now the hands of my daughters, Naima, Tyson, and Mabel, and those of my grandson, Flynn, live there, navigating sound.

AN UNCONVENTIONAL CHILDHOOD

Stockholm was the beginning of a new musical journey for Don, but still he missed New York's relentless rhythm, the food, the language, and the dialogue he shared with his peers. His soul needed all of that. The city called, and, in winter 1966, he and Moki answered. We moved into a loft at 107–109 Broadway, Williamsburg, in Brooklyn, that the mighty saxophonist Marzette Watts arranged for us.

I still remember the dry heat and sweet cardboard tang of the stairways—a New York building smell. Sitting in the kitchen and hearing the traffic from the bridge. When the J train passed, heading out into the depths of Brooklyn, the floor shook. Climbing the stairs, in my red shoes and a red-and-white striped vest, my hands reaching for the handrail; the smell of cigarettes; the painted walls basking in muted yellow light; the sound of the cats rehearsing burning holes in my ears.

Only musicians lived and worked there. Everyone, it seemed, rehearsed in that building. Ornette Coleman; John Coltrane and his drummer Rashied Ali; Elvin Jones; Albert Ayler; Marion Brown—and countless others, practising in different parts of the building. "Coming down the street, you could feel it shivering and hear it screaming from all that free jazz," Moki wrote in her journal.

Those men who loved their instruments as much as their kids or mothers, and way more than some lovers, always fussed over me. I felt safe there. I have been told that John Coltrane thought I was cute. I like that. Don was so respectful when he talked about him, as if Coltrane had something holy in him and playing with him brought him into that holy place, too.

Williamsburg was the hood, with people of colour from all corners of the world—Puerto Rican and Dominican migrants, African Americans and people from the West Indies—many of whom had flocked there to work in the factories and the Brooklyn Navy Yard after the war, along with European refugees, especially the Orthodox Jews of the Satmar Hasidic sect from Hungary and Romania. But by the sixties, heavy industry was in decline and unemployment, crime, gang activity, and the drug trade were on the rise. Those with the means to move out of the area often did, and the low rents allowed people like my parents—those other migrants, impoverished artists and musicians—to move into streets lined with bodegas and barber shops.

Under the Williamsburg Bridge, full lives were being lived—every tiny part of New York was occupied, used, abused, loved. Nuyorican salsa bands rehearsed underneath, reverberating in time with the traffic and trains. I still melt inside when I think about the sound—an echo from another life.

But life in New York was hard, and that was a shock for Moki. She was twenty-three years old, in a strange city with very little money. She was working on her designs and had begun to sell a few pieces to a design store, but her earnings didn't stretch beyond rent and feeding us. We may have been living in a building where divine music was being made, but it was old-school New York. Real but rough. It was freezing. My bronchitis was born. I saw my first water bug, which Don called "ugly." Even now, whenever I hear that word, that's what I see. We were so far from Sweden and Moki was heartbroken. She wasn't prepared for the discovery that, in New York, her heroes, Don included, lived hand to mouth, in squalor. Most jazz musicians in America were poor. They had nothing. Jazz is one of America's greatest legacies, but even today it isn't honoured enough. There was to be more heartbreak, too. There, in Williamsburg, Don's demons returned to claim him.

I cannot remember my parents' bed catching fire. I do not remember my mother jumping up from her sewing, the smell of burning cotton drawing her into the bedroom, pulling Don up, throwing the mattress in flames out the window. I do not remember being in the cot right there beside the blaze. I was sleeping. Then I was crying. I cannot remember, but Moki told me. Until that day she did not know about her man's bit on the side, a snake that went by the name of heroin—a hero-in pain.

Just before the fire, the fashion photographer and film-maker Bert Stern (of the 1959 film *Jazz on a Summer's Day*, which documents the 1958 Newport Jazz Festival) had offered to sponsor Moki as an artist-designer for the iconic midtown Manhattan department store Henri Bendel. Her career was about to take flight. But on what should have been her first day, she called Bert to tell him that she wasn't coming in.

"I can't," she said. "I forgot my scissors in Sweden. I have to go get them." She never went back to the store, but she always said that Bert Stern's recognition of her talent gave her the courage to choose to combine motherhood and her work with Don. While Bert's offer was a huge chance turned down, it was also confirmation of her value and identity as an artist.

That day—yellow cabs on the bridge honking, a saxophone playing two floors up, the tears of a crying child mixed with her own, the lingering stench of smoke in the bedroom, and the presence of death staring her in the eyeballs—Moki made a pact. In that duel between life and death, she chose life. The flip side of that deal was always looming, but right then, she had to make a commitment, not just to keep Don alive, but to keep our family together.

She knew she had to get Don away from New York. They would

return to Sweden, where she would pour her energy into the existence they could make there together—with love, art, music—a space full of colour and hope. A certain kind of beauty.

My parents set out to create their own world—a flying carpet strong enough to hold us together and withstand any form of ugly that was staring us in the face. Keep Don out of trouble. *We can fight this*, she determined. Moki—the warrior, the mother, a creator herself—became our protector.

MOVEMENT INCORPORATED

On our return to Sweden, Moki threw herself into painting, gripped by a creative fervour. A certainty had formed in her mind that she and Don needed to elevate their home and working lives to match the heights of the new music and art they wanted to make. She kept painting, working on pieces of paper and board, which she'd hang on the walls. This was our home—a work of art in progress. She produced a dozen pieces within weeks. One of those paintings was on the first album cover that Moki made, for *Where Is Brooklyn?*, which Don had recorded during our short time in Williamsburg. Our building is in the picture. The music born there is in flames, burning up, spilling out of hearts on fire.

Moki also painted big yellow flames licking up the dark blue walls of our Gamla Stan kitchen. She used bright strong colours like other people used white and beige. She was moving away from repetitive textile patterns in her paintings, experimenting with a new eloquent language in bold colour palettes: hands, flamboyant birds and exotic creatures, sunbursts and skies all spilled from her paintbrush and onto the walls. She said, "Rooms are our place in space, something fantastic that one doesn't have time to think is boring." She was always sewing on her machine, and crocheting, making our clothes and even the bags we stuffed our belongings into when we were travelling.

Don was also in a space of discovery, composing, studying, exploring limitless possibility. There were always different musicians coming to the house, like Maffay Fallay and Okay Temiz, who taught Don the music and rhythms of their Turkish homeland.

Day and night, playing, practising, improvising, laughing, exploring, creating, living.

My parents were developing the idea of family and home as a creative and collaborative journey that you *lived*, an experience rather than a static reality. There was to be no division between the making of art and the making of dinner. Don and Moki understood that it was the *now* that mattered. They fought to expand our lives, to make them bigger and richer by bringing people together. The dream was to create *a world more beautiful*, a life less paranoid, more embracing of other cultures, full of spirit, letting their creativity add to the universe rather than just taking from it. The funds were often limited but the resources and potential endless. They conjured a lot—created a boundless universe of their own—from very little. Passion, creativity, inspiration were a force and a privilege, because for them there was a choice.

I was raised amid all that energy and movement. Sharing space, each of us doing different things, influencing each other with interesting collisions. It was the together part that was inspiring. Moki hung a red wooden swing in the doorframe, where I would rock in time to the music. Sometimes it was Don who was playing; sometimes the music came from the record player, which sat low on a wooden crate painted blue. As soon as I could reach, Moki showed me how to lift the arm gently to put the needle on the record and make it play.

I sometimes liked to stand sentry in the tall windows of our apartment, their windowsills deeper than my feet were long. Taking the big step up to stand in the frame, cold air would nip in, bite my cheeks, and make them red. From my vantage point two floors up, I'd keep watch over Gamla Stan, my naked toes gripping the shiny paint on the sill. Two blocks down lay the sea; a few blocks over to the left stood the king's castle. When Don was home, he might take me to watch the changing of the guard, pushing me in my carriage over the cobblestones, which would make my voice vibrate. We liked the rhythm of drums echoing in the courtyard of the palace. Don wrote a song inspired by the sound, called "March of the Hobbits."

Sometimes I sat on Moki's lap and pressed on her belly. I couldn't understand how I could ever have fitted in there, but I knew that we fit together. I loved her hands on me, or her arms around me, but I also liked it when she let me go. I felt free because I knew she was always there, working in the room behind me, sitting at her sewing machine on the low table that had its legs sawn off because she liked to be close to the floor.

That first winter back in Stockholm, Moki brought me to the ice rink in Kungsträdgården park as soon as it opened. I knew how to skate already. Once when I was staying with my grandmother in Rinkaby, she'd taken me across the train tracks outside her house where a big puddle had turned into ice after a cold night. She tied a pillow around my bum and I held her hands tight until my feet in the skates stopped bending and slipping and the pillow couldn't get any wetter, but I could stand alone.

Moki and I walked all the way to Kungsträdgården. I had a winter coat made of fur, soft and fluffy like a white rabbit, with hairs that tickled my nose. It had red binding around the wrists and along the zipper, which Moki closed tight all the way up to my face so my ears kept warm. I didn't need a pillow anymore. I just ran out onto the ice by myself, but I could always see Moki because she didn't look like anybody else. *Maybe she is perfect*, I thought.

Because it was the opening day, a man was taking photographs at the ice rink. He was talking to Moki. The next day I was in the newspaper. My grandmother cut out the photograph of me and framed it.

When I was about three, I started nursery so that Moki could study and work more. I didn't like it when the lady there tried to make me go to sleep. She seemed to not like me. I was happy when Moki picked me up.

"How was it?" she asked.

I told her that I didn't want to go back.

"Why, Neneh?" she said. I liked the way my mother said my name.

"The lady didn't have kind eyes," I replied.

The next day, Moki went to the nursery, looked the lady in the eyes, and came to the same conclusion as me. I never went back.

"Neneh, *du är Klok*," she said. "You were right." After that I had a babysitter called Tant Nora. She gave me a rag doll with long black yarn for hair and a red silk dress, which I still have today.

I loved that Moki thought I was wise. We were connected. Maybe the bond between us was an invisible cord that remained after the doctor cut our physical one. Love. I was so happy there, in Gamla Stam, as a child.

•

With money to make and concerts to play, Moki often took me on the road with Don. We journeyed across Europe and moved in and out of temporary homes more often than I can mention. And more than I ever realised at that time, my parents' choices were as much political as personal. They chose to move beyond the mainstream. Our itinerant lifestyle meant it was important for Moki to practise her art in mediums that were as portable as possible—textiles and painted paper hangings that could be rolled up and taken on tour. She would continue to work wherever we found ourselves, and her artworks made our temporary lodgings a home. Wherever we landed—Brooklyn, Stockholm, Paris, Milan, Amsterdam, Berlin—every space that Moki inhabited was an organic, living, constantly evolving work of art.

We briefly lived in Paris, in 1967, when Don had a residency at Le Chat Qui Pêche. They weren't really into children in France. I was only three, but that was the first time I remember feeling melancholy. I noticed other people's unhappiness, and that everybody cleaning the streets was Black. Feeling their disappointment and hopelessness, I started to think about what they had imagined they were coming to before they arrived in this city with its streets that reeked.

Moki was tired of the dark, airless, smoky, male-centric, sometimes seedy inner-city jazz clubs. With a small child in tow, maybe she realised that this lifestyle was wearing on all of us. It was particularly destructive for Don, and not only because the shadow of his addiction was always there. His work was reaching a new elevated plane but still he was treated badly, endlessly ripped off by club promoters and record-label managers.

Money was a constant problem. Don was hardly materialistic, but he was acutely aware of the struggle to access his earnings. The business was endemically racist; all the big managers and record-company men were white. The musicians didn't own the rights to their records and the royalty system was rigged so that even if they had hits, they didn't see the profits. They were often paid in cash—pin money for clothes, rent, and food—while the long-term assets went to the record-company owners. Don and Moki wanted to take the music out of this corrupt commercial environment and into a community of mutual respect, to give creativity another dimension in which to live.

Back in Gamla Stan, they began to imagine a way of working together in which Moki's art could interact with Don's music as part of a collaborative experience. Performances would take place in all manner of venues, from museums and art galleries to educational spaces or the home. My parents would integrate family life into their creative endeavour and, likewise, other families and children could form part of the audience or join in. Don and Moki were committed to radical theories about child-led education and believed in the value of lifelong learning for everyone. Big, new ideas. They called their project "Movement Incorporated."

Don referred to "collage music" to describe his jazz quintet's use of improvisation as the sole basis for their work, but Movement Incorporated was how he and Moki described their performances and workshops. The aim was to incorporate visual arts and music, professionals and amateurs of all ages and backgrounds, and music of many different global traditions.

Movement Incorporated lasted only from July to September 1967, but during that period my parents established all the fundamentals of the joint artistic practice to which they would devote their lives over the next ten years. The project was political and idealistic, overturning the hierarchies and conventions—of race and sex, artistic forms and approaches—that governed their lives. Don always refused to claim authorship of the music they made, saying it had been produced by the collective. He also acknowledged that Moki's art created the conditions for the collective to operate. Don and Moki were more than a partnership; they were a centre of energy.

They held their first concert on July 19, 1967, at ABF Hall (Arbetarnas Bildningsförbund Huset) in Stockholm. I loved the bustle and freedom of being on tour with them around this time. Moki made posters, designed the stage, and made huge, brightly coloured paintings to hang as backdrops and on the walls. They replaced the hall's chairs with carpets to encourage the audience to sit on the floor alongside the musicians in the centre of the room and lit the venue with candles. During the performance, the smell of incense filled the air, while Moki made live paintings and prepared food to share with everyone. Don was joined by Swedish, American, and Turkish musicians and played both his cornet and an Indian flute. The event sold out and was a great success. It was happening.

Buoyed by the reception they received in Stockholm, my parents rolled up all the carpets, paintings, and wall hangings, packed everything into a borrowed car, and we travelled together to Copenhagen, where they performed in a beautiful old hall at the Academy of Fine Arts in Charlottenborg Palace. Don invited professional musicians as well as people he met in the park to join him on his magic carpet, and Moki set to work making more posters. On the night, along with the music, they showed an experimental film by a Danish Situationist, and a friend of Don's staged a magnificent firework display.

Next stop was Paris, again, where they hoped to repeat the experience, but with no clear plans and no suitable venue, we soon ran out of money to pay for our hotel. Faced by the prospect of being cast out on the street, Don took his cornet and one of Moki's paintings to the Place de l'Odéon and started to play. A French television producer approached him, they got talking, and, the next morning, he, Moki, and two other musicians were in a TV studio preparing to perform under the title of "Movement." That is how my parents came to be part of the premiere of colour broadcasting in France. Moki said that there, up on a ladder painting huge panels for the set, she suddenly knew she was pregnant. My baby brother was inside her.

He was born on May 7, 1968, in Stockholm. Don was away doing some gigs when my brother arrived, three weeks early. The first time they met was in the hospital, when my new baby brother was two days old. Don picked him up, apparently fast asleep, but the baby immediately opened one eye and looked straight at him. Don greeted him with, "Hey, Eagle-Eye."

Don's people carry First Nation Choctaw in their bloodline, Choctaw being one of the tribes that took in escaped and freed slaves. He carried his heritage with dignity and named his son with an eye to all that history.

Five months after Eagle-Eye's birth, we had to leave the Gamla Stan apartment. The medieval town was being renovated. In the crusade for a spanking-new Sweden, everything had to be *renewed*, made modern, clean and streamlined. They gutted the old dwellings, discarding their contents as garbage—the old bathtubs, *kakelugnar* (traditional Swedish tiled stoves), and other antique fixtures now represented poverty. They just chucked them into the streets. Today you pay a fortune for these original vintage items.

My parents always regretted giving up the apartment, but once it was renovated the rent would go up and we couldn't afford to keep it. So, as it turned out, we were leaving Stockholm for good. With nowhere to call home, we went back to New York, this time ending up in a house in Congers, a suburban hamlet north of Manhattan.

As an interracial couple with me and Eagle-Eye in tow, Don and Moki were not much liked in the area. But Moki loved that house. She painted it from top to bottom in bright colours, just as she had done in Gamla Stan. I remember the smell of our toy box. We still have it; it's used now to store firewood. It sits next to the big fireplace in the living room of the Swedish schoolhouse that we would later move to. Every time I stick my head in there to get a fresh log, I'm taken back to Congers.

That summer, I flew on my own to Sweden to stay with my grandparents for a couple of weeks. When I returned, I was gutted to find that Jan and David, Don's kids from his previous relationship, had been to visit. Don and their mother, Carletta, had met in high school and got married very young. But when Jan and David were infants, Don had moved to New York, so they were being raised by Don's mother, Grandma Daisy; her mother, Nana; and Don's sister Barbara in Watts.

I studied the Polaroid photographs of them riding the new bikes that Don had bought—shiny new Choppers with tassels hanging from their big, lowrider handlebars—staring at those two children who were my older brother and sister, so desperately wanting to know them.

One day at the end of that summer, I was sitting with bare legs on a thick wooden bench in a neighbour's yard when I got a splinter embedded in my thigh. Moki soaked my leg in hot water and tried to get it out with tweezers, but it just went in deeper. We tried for days. Eventually, we went to see a doctor, which was a *really* big deal for us as we did not have health insurance. Any time we left Sweden to go to the States, Don and Moki would say, "OK, that's it. If anybody is gonna get sick, get sick *now*." On this occasion, however, we went to the clinic. I sat in the waiting room on my dad's lap. A nurse came in, lifted me up, and took me into the doctor's office. Everything in the room was cold, sterile, white. Immediately, I started to scream. I knew he was going to cut into my leg. The nurse put me down, stonily strapped me to an examination bed, and then, without any anaesthetic, the doctor started digging away at my thigh to remove the splinter. There were no words of kindness from either nurse or clinician, no attempt to soothe.

Afterwards, looking up at a big jar of lollipops on a shelf, the doctor said to me, "I'm not gonna give you a lollipop, because you weren't a good girl." That was how I experienced racism as a five-year-old child.

The people in that clinic did not like my dad, and they did not like me. And they did not want us there. My dad picked me up. I don't know what he said to the doctor, but I felt his rage. It was a contained kind of anger. I felt defended, protected. Moki and Don marched out with me in his arms and took me to the nearest store and bought me a big lollipop with pink bubble gum in the centre. But the trauma remains: to this day I hate sitting on wood with bare legs.

Some other crazy racist shit went on in Congers. A stranger threw something at Moki when she was out on the porch—a hard object that hit her on the head. That was how she was made to pay for living with a Black man in small-town America in 1969.

In early fall, the owners announced that they were selling the house. We were homeless again.

TO TURKEY AND PARIS IN "THE BUS"

We packed up and flew back to Europe carrying all our luggage—countless grain sacks full of fabrics, trunks for the tapestries, the typewriter, Moki's sewing machine, paintings, records, and our clothes, crammed into a multitude of her handmade multicoloured duffel bags. Then there were all the instruments—my mum's tambura, Don's flutes and horns. And, of course, one or two essentials: a few jars of Skippy peanut butter; big bags of curry powder, turmeric, and cumin; bottles of sesame oil. I was on foot, while Eagle-Eye travelled in his big, old-fashioned yellow baby carriage.

In Amsterdam, Don and Moki bought a fully equipped blue '62 VW transporter van for $200, which we called "the bus." The owner had already fitted it with a bed, but soon, with Moki's embellishments and modifications, it became unrecognisable. We drove north for concerts in Norway and Sweden, collecting my scooter and Okay Temiz on the way. Then we headed for Istanbul. Apparently, Okay's bags were stuffed full of porn magazines that he was taking to sell on the black market there for a fat sum of money. The journey seemed to take forever, although it was probably only a week or so. In Istanbul we met James Baldwin. Mr. Baldwin had lived in the city for a while and, at that time, was rehearsing John Herbert's play *Fortune and Men's Eyes* in a nearby theatre. We sat outside at a café, ordered coffees, fresh lemonade, and mint tea, and talked with him for a while. He asked Don to create the music for his production. I remember James Baldwin for his kindness. Sitting there on an Istanbul sidewalk, he did not address me through my parents but directly to me. His eyes were good and they were warm. He was magnetic.

We adopted a cat, orange and with long fur, perhaps an Angora: a real Turkish treasure. When it was time to go home, Moki packed us all back in the bus and the cat came too. The plan was to stop off in Paris to hear some music. I wasn't thrilled about that, but my parents told me we were going to do something extra special. That night, we stayed at a hotel and got all dressed up.

Washed and scrubbed clean, my brown skin was greased, shiny. I wore my brown sleeveless corduroy dress with its black cotton lining printed with camels, a fresh pair of white ankle socks, buckle shoes, my legs bare and sturdy. My shoulder-length hair was gathered up tight in a bunch high on top of my head, pulling at my eyes, pulling at my forehead. Moki tied a yellow bow on top. I felt beautiful.

This was my Miles Davis outfit. We were going to meet a king.

Inside the theatre it was dark and quiet, with solid wooden floors. Don was looking for the opening in the curtain on the stage, holding me by the hand—that made me feel special, too. Miles liked my ribbon. Dressed in snakeskin, he lifted me up and set me on his knee. The snakeskin felt weird on my bare legs. His raspy voice close to my ear, he said, "Look what I got for you." He pulled a Toblerone bar out of his snakeskin trumpet case.

Miles was a leader—but so was Don. Miles did not always speak kindly of my dad and his music. He did not want to like the free-jazz crowd, perhaps because he was not leading the movement from the front. But Don didn't think about Miles as a rival to bring down. The world that Don and so many musicians of his generation were exploring was more collective, less ego-driven. It was all about freedom. Perhaps Miles eventually changed his mind about the new jazz men, because Don told me, years later, that the two of them had bumped into each other at an airport and Miles had said, "Hey, Don. I sound a bit like you now, right?"

Before we left Paris, Moki took me and Eagle-Eye shopping for fabric in the Barbès district to the north of the Gare du Nord and Montmartre, its streets a long way from the Champs-Élysées. The budget department store Tati, the biggest and best tat shop ever, took over nearly a whole block. The pavements were cluttered, loud, messy, alive with the sounds of Arabic and African languages—Wolof, Bambara, and Ewondo. The people spread out, making no excuses, no polite banter.

For Moki, the many cloth shops along the steep hills of rue des Poissonniers and rue Doudeauville were treasure chests; they sold African waxed cottons in joyous combinations of bright primary colours, alongside delicate Italian silks and satin jacquards. I could sense Moki's heart beating faster as she scanned the array of fabrics on the shelves and the rolls of cloth stacked haphazardly in every corner. She would vie for attention and for the best price, banging heads with all these imperious ladies in djellabas pushing us aside, just about climbing over us to get a feel of a yellow silk, seeming harsh but then cracking a dazzling gold-toothed smile. Those women must have looked at my white mother and wondered, *What is she doing here, this woman who is not dressed at all like a French white lady?* On her own and with two brown kids—she really stood out.

Bored with waiting for Moki, I'd pretend I was speaking to Eagle-Eye in an African dialect—we were from Mali. We became other children of other people—of the women on the bustling hill in Barbès—babbling away in an invented language.

I felt some embarrassment about my mother being so different wherever she went, but I was also fiercely defensive of her. Now I admire how she couldn't help but just be herself. She wore her hair cut short, hennaed to a dark-toned red, a string of blue glass beads around her head. A long dress under a Bedouin cape. That cape, laid on a bare floor, became our bed, or a resting place for us on the stage during my parents' performances. In the bus, it was a bedspread. When we arrived at the next city, it was a vessel in which to smuggle our kitchen—a two-ring electric stove, pots, pans, and utensils—into a hotel. Wherever we laid Moki's cape was our home.

HAZY DAYS IN THE USA

In early January 1970, Don took up a post as a visiting lecturer at Dartmouth College in New Hampshire. On our flight from Sweden, we took the Turkish cat with us, hidden in a Pan Am bag, which Moki casually hung on the handle of Eagle-Eye's pram. Moki loved that cat.

Our home was a new-build red-brick hunting lodge outside Norwich, Vermont, across the Connecticut River from the college. The house was set back from the road along a drive with a picket fence, and beyond the open fields stood a red, oval-roofed farm like a Fisher-Price mirage. We had not lived like this before. It was the first and only time my parents enjoyed the luxury of a salary every month. Moki bought Pampers for Eagle-Eye. I would put my face in the packet, drink in that intoxicating manufactured baby smell.

I was almost six, so I went into first grade at Norwich elementary school, where the Stars and Stripes stood at full mast every day. After school, I'd play outside in the snow, scooting down the slope in the garden.

We had a brand-new brown GM van in the drive and a washing machine—another first. When the plumber came to install it, his eyes had to reset. Our home was not what he was used to. In the big main room, there was no pile carpet, no La-Z-Boy chair angled towards a television set. A low double bed stood up against the fabric-covered wall, the child's swing hanging near the record deck.

Moki led the plumber in. On the kitchen table sat her sewing machine—it followed us wherever we went—fabrics spread out in haste. The plumber went to work. When he was done, he asked Moki for a towel to dry his hands. Moki gave him the first thing she could reach. "Sorry, ma'am," he said. "I can't use this." He handed her back the star-spangled banner in old, ripped linen. I can't help but think that Moki knew exactly what she was doing. The plumber walked out without a word.

The Vietnam War was in full force, student uprisings a daily matter. Young voices finding their power. When the U.S. entered the war in 1961, thousands of inner-city young men were drafted. The social, economic, and political disparities were glaring; the same young people who were often let down and abused by the legal system were now being sent to fight in the name of the very laws that were used to abuse them. Meanwhile, their more privileged contemporaries took advantage of educational and business options. There was civil unrest across the country.

Change had to come, and music played a huge part in the cultural shift. Don's engagement at Dartmouth came at the right time. He taught two classes: one for music majors and an "open" class with 150 students. His spirited, loving, passionate way of teaching inspired them all. Lots of kids who were majoring in other subjects moved over to study with him, some altering the course of their lives forever. His big project was to create a student "opera." Moki was also involved, planning costumes and set design. At home, it was an open house at weekends, with set- and costume-making, rehearsals, music playing loud on the record player, and huge meals cooked by Moki, of course.

It was in Vermont that I started properly listening to records and understanding that the music affected not just how I felt but the mood in the room. Even at a young age, I realised that reality wasn't static. Music provided a means to find myself but also an escape route; a way to disappear and get through things that I found tough. It created space inside me, away from my limited sense of myself. Snug in the swing, I swung higher, harder, to Sly and the Family Stone and their revolution; the Rolling Stones's *Let It Bleed* with the birthday cake on the cover; and Aretha Franklin's seesaw love. I sang, I swung. *Diana Ross Presents The Jackson 5*, with the gold and Motown-blue cover that I loved to shreds. I like that my parents thought I needed those albums when I still only had milk teeth. I came to life, became real, found my heart inside those songs.

At the end of term, Don and his students performed their opera in the university theatre. The energy was vibrant but quiet, dry ice rising over an ocean of voices coming from somewhere inside the sunken stage floor. Slowly, as the stage ascended, the vibe changed, the music became effervescent. The performers now level with the audience, Don started to dance. Mesmerised, my feet dangling from the front-row seat, I suddenly noticed Eagle-Eye on the stage. I was confused because he had been just there, next to me in Moki's arms. But he had taken off, climbed the stairs to get to his dad, his chubby little legs in tights over his Pampers. Don danced him in. The event was a fabulous success, with the students excitedly bringing their proud parents to meet "Professor Cherry, Moki, and their family."

My parents, though, were disillusioned with the States. The pervasive racism, the evaporating glow of the brief economic reprieve, and, above all, the U.S. intervention in Vietnam and bombing of Cambodia played a part in their decision to return to Europe. For the next eight years our main home would be in Sweden.

When it was time to leave, we took our life with us:

My mustard snowsuit
The brown GM van
The painted furniture
The records
The toy box
The orange Turkish cat.

THE SCHOOLHOUSE

When we drove into the yard at Tågarp for the first time, there was a rainbow over the former schoolhouse. Don said, "This is it, baby." My parents bought it on the spot.

It was early August 1970 and we had been driving around Skåne County looking for a place to call home. Thanks to Don's salary from Dartmouth, he and Moki had been able to put some cash aside: Moki dreamed of a place big enough for us as a family, a place in the world where they could find peace. Tågarp Skola was right in the middle of the sparsely populated village, at the apex of a triangle where the small dirt road split into two. They met the owner and, within half an hour, sealed the deal over a bottle of *brannvin* (schnapps). A few shots, a handshake—done! We moved in on September 9, my parents full of ideas for this new adventure. Moki was twenty-seven; Don was thirty-six. They were both still so young.

The building had eleven wood-burning stoves and no insulation, but with two huge schoolrooms and two teachers' apartments, there was more than enough space to house our family, any number of visiting friends and musicians, and all my parents' dreams and ambitions. Here at last was the embodiment of Moki's maxim: "The stage is home and home is a stage."

Don's piano with the golden throat had travelled down to Tågarp with the rest of our stuff in the van, but it was too heavy to unload. So for a while it stayed there and, much to the consternation of our naturally curious new neighbours, Don went out every day to play it. Finally, Moki called in a team of professional movers and we all closed our eyes and held our breath as they hefted it up the stone stairs into the house.

Moki scrubbed the old building from top to bottom with pine-scented *såpa*, green jelly soap, and began the long process of painting all the rooms—each in a different colour. The schoolhouse was one of Moki's greatest works of art. She painted every inch, every wall, every floor. One classroom became her studio; the other, which once would have been the larger classroom where the older kids were taught, was where the piano found its resting place, so it became the music room and—no-brainer—a living room. At the front was the green room, where we kept the record player, and again, Moki hung my red swing in the doorframe. To the back was the wooden outhouse with three different-sized toilet cubicles for the schoolchildren.

Moki and Don wanted an independent, healthier, more natural life, and an important step was to prepare the ground so we could start growing our own food. A local dairy farmer was one of the first people to help, when a lot of our neighbours really didn't know what to make of us. He saw Don and Moki attempting to tame the garden and showed Don how to use a sickle. He hacked away at the tall grasses and scrub; then, finally, Moki started to dig the soil.

It took time, but Moki did eventually manage to make her beautiful kitchen garden and grow food. Right up to the last years of her life, she would make the garden bloom so we could eat our own homegrown organic vegetables: potatoes, herbs, tomatoes, zucchini, squash, spinach, chard, and mangold, lots of lettuce and some kale.

Our area, Göinge, was lost in time, real deep country, slightly cut off: all the guys in dungarees, everyone wearing clogs. One of our neighbours still had a workhorse. The big summer happenings were the flea markets. Moki found pretty much all the furniture for the schoolhouse at those events: she had an amazing eye for forties and fifties design. Back then, Eagle-Eye and I were less than impressed by her thrift-conscious buys: when she arrived home with her treasures, we would groan, "Oh my God, why can't we just go to IKEA like everyone else?"

On New Year's Eve 1970, Don and Moki threw a huge party. There were people sleeping all over the house, including dear friends of my parents from Stockholm, Steve and Anita Roney and their children, Nunu and Shanti (and, later, Marimba). Steve ran a gallery in the city and presented experimental films and non-Western music at Moderna Museet. Not long after, they bought a house in the next village, Tofta. Our friends Jack and Kerstin McNeil and their daughter Hanna followed soon after, buying a house in Farstorp. Our families have been a little trinity down there ever since, and all of us kids grew up together. Whenever Don and Moki both went away, Eagle-Eye and I stayed with one or the other.

People were always coming and going; the doors of the schoolhouse were permanently open. Some stayed overnight, others much longer. One year when we got back from one of our journeys, we discovered a funny man called Mannfred living in the outhouse. He had ridden all the way from Germany on his bike. He stayed for a summer, barely speaking a word, but every day he worked like a maniac, digging up rocks and taming an area possessed by prickly raspberry bushes at the back of the garden. On many nights dinner was for twenty people. Some visitors started ambitious projects, eager to contribute to the living organism that was our home, but many of these were never quite finished: a ceramic oven, an outdoor kitchen, a tipi frame that never got its canvas. I can't understand how Moki had the energy to make all the beds, cook dinner for everyone, to constantly toil to make our world more beautiful.

A couple of years after our arrival, things got really crazy as the number of houseguests rose, along with temperatures and tempers. One morning we woke up and found that someone had taken all our saucepans and hung them up in the apple tree. Everyone seemed to be splitting up with their partner or having a nervous breakdown. Someone's kid brought chicken pox to the house and I caught it, so I went to stay with my grandparents. I'll never forget lying in their garden in a deckchair in a bikini, my grandmother doting on me, crossing my legs and looking up at a plum tree, thinking, *Jackpot. Bye bye, Tågarp.*

Mormor and Morfar's home in Rinkaby was a refuge, my reliably safe, stable place. And, joy of joys, they had a TV. I loved to eat things there that I didn't eat anywhere else: *filmjölk* (buttermilk) with oats topped with cocoa powder and a spoonful of sugar; thinly sliced bread with liver pâté and sweet, sliced pickles, cut into dolly-sized bites. Such was the love of my grandma.

•

I started school in Farstorp. When I went to register with my grandfather, in the autumn of 1971, I wore a beautiful fake-fur jacket with patent brown edges, a flowery ruffled dress, and I carried a little handbag on my shoulder. My outfit was brand new and I felt pretty. But this was accompanied by another, even more acute sensation, and it is that which anchors this memory so firmly in my head: the sense of being different.

We were different for many reasons: Don was a foreigner; we often wore Moki's homemade creations; we made our living from avant-garde art rather than farming; but, above all, we were the only ones in our neighbourhood of African heritage. That didn't mean I wasn't also Swedish. I spoke Skånska, the local dialect, without an accent, and that's the language I still use when I'm there. Skåne had been Moki's family home, after all, which was why I used to get so angry with some people who stared at us as if we were aliens. I wanted to be undefeated, not beaten down by people's judgement of my Blackness. I stared back when they looked, answered back when they made thoughtless comments about my skin. They said it so flippantly but every time I heard it, I felt it like a cut. Even when I was very little, drunk men would want to touch my hair. Then they'd say, "You're so brown! I bet you don't need to sunbathe, do you?"

One time, Moki left me in my buggy outside the post office while she popped in. When she came out, an old lady was peering at me.

"What do they eat?" the woman asked, in a thick southern accent.

"Bananas, of course," Moki replied, without missing a beat.

At the little country school in Farstorp, I was conscious of my flat nose and my flat forehead, so different from those of my classmates. I would stare at their faces, entranced by how the girls would flick their blond hair, blow their fringe off a perfectly pert button nose.

Our teacher read to us from classic Scandinavian storybooks: *Pippi Longstocking* by Astrid Lindgren and *Mrs. Pepperpot in the Magic Wood* by Alf Prøysen, about the little old woman who shrinks when she gets stressed. But there was one book of old Swedish fables that had a story about someone arriving on an island full of Black children. That word again: *neger*. The illustrations were of jet-black kids, the colour of no one, with huge bright red lips the colour of mean nail polish and, of course, their naked bodies dressed only in grass skirts—the same depiction someone might make of cannibals dancing around a stew pot.

A different teacher picked up that book years later. I was older. I had a crush on a boy in my class. Sitting at the back of the classroom, I remember my humiliation. I knew the story and what was coming: the teacher was going to read that word aloud. When she got to the bit about the boat pulling up on the shore, the jet-black kids of this desert island standing there in a line to joyfully greet the great white travellers, in unison the whole class turned around and looked at me. I wanted to dissolve, but I froze like stone.

I knew everyone in the tiny school and had lots of friends. It's not that I was not accepted, but the anticipation that at any moment I could be singled out caused anxiety and made me feel vulnerable. I struggled with being seen as different. I have a deep relationship with my country, yet I have habitually over-explained being Swedish: "Oh, I have a Swedish passport, my mum's Swedish but my father's African and my stepdad is American . . . "

There was also a part of me that defended who I am, that fought to be seen for who I was. Standing in line at a school sports meet, feeling the eyes of the girls from the other school on me, I heard someone say, "I bet she'll be really fast because she's Black." It felt like an upgrade, a scary thrill. I wish I could say that I left them all in the ditches behind me, but there were one or two that were faster. The gold medals were never mine. Among my peers, I worked hard at never showing those vulnerabilities. But I was always on the periphery, always aware of my difference.

•

Early one September morning, not long after we moved to the schoolhouse, I was sitting on Moki's lap looking through old photographs—big black-and-white prints. It was cold and windy. I was wearing a striped nightie.

"Who's that?" I asked about a face I recognised but did not know. It was a photograph of a Black man wearing a striped top.

"That's just someone I know," Moki said. We continued looking at the pictures, but she returned to the photograph I'd asked about. I could feel her shaking. "Neneh, there is something I have to tell you," she said. "This man is your real father."

I felt sorry for Moki because I could tell she was scared about how this news would affect me. So I said, "It's OK, Mamma." But my foundations shifted to their core. I had believed one thing and now I knew another. I worried that Don might hand me over to this new man, or that he might love me less than my little brother. But Moki knew that Don was my daddy, and he continued to show me that he was. It was Don who brought me up, and he was devoted to me.

Don and Moki must have discussed the need to tell me the truth. It was never going to be a big secret; it was simply that Moki had been waiting for the right time. She and Don had just bought the schoolhouse, and their focus was on nurturing family life in Sweden. I understand how important it was for Moki that I should know about Ahmadu, but I also know that her strongest instinct was to protect me. She knew that Ahmadu was complicated, unpredictable, not truly able to be there as a father, and yet she only ever talked to me about him with love.

After I was born and Moki had asked Ahmadu to leave, he met Maylen, a former dancer, and they had two children together: my sister Titiyo, who is three years younger than me, and my brother Cherno, who is six years my junior.

A few years ago, I found an unsent letter from Moki to Ahmadu and Maylen. It was written on a sheet of the butterfly writing paper I collected as a child, as fresh as if she had penned it the day before. She wrote what a wonderful child I was, that Ahmadu and Maylen really should get to know me. But, for a long, long time, Moki's efforts were in vain.

•

When I was nine, the autumn after the crazy summer in Tågarp with the chicken pox and the saucepans in the tree, I learned of another surprise addition to my family. We had just gone back to school and I was at a friend's house. When I phoned to tell my parents that I was going to be back later, my mother told me, quite matter-of-fact, that I had a new baby brother called Christian: he lived in Denmark and his mother was called Lune. It had come as a shock for Moki, too. Now Christian and I are very close, but it wasn't so straightforward in the beginning.

I remember riding my bike towards Tågarp, not knowing what I was going home to. I didn't fully understand what was happening. As children, we sensed and heard things, knew some things were going on around us, but a lot of the detail was filtered for a child's ears, then filled in later. Moki and I talked a lot over the years. And, of course, fidelity was not the main issue with Don—heroin was the mistress that had its claws in him.

It was soon after this latest family revelation that Moki and Don took me to meet Ahmadu at his apartment in Stockholm. It was a strange and difficult day, but I am so thankful that we went in alliance, as a family. Don was the person I called Dad and he was always there. He was sweet, polite, and so respectful of the importance of my knowing my biological father. Ahmadu greeted us with love and no awkwardness. The apartment felt cosy and welcoming, with a deep presence of West Africa yet definitely still Swedish, lots of houseplants, warm lighting, and the sweet smell of spiced stew and rice cooking on the stove. We sat at the table. Ahmadu went into the kitchen and cried.

When I saw Ahmadu and Moki together, it was plain that there was no lack of love and feeling there. It made me feel uneasy. I saw something in Moki that I didn't recognise and it freaked me out a bit. Don took deep breaths. You can't own the sacred space that lovers share, even after love has changed direction.

When I was a bit older, about twelve, I would spend some of the school holidays with Ahmadu and his family at their home in Bergshamra, to the north of Stockholm. My sister Titiyo and I became very close. Both of us had little brothers, neither of us had a sister, and we really wanted to love each other. Maylen and I also got on well. I spent more time with her than with Ahmadu, who was always on the road. He played in bands and made his money touring across Sweden, lecturing on African culture and music. Knowing him, and knowing what was no doubt going on while he was away from home, Maylen seemed to struggle. Ahmadu was a generous loving spirit, but his infidelities meant that he was stressed, constantly having to cover things up. He would be distracted and edgy when he came back. Lies can do that to you. He avoided her and dodged the difficult questions. And in his inability to be accountable, there were times when he appeared to gaslight her: *What is the matter with you? Why are you getting hysterical?*

Ahmadu and I were close, the kind of closeness that comes from shared DNA and blood. It was a recognition that existed without words. But I had to grow to love him. Ahmadu was so moved and happy when we did finally get to know each other that, at times, I found his emotion quite overwhelming. He had a lot of remorse about how everything had turned out and the lost years of my childhood, and though he didn't exactly make things easy for himself, he loved all his children deeply.

ORGANIC MUSIC

The seventies, in our household, were a time of organic music, Tibetan Buddhism, and lots of brown rice. Moki and Don's project was evolving into a mission to bring music, art, and communion into everyday life, not just for our family but for everyone. They were wildly creative but very disciplined in their approach, and their generosity and enthusiasm touched many.

For Eagle-Eye and me, our parents' work was simply life itself. There wasn't much distinction between them. Sometimes there was no distinction at all. In 1971, the director of Stockholm's Moderna Museet, Pontus Hultén, invited Don and Moki to participate in the exhibition he was curating, *Utopias and Visions 1871–1971*. They packed us, and all their art materials and instruments, into the van and we drove to Stockholm to live in the museum for three months. I had a little black kitten that I couldn't bear to be parted from, so she came too. I made a cosy bed for her in a cardboard box.

The museum was on an island, in what had been an army barracks, with beautiful gardens at the back. We slept and ate in two rooms, which Moki fitted out with mattresses, fabric, and cushions. She brought our two-ring gas stove and cooked all our meals there. Our days were spent in the geodesic dome that Bengt Carling, a family friend, built in the gardens. The space was open to the public, and Moki and Don invited people to join in with whatever they were doing. Don played the piano, flute, and trumpet and sang with a rotating ensemble of collaborators from the tribe of musicians from Sweden and artists from farther afield who happened to be passing through town. The Japanese experimental music group the Taj Mahal Travellers were on their first European tour and came to join us.

Moki set up her sewing machine on a table and started to work. She made costumes for the performances and soft cushion-like sculptures. She hung tapestries from the ceiling and walls, filling the floor with tall leafy plants. Bathed in the serene white light of the dome, a white birdcage dangled from a chain and, of course, there was a grand piano. In the centre of the space she painted, with intense focus, an intricate seed on the floor that, over the course of the summer we spent there, grew into a great big mandala.

It was like living in a playground, with extra art. I had the run of the place. I used to pretend I was one of the museum guards, hanging out with whoever was in the dome and roaming the galleries telling people, "Don't touch that!" When no one was looking, I stroked *Monogram*, the famous piece by Robert Rauschenberg—a stuffed goat with a paint-splattered face and a tyre around its middle. And I giggled at Dalí's extended bum-cheek painting.

The *Utopias* exhibition was a game-changer for Moki and Don. It was a validation of what they were doing, and it led to a flood of other projects. They made a children's series for Swedish TV called *Piff, Paff, Puff*, which was filmed at the schoolhouse. Eagle-Eye and I, and other local kids, all took part. Then there was Moki's first solo exhibition, held in 1973 at Galleri I in Stockholm, and another commission from Pontus Hultén, who by this time was the inaugural director of the Pompidou Centre in Paris. In 1974, he invited them both to create the first *atelier des enfants*, an educational space for children, building on what they'd done at Moderna Museet.

Don and Moki believed that music and art were life-giving and life-changing, and that creativity was a human instinct common to all cultures. It lived in every single person and could be accessed through play, experimentation, and collaboration. They took their workshops all over Sweden, funded by Sweden's Ministry of Education, to schools from the far north to the very south. They thought that children were more capable than adults of listening to music and grasping its essentials, because their imaginations had not yet been dulled. Don said, of his own playing, that he always tried to recall the feeling of being given his first trumpet by his mother. "That's what music is really about," he said. "That infant happiness."

•

Tågarp Skola was a place that drew people in and brought them together. It became a collaborative environment where people could gather and find space for the creative process.

I think some people assume my family existed in some sort of hippy paradise, but a commune the schoolhouse most certainly was *not*. Don raised us with some of the family values that he had grown up with in his Black family in Watts, LA—standards of behaviour passed on by his mother and grandmother—and that sometimes meant strict. The inner sanctum of the home was sacred, and his firm hands of love and guidance held us tight. Any number of friends could be at our house but, at a certain point, Don would tell them to go home. It was time for me and Eagle-Eye to clean up and be with our family.

On warm summer evenings, we'd all eat dinner outside in the long grass. Once those plates were clean, my parents and their various friends and collaborators would play and play long into the night. For me and Eagle-Eye, it was impossible for this sound and energy not to enter our consciousness. There was something about being at Tågarp, close to nature, that meant that creativity could take root and flourish. I look at Moki's artwork for Don's *Organic Music* album, its dreamlike imagery, a self-portrait of my mother in front of the Moderna Museet dome, Don sitting in the grass playing the tabla among abstract foliage that is almost our garden. It tells the story of those times. They had succeeded in taking music out of cramped smoky basements and releasing it into the wild.

•

Around this time, Don and Moki discovered the Karma Kagyu school of Tibetan Buddhism. When Kalu Rinpoche, a Tibetan Buddhist master, came to Sweden, we travelled to greet him at the airport. The practice of meditation and praying was a meaningful commitment for Don and Moki in their search for a spiritual consciousness in music and art. And in Don's fight with addiction, meditation gave him strength. It influenced everything, from the work they were making—Don used a lot of Tibetan Buddhist mantras in the lyrics on his albums *Relativity Suite* and *Brown Rice*—to the clothes they wore and that Moki made for us. She had Tibetan boots and they both wore those Tibetan hats with the flaps. We even had a Nepalese temple dog called Singema.

We used to go to Copenhagen to visit Ole Nydahl and his wife, Hannah. Ole had been around on the jazz scene, but in 1969 he and Hannah had travelled to Nepal, where they met and studied under the sixteenth Karmapa, the spiritual leader of the Karma Kagyu line of Buddhism, as well as Kalu Rinpoche and the Dalai Lama. Since 1972, they had run a Karma Kagyu meditation and teaching centre, the first in Denmark. Now Ole was known as "Lama Ole." That's where we went to pujas, the ritual ceremonies with meditations, chanting, and offerings to the Buddha.

On one occasion, everyone was crammed in the room, waiting silently for the puja to begin. First, in walked the monks, and then Kalu Rinpoche was led in. Everything turned very still. There was a sense of the air itself hanging in suspension, people doing prostrations, and me and Eagle-Eye sitting there, not really knowing what we were doing, but knowing, somehow, that this was something or someone special and we must not move a muscle. There was honour and a beautiful sense of self-preservation in those ceremonies.

The monks, some of them barely into their teens, intrigued me. They acted serious, but then their faces would break into huge smiles when we spoke to them. I tried to imagine how they lived, up in their monastery in the Nepalese mountains. I dreamed of going there.

"Can girls be monks too?" I asked.

"Yes, but they are called nuns," was the answer.

Back at home, Eagle-Eye, Nunu, and Shanti Roney and I would play pujas. Eagle-Eye would always be the Holy One.

•

Moki cooked in the same way she painted or cut fabric—with spirit and love—and there's no doubt I inherited that passion from her. If Don had been away, she would cook something special to celebrate his return. Those meals—the flavours, the scents, the expectation, and the sense of harmony in the house while the preparations were in progress. There was a sound, too, that went hand in hand with the warmth and the smell of Moki's cooking: Brazilian Cuban music playing on the stereo.

While Moki wasn't wed to many of her homeland's customs, she loved *some* traditions. She had a deep respect for Sweden's version of soul food, *husmanskost*: steamed cod, boiled meats, hearty stews like *dillkött* and *kalops*, using the best basic ingredients and proper cuts of meat. She made the most delicious gravlax, a dry-cured salmon marinated in herbs. She was also quite a bold cook. One year the frost came early and the tomatoes in the greenhouse were going to go bad, so she made a green tomato chutney from an old Indian cookbook. I still have that book, a little paperback with no pictures, its pages now hanging by a thread. Eagle-Eye and I still talk with friends about that chutney, and the recipe is still used by our family every year at harvest. None of them, not even aunties Lil and Kerstin, who make an amazing version, has ever come up with anything that tasted quite as good as the one Moki made that year.

She made an incredible lamb stew with anchovies and red wine, and created another of her great dishes from a description she read in Louis de Bernières's *Captain Corelli's Mandolin*. In the novel, when the communal wood-fired ovens had been lit for baking bread, the villagers placed this lamb dish with potatoes, sliced tomatoes, and olives, seasoned with thyme, in the embers and left it to cook for hours. Moki's version sings to me anytime I think of it: a simple dish, but quite simply divine.

I can still see her, making a beef-rib recipe from an old cookbook by the Swedish chef Tore Wretman, her hands rubbing the dry spices—ground juniper berries and cloves, salt and pepper—into the meat, treating the food with such care. She was always fully engaged with the process, having a relationship with what her hands were doing, really taking time to do it thoroughly and mindfully. You could taste all that in her food, the sauce whispering her secrets.

Moki had a palate and an eye for fine things. As she would say all her life, "I'm a fiend for beauty." But she was not a snob in any sense, least of all a food snob. The word "passionate" springs to mind—she enjoyed a classic restaurant, but not necessarily as much as she would rice and beans in a little Cuban joint on the Lower East Side. Where the food came from and how it was executed mattered far more than the grandeur of the eatery. She didn't like things that were made without intention or feeling.

HAVEN, HEAVEN, HEROIN

The first time I saw the track marks on Don's arms we were in the parlour in Tågarp, which Moki had painted purple in homage to the autumnal heather. There were candles lit and the open fire was crackling. I was on the couch, facing the fire. Don was standing in front of me, warming his back. He rolled up his sleeves and, as he did so, I saw his bare arms.

"What's that, Daddy?" I asked.

"That's where the snakes bit me," he replied. He told me about going to jail because of those marks the serpents had left. I saw that he was showing me something, but it was not everything. Those track marks were souvenirs from a life, but they did not define him.

I know a story can contain some dark threads without them dulling the brighter colours. Don grew up under segregation in the fifties, sixties, seventies, and on and on. I can understand the shock of landing back in the blunt reality of life after flying so high in music. The heroin would return him to those friendly skies, but it left its marks on all of us.

I read Moki's journal about buying the schoolhouse. She wrote that her investment in being in the middle of nowhere in the Swedish countryside was, in large part, to keep Don away from drugs. He probably would have been able to get heroin in Stockholm, even in Malmö, but he did not have the same relationship with those city streets as he did with New York's. Of course, they both wanted a space big enough to house their creative dreams and ambitions, but I had never thought about that element. Moki put her energy into creating a place that could contain everything. The home would be a whole world in itself—children, family, her art, Don's music, collaboration, the dreams, the inspiration—everything could happen there in Tågarp.

She was only partially successful. Don wanted to be free of his addiction and was incredibly strong—so long as he was away from the States. He would have lengthy periods in Europe when he was clean, but throughout his life he'd want to get back to the U.S., and within two or three days of returning to New York he'd be gone again, taking whatever little money he and Moki had with him.

•

My parents took us to New York every year, often for months at a time. We were drawn back. Don needed to be there for the music—so many of his peers were there. And Moki's creativity thrived there, too. On our arrival in the Big Apple, until my parents found us a place to sublet, we would often check in to the Chelsea Hotel. It was pretty shabby at that time. Patti Smith, Bob Dylan, Uncle Abdullah Ibrahim and his family, Sid Vicious—the guest list at the Chelsea was endless, but the building also housed old ladies in twinsets with tiny dogs. It was an affordable place for all sorts of people to take refuge.

We would set up home in one double room with a bathroom and a kitchenette—classic New York. And a television, of course. The beds were covered with candlewick bedspreads with textured caterpillar frills in a sludge-green colour so ugly it has no name. Moki would rip them off the moment we arrived and replace them with our fabrics.

Stanley Bard was the notorious manager of the Chelsea. He had the craziest art collection because so many broke artists paid him in kind. At some point, in the first few days, we would have to make a deal for our rent.

"Hey, Mr. Cherry! What can we do for you today?" Mr. Bard would say.

Don would tell us, "Look as sweet as you are and a little bit hungry—and be quiet."

The hotel was my playground. I would take off and go wandering around the building. The only place I would never go were the apartments at the top. There was a rumour that someone who lived up there kept a roomful of snakes and lizards. I liked to hang out with the chambermaids, every one of them a Black woman. One day one of these ladies, wrapped in her big blue housecoat, was making a steak sandwich on a small white hotplate in the housekeepers' room. I was like a zombie, following the scent of the cooking meat along the corridor. She saw me standing there staring and let me have a little piece. I will never forget it: her voice, her kindness, the way she cut off a corner of her sandwich and simply handed it to me without making a fuss. "Here, baby. You better have some of this—you look like you're starving!"

I'd ride the elevator all day with the "elevator man"; then, back in our room, Eagle-Eye and I would get into the wardrobe and pretend it was a lift. One of us would be the elevator man and the other would say, "Third floor, please." We made a playground out of wherever we were, creating whole worlds in those poky rooms, 23rd Street in a ruckus down below.

The first few days in New York usually had a holiday feel. We would walk around, sink back into the city, go and say hi to everybody, eat up the sounds, and taste the moreish American food. We would go to the corner deli to stock up on essentials for the kitchenette. Don took the lead on the catering front. This was his stomping ground, and he wanted to taste all the flavours he knew so well. We loved that, because he gravitated towards Twinkies and peanut butter, loaves of Pepperidge Farm bread and those square, plastic-wrapped orange cheese slices that came in packs of ten. He would get Land O'Lakes butter, in sticks wrapped in white paper like parchment. We would smear it on to the squishy raisin bread. Next came the joy of peeling the processed cheese off the thin cellophane film, the way it would instantly break out in a light sweat, tiny glistening beads forming on its surface. And then, carefully placing my cheese on top of the thickly buttered bread, I would take my first wondrous bite. The effect of that nondescript, rubbery cheese and the cold butter on the soft raisin bread in my mouth, all washed down with a glug of cool Florida Fresh Tropicana orange juice from a glass bottle, was glorious. I can taste it now.

Moki would take us walking in SoHo, which in those days was the fabric district, still mostly industrial. She always carried a pair of sharp fabric scissors in her cloth bag. There were faulty bales left lying on the sidewalks and whole dumpsters full of treasures—scraps of cloth and ends of rolls. Moki would climb right in, her scissors at the ready. She made a lot of her clothes, tapestries, and backdrops entirely from the oddments she gleaned on these outings.

Walking in New York with Don was always an adventure. Usually, our journeys took us back to familiar faces and places. Most of the tribe lived downtown. On a corner in the Bowery lived the writer and publisher LeRoi Jones, aka Amiri Baraka. He was always happy to find us on his doorstep. "Hey, Don! Moki! Y'all back in town?" Then we would go to Marzette Watts's loft on the Bowery. He, I discovered, was married to two sisters, both thin and white with short hair. Next stop was Sara Penn's shop on First Avenue. Dark and warm, jazz or African music on the record player, incense always burning, Sara's store was packed with kimonos, mud-cloth and indigo wraps and clothes, musical instruments and jewellery from all over the world. The objects on sale were ever-changing, but I liked the way Sara and her shop seemed timeless: the musky amber scent, the tear in one of her earlobes where an earring had been ripped straight through, still the same every year.

Lastly, we would head on down to see Ornette. Ornette was an expert in many things—even in SoHo he led the way as one of the first to take a loft. Since the late sixties, he had occupied the whole building at 131 Prince Street, which he called "Artists' House." Downstairs was a performance space. Ornette lived upstairs. He had a pool table. We loved that. He would sit in his studio holding his sax in his lap, music stands all around. His voice was soft with a kind of lisp. Don and he were equals, brothers, but in Ornette's company Don changed in a very touching way, becoming quieter, with a calm respect.

On our first Sunday in the city, we would go shopping with Don and Moki on Orchard Street on the Lower East Side—in those days it had a bustling market at the weekends and all the city's best discount stores. Every year, religiously, my parents would take me and my brother to buy a brand-new pair of bargain OshKosh dungarees. Then we'd go to one of the discount shoe stores and get a new pair of Converse or Keds.

That area was home to a lot of Eastern European and Russian Jews, the streets lined with Jewish bakeries, restaurants, delis, and pickle stores: Yonah Schimmel Knish Bakery, Guss Pickles, Russ & Daughters, Veselka. On Sundays, when the street was heaving with people, the air would be smoky from the shish kebabs grilling on hot dog carts, burning my nose, making my eyes and mouth water. Hungry after our shopping trips, we would stop in at Katz's famous deli and order one of their legendary pastrami sandwiches, to share, with their outlandishly long French fries on the side. I loved to look at all the photographs covering Katz's walls, and the garish price tags and signs over the counter, especially the one that said, "Send a salami to your boy in the army."

Landing in New York after the quiet of Sweden, the sudden rush of being in the city was overwhelming, energising, exhilarating. The city felt so deadly and alive, the streets sweating and dressed in a layer of grime. Car horns beeped; police sirens blared. The New York buses had a sound all their own, the constant hum of the diesel engines reverberating between the tall buildings on those dense, narrow streets; apartments lived in by Puerto Ricans, Dominicans, Cubans, Haitians, Italians, Polish, Irish, Black and Brown people. Everyone talking all at the same time, salsa playing in doorways and bodegas and blasting from the window of a big Cadillac passing by, Minnie Riperton telling us how loving is easier than breathing.

This, for me, became the soundtrack of New York. Everything all at once, scrambling to be heard, a mess, but all in tune at the same time. The smell of food cooking in the apartment buildings: sauerkraut on one landing; the sweet smell of Palmer's Cocoa Butter mixed with cooking beans, fat-fried chicken, and rice on the next. I wish I had a jar labelled "New York in the Seventies" that I could open and spill onto these pages with the smells, sounds, life, blood, and energy of back then.

After the hectic rounds of the settling-in period, there would be gigs and rehearsals or workshops to prepare. Moki would once again unpack the sewing machine and the familiar hypnotic hum would fill the room. When my mother was working, her focus had a palpable intensity. The air around her head changed, like it was sucking her into a portal. Sitting with her back very straight, her head slightly tilted down, she was there beside us in our room, but somewhere else, too. So I would wander the corridors or play with Eagle-Eye, absorbed in our own imaginary worlds.

I believe that Don took me out walking to share his truths. He is one of the few people in my life who was always entirely and straightforwardly frank with me, whether I wanted to hear it or not. He would say, "When you do something bad, it comes back to you." He talked about karma, and it was as if the pieces of a puzzle found each other in my childish brain. *So that's what the bad feelings in my gut were when I had done or said something unkind.* Other things

Don taught me—about love, integrity, truth—without having to say a word.

Over at Astor Place, Don usually bumped into old friends. "Hey, man, I ain't seen that cat for a while. Last time we hung out, we smoked some bad shit," he'd say, laughing. My brother and I, snatching a glance at each other, thinking, *That's funny. They smoke shit?* After a catch-up and chat, we would cross over Broadway, past the subway stairs on the corner, warm, dry air blowing up a baked newspaper smell. Farther up on the corner of 8th Street and Sixth Avenue, there was a Gray's Papaya where we sometimes had chili dogs and papaya juice. On the other side, there at Greenwich and Sixth Avenue, was the New York Women's House of Detention, a grim dark cathedral of a prison. Once, Don took me to stand outside. We walked as close as we could. Then he reached into his shoulder bag for his flute and played for Angela Davis, who he said was "staying there a while." This was Don telling it how it was about many things: womanhood, racism, inequality, his love for Angela Davis's being, her words, her life. "Understand, be here and meet this tremendous, unstoppable, passionate, intellectual Black woman." We made that walk several times, paying respect to a queen in her tower. The sound of Don's flute must have soothed like medicine inside those prison walls.

One night, after a date with Don to see Earth, Wind and Fire at Madison Square Garden, he took me to eat at the Pink Tea Cup, one of the few soul-food restaurants downtown. Light pink walls, dusky with grease, pictures all over of some of the greats who had come through their doors: Malcolm X, Aretha Franklin, James Brown, Muhammad Ali, and more. A jukebox in the middle of the room, sweet music playing, mamas in the open kitchen. I had fried chicken and sides of greens and black-eyed peas; probably some sweet potatoes, too—food that would honestly save any lost soul, leaving me feeling warmed and loved.

But there was another piece to our New York puzzle. With horrible inevitability, one day or the next, Don would announce that he needed to go "take care of some business." He would leave us, disappear, go uptown to Harlem, and get high. All we could do was wait. Hours became days. Moki would become desperate, her anxiety levels through the roof. Sometimes throwing up was her only way out from the stress. It was terrifying, both the not knowing where Don was and whether he was safe, and watching Moki in such pain, barely able to control her fear or shield us from it.

One winter, when we were living in a sublet on 9th Street, she became ill with a dreadful flu. The atmosphere in our apartment grew heavy with worry and sickness. Eagle-Eye and I went out to play ball in the long, straight hallway, and that's where our fairy godmother, Wendall Harrington, found us and invited us to hers. We went to check with Moki and then Wendall took us upstairs, where she made a pot of chicken soup for our mother, full of heart and goodness, vegetables and succulent meat. That's when I first discovered I have a taste for chicken heart. After that day we could go up there whenever we wanted. She made cookies, dished up Pop Tarts. She let us watch TV. *A lot* of TV. Inside that box with its alien-insect antenna, we found security. Eagle-Eye and I knew all the right channels and their daily schedules by heart: *Soul Train* on a Saturday morning came after *Fat Albert*, one of the few all-Black cartoon shows. We tuned in for *The Woody Woodpecker Show*, *Popeye the Sailor*, *The Bugs Bunny Show*, *The Munsters*, *The Brady Bunch*, *I Dream of Jeannie*, *The Partridge Family*, *Gilligan's Island*. These programmes took us to Kool-Aid-coloured worlds, full of American promise, goof, and suburban mush, and held us tight. The commercials sold us Captain Crunch, G.I. Joe, Wise Potato Chips, and Wonder Bread, the softest squishiest bread, every loaf "wrapped warm from the oven," and my brother and I sang along to all the ads. We knew every word by heart.

•

We always travelled home to Sweden at the beginning of May, the early days of spring. I still get a feeling of wistfulness around that time of year, a memory that is awakened by birdsong, the smell of the garden stirring back to life. There would be a time of transition, of coming back and readjusting. We would unpack our bags, reaching first for the vinyl records we had brought home with us, music we had discovered on our stay. We also carried home the clamour of New York. Having longed to be back in the wild—this other freedom—we now hankered for that noise.

For the first few days, Don would retreat upstairs to the meditation room (which we always referred to as the "puja room"), to be sick, to kick it—to go through the process—cold turkey. Sweating, crying, throwing up. He was weak to the drug—but strong enough to stop when it was time. Moki would go up and come down again with a bucket full of excrement and vomit. We didn't ask any questions.

As soon as we got back to Tågarp, Eagle-Eye and I would be running wild outdoors. We played barefoot in the woods and fields, building moss castles and pretending we were cows. And soon, this contrast world would once again seem normal.

After a few days, Don would re-emerge—back in his body. Fragile but present. Warm and beautiful again. His hands—his fingers—are so clear in my mind. I always seem to retain such strong impressions of the hands of those that are gone. He would stand in the window at the front of the house, the floor there green with dark blue baseboards. In those days the record player was in that spot and we would listen to Chaka Khan, Stevie Wonder, the Temptations, and Earth, Wind and Fire. Picking up the needle, with a tear in his eye, Don would say, "Let's play 'Devotion' just one more time." The sound helped us to express the things we couldn't say with words. It was then that we had the deepest exchanges. There we felt pain, joy, longing for more, longing for less.

Music has been my constant companion, carrying me through the chapters of my life. The different eras are defined in the words, notes, tones, and melodies of the music as the dial moves around, up and down, through different sounds. Sometimes the songs tell it better than I ever could. A tune can throw me back in time to a place and a feeling, squeeze my heart to a standstill. Some of my deepest moments of belonging are within the walls of the music that unfolds around me as I dance, swaying, rocking, following my body. Just then, for a minute, three minutes, five minutes, everything makes sense. The beat did it, it had me, said it all. Music is the key.

•

In 1974, ABBA's *Waterloo* album came out. I had a friend from Malmö called Bodil, whose family had a weekend house down the road. Bodil and I spent most of our time outdoors every summer, but that year we prepared a show in which we mimed all of ABBA's songs. We worked ten hours a day on this performance.

I had a little transistor radio that Don had bought for me in New York. Under my pillow I had it tuned to Radio Luxembourg with Tony Blackburn. Bodil and I also used to listen to Radio Caroline, the offshore British pirate radio station. She was into the quintessentially British pop bands of the seventies, glam rockers like the Sweet and the glitter-stomping Slade, so I listened, too, while we played with Barbie dolls, pretending to be their wives.

I didn't have the money to buy lots of records but I did own a Donny Osmond album. All the girls at school were obsessed with Donny Osmond, so I went out to the record store in Hässleholm and bought it with my own money. I felt such a sense of achievement—as if I had joined the posse. But I will never forget Don's expression when I brought it home. He never said about any record, "You can't play that" or "This is shit." He didn't need to—his face said it all. Not sad, disappointed, or with disapproving eyes, but just with a very knowing look that said, *OK, Neneh. Have your five minutes with Donny, but this ain't it*. Sometimes he would say, "Oh, yeah? Well, here's another version of that song" or "Listen to this. These people have taken it from here." But he understood why I had bought Donny's bubblegum pop album, why I *needed* to have it. The lure of the music that my peers loved was too powerful to resist. I was following a stream, trying to fit in, but also trying to figure out who I was. He knew that.

HEADING WEST

September 1976. I was twelve. Don had rented a tiny unfurnished studio apartment on 14th Street in New York, a beehive of activity. One room, high ceiling. We had fold-up metal chairs and slept on mattresses that got packed away during the day. Moki found a card table on the street and this became our dining table. The toilet was a bunch of stalls down the hall.

The studio had huge windows with wide ledges. I would go out and sit there, dangle my legs, watch life pulsing hard. I would make up stories. Some of those tales have made it inside the songs I have written. I was particularly fascinated by the card hustlers. A dude shuffling, slick as a water rat. Two lookouts, one on the corner of University Place, the other farther up on 14th Street. A couple of guys in the crew, sidling up to watch. A cute woman reeling them in: "Come on, honey. Let's make your day." Pick the card: "Where's the red? Where's the red?" Once they were hooked—one win on the house—then bang, they'd do them. I watched it all unfold from my ledge.

Every day I took trips down to the stores, looking and longing. Not exactly sure what I was looking for, shedding the forest or seeking something to belong to: my culture, perhaps. In New York I could disappear in a sea of people of different colours—but in *my* colour. I could spread my wings and absorb Black culture.

There was one shop I always visited that sold small stuff: jewellery, hair accessories, cheap shit. Sometimes if I had some change, I could buy something. That's where I saw the girl in the light blue corduroy suit, with a white shirt and pale blue desert boots.

A little older than me, maybe fifteen or sixteen, this homegirl, this young teenage star, was the most beautiful girl I had ever seen. She had glowing dark ebony skin and the most amazing hair, like a crown—pressed, shiny and sleek, pulled up eyebrow-lift tight in a bun in separate rolls, all defined like it was an amazing cake. Divine. Long nails with clear polish and lots of silver bangles with lion heads at the ends—the look worn at the time by the coolest, strongest-looking girls. I wanted those bangles so much but could never afford them. I took in everything about her so I would never forget that beauty—how she carried herself, like a princess. She will never know this, but she was an absolute inspiration to me. I bought my own light blue corduroy suit and a white shirt. I could not even dream of doing my hair like hers, but I did my own version. That felt good, like finding *me*.

The sun was shining; we were off uptown to go see the bass maestro Charlie Haden. Don and Charlie had started out as band members in the Ornette Coleman Quartet, but would go on to play together throughout their lives. Eagle-Eye, Don, and I took the train to 96th Street on the Upper West Side, where Charlie lived on the sixteenth floor of a high-rise with his family: his wife Ellen, eight-year-old Josh, and the triplets, three robust girls, still babies, lying on the floor. As you entered the apartment, they would all roll over at once.

Eagle-Eye and I were excited. It was always fun to go visit other kids, even if they were younger than us. But Don and Charlie had some business to take care of in the bedroom.

"Hey, Neneh," said Charlie. "Can you stay with the kids for a minute?" Charlie's mouth had a little lean to one side when he spoke. I was happy to take responsibility. But they were gone so long. I went to the window and looked down. It felt unusual being so high up in the air. I started to understand that something was not right. The sun glaring against the buildings' facades felt ugly and hard and wrong. I felt a dread come over me. I wished it would rain. I tried to ease my misgivings by playing with the children. I was in charge, after all, so I held it down.

The brothers in the bedroom had been examining their veins, playing that game. On the sixteenth floor on 96th Street, death came into the room, sitting on Don's shoulder. The snakes were up in his veins, awake. And the sun would not stop shining. Don was high—*really* high. I saw and felt it for the first time. And I knew that it could kill him. That made me grow up.

On the journey back downtown, Don sat opposite Eagle-Eye and me on the long seat of the A train. He was nodding like he was sleeping. I took responsibility, kept calling him back out of his stupor. I did not want anybody to look at him and pass judgement; strangers who did not know, who didn't understand who he was, condemning him, when it was so much more complicated. I knew who he was and who he wanted to be.

Somehow, intuitively, I knew that he couldn't help it. I understood that sad thing in him and I forgave him from the minute I knew he was taking drugs. I think that's why I chose to be his protector. I didn't want to be angry about it. I just wanted it to be OK, so I was compelled to say, "It's OK. I forgive you. I am of you—I am of you—I am of you—you are allowed to be imperfect. It's OK."

But everything changed that day—the bliss of unknowing was no longer possible. This new truth was ugly, and it hurt. Eagle-Eye worshipped Don, and Moki and I, united in an unspoken agreement, committed to preserving his innocence. That was a strong instinct that needed no contemplation. I put myself in front of my brother, like a porous wall soaking up the toxins, and when I turned around to face him, I smiled with my eyes. I didn't want him to see what I knew. My anxiety levels were high and muted all at once because that is how we adapt. I normalised the constant fear that Don was going to die. He walked with a dark angel on his back. I decided to never judge him, so when Moki got really freaked out, struggling to breathe, when he didn't come home or when we thought he was lying dead somewhere, I didn't get angry with him, I got angry with her.

After that afternoon, I started staying awake at night. I needed to keep both eyes open. Seeing Don in front of the stamp-sized TV watching a late movie or basketball game, sometimes he would look like he was sleeping, floating away.

"Are you all right?" I would ask, pulling him back.

Nod, nod, nodding. The drugs would make his teeth grind. I guess he had been in this state around us before. In fact, I knew he had, but these odd mannerisms now registered for me. On the lookout, I saw and heard the signs.

Not many days later—just me, Eagle-Eye, and Moki in our room. It was late evening, time to eat dinner. We unfolded the card table and the metal chairs, and laid everything out together, complete with cloth. We sat down to eat. Then we heard steps in the hallway—Don was home! He came in carrying the washing from the laundromat and his trumpet. But something was not right.

"Don, what have you taken?" It was so bad that Moki had no time for any coded exchange to shield me and my brother. Our little space froze. I do not know how long we were there, immobilised, before Moki gave me a dime and told me to run down and phone Wendall. I sprinted to the telephone box on the corner of the street, dialled her number: "You have to come now. Don is sick."

I went out onto the window ledge, walking back and forth in panic, trying to breathe, watching for Wendall to come up the street. Moki was pacing the little space of our room, Don in her arms, keeping him moving. He threw up. Eventually, Wendall arrived. I took Eagle-Eye out around the corner and waited in a falafel joint. Wendall joined us, bought us something to eat. Then she swept us over to her apartment on 9th Street, tucked us in, lulled us to sleep.

The next morning, Moki called to tell Wendall that everything was OK. We could come back home. When we got there, Don and Moki were lying close together on their mattress, shipwreck survivors after a heavy storm. Don looked reborn, Moki tucked in next to him, a sheet covering her naked body. A new day. They were thankful, happy to see us. I didn't want to ask any questions. Seeing them together in bed, in love, was relief enough. But I knew that during the night they had just about clung on to the ropes on the life raft.

Moki and Don told us that they were sending us to LA to be with Don's mother. They said they loved us and it was better for us to be there. They took us to JFK a few days later. I was wearing my light blue corduroy suit and white shirt. Grandma Daisy lived with her mother, who we called Nana, on 130th Street in South Central, just off Avalon Boulevard. Meeting her, Nana, Don's sister Aunty Barbara, and my cousins taught me so much about the things that matter. They showed me that in the face of hardship and disappointment, resilience and love keep people together, and that family, however it's made, of blood or not, is *everything*. But it is not always simple.

Don's uncle Ernie picked us up from the airport in his big old Cadillac.

LA sun shining, taking in this new landscape, I asked him, "Where's the city?"

Uncle Ernie said, "*This* is the city."

Ernie was Don's favourite uncle. On the drive, he told us that he had once travelled the world with the merchant navy, been to Brazil, Cuba, Colombia, returning on leave with records in the trunk of his car—and some rum, to get the welcome-home party started. He told us that Don and Barbara would dance. Laughter, joy, music: Ernie brought just that to the party. Those records he brought home were a big part of opening Don's ears to different rhythms and energy, a whole world, the endless possibilities of music.

The moment we pulled up at the house, Grandma Daisy and Nana appeared at the netted porch door with the dogs, Poopy and Popcorn. The neighbourhood looked so tidy and nice. Everybody had separate houses with lawns out front, so different from New York.

Some boys were sitting on a stoop across the street. It was the neighbours' sixteen-year-old son, Larry Woods, and his friends. As I stepped out of Uncle Ernie's Cadillac, Larry and his crew welcomed me with a playful serenade of "Cinderella, oh, Cinderella, Cinderella." Awkward, shy, green—embarrassed, but kind of liking it. New York felt a million miles away, a mirage in the heat of LA's late-afternoon sun.

Larry stood up, crossed the street with a swagger. He was wearing baggy brown cords and a matching brown cap, and held a cane in one hand—not for a bad leg, just for effect. His boys, Dino and Ernest, followed close behind.

"Hey! My name is Larry."

"I'm Neneh."

"Nana?"

"No, Neneh."

"Oh, yeah. I heard you came from, where is it, Sweden?"

At that moment, for once, I felt utterly Swedish. As if I had dropped in from another planet. A little girl, just catching sight of my womanliness.

Soon it was dinner time (in our family, no gathering or arrival of guests is complete until we eat). After Grandma Daisy said grace, we drank cool, sweet homemade lemonade out of large plastic tumblers. We gulped it down greedily and had more. We ate greedily too, a big plateful of meat loaf, string beans, mashed potatoes, and gravy.

Chuckling, Nana said, "I made the meat loaf. That is the only thing I like to cook now, so it's the only thing I cook."

The little house had a living room, two bedrooms, a bathroom, a small kitchen painted aquamarine blue. Eagle-Eye and I were to share the foldout couch in the living room. Later, as I helped Grandma Daisy prepare our bed, I was exhausted. I just wanted to lie straight down but we did it properly, pulled and tugged, got the sheets just right, tucked the blankets in. I was lost on this new ground, my soul still in transit, yet to meet the bit of me that was there waiting. This whole day, which had begun in New York, felt like a dream.

Grandma Daisy put my hair into two braids and tied a headscarf around them, tight. Then, my eyes fuzzy from tiredness, it was just me and Eagle-Eye. We always had each other and here we would be fine. In our grandma's house we were bound by love. I missed my parents. I missed what I knew, but I wanted to be in this new place, too. Eagle-Eye's body turning in the bed like a clock, his little skinny bones next to mine, annoying but safe and familiar, I plummeted into sleep. I dreamed about Moki.

FIRST LOVE

The week we arrived in Los Angeles, Stevie Wonder released *Songs in the Key of Life*. I know every note, word, rise, and drop on that album. It was everywhere, inside everybody. For me, it became a private matter, took bits of my heart out and unlocked my own story in the narrative of its songs. Like so many others, I was the girl with the ebony eyes. The "Ordinary Pain" was my pain.

But being in LA was a revelation for the other senses, too. I remember the strange soft light of this desert city: red sunsets, smoggy, clogged, and beautiful. For a place so polluted, it smelled so good. Everything I ate tasted otherworldly, the flavours somehow intensified. I felt my body, my brownness, the touch of my clothes on my skin. The time spent there was a vital lifeline. Starting to consciously push outwards and yet looking in at the same time, feeling, needing, wanting, I found parts of myself that were starved and lonely. I needed to be where I was Black, to feel that sense of inclusion.

The arms of Daisy and Nana, our grandmothers, enfolded me. There was instant love and the feeling of being home right there in that embrace. I let go, found my groove, latched myself to something of the soul, plain and strong.

Don's grandma Nana had lived in a little house in the back garden since the Watts riots in 1965. She had been a nurse, played piano for silent movies, ran speakeasies, was famous for her Choctaw beer, and married four times. Her last husband was a white man. I heard she had loved him most of all, but after the riots they couldn't make it. He could not live there, and she could not leave her home, which was then burned to the ground.

We got to hang out with our cousins, my sister Jan, and brother David, Don's children with Carletta. Music again was our bond: the tunes on a record player in the house, the songs that followed us on the car radio out driving. The family paraded Eagle-Eye and me around the hood like mascots to meet-and-greets with the friends and neighbours of the whole Cherry tribe. I loved driving with Aunty Barbara and my cousins Karen and Lisa, the radio blasting out Johnny "Guitar" Watson's "Ain't That a Bitch."

"Hmmm," Aunty Barbara would say. "Don't sing that, it's bad. Listen to 'Superman Lover.' Sing that instead. That's nice."

I got my hair done at Aunty Mabel's beauty parlour. My natural curls were replaced by loose straightened hair, which was then re-curled: not pressed but stressed by the dryer. It was the first time I wore my hair like that, and I felt like I had joined the sisterhood. This was the depths of the seventies when Afros, naturals, and beaded braids were all the rage. Everybody was looking for lost roots and so much was expressed through taking pride in our natural hair. And yet there in Watts, suddenly rid of my unruly bush, it felt new, strange and cool.

I started sleeping with candy-pink foam curlers, wearing them for most of the day, covered in bandanas of different shades. The curlers were the shit: a fashion statement in themselves. Because of my mixed blood, everyone commented that I had "good hair." This made me sad, singled out, embarrassed. I didn't want my hair to be better than Lisa's or anyone else's. It was not better. What is better hair? When I think about where this seed sprang from, a fury starts to grow in me.

Dangling on the brink of adolescence, I was at an age where I was longing, though it's hard to say what I was longing for. For love? For contact? Needing to be needed? I have watched my own daughters reach that age, staring into empty space, dreams flickering behind their eyes. I fell in love for the first time and, as happens with those agonising first crushes, I fell hard for Larry Woods. His eyes cut into me, saw bits of me that, in a way, I had no idea I possessed.

Larry reeled in my innocent ass like a cat playing with a mouse, though no doubt a bit more gently. We started talking through the fence. His sister Janita and I were around the same age and we hung out, too, doing the funky chicken outside their house in our slippers—I had fluffy yellow fake-fur house shoes in the shape of baby chicks. There were steps to learn. Everybody was down with the latest dances, the music oozing out from every corner. I felt different and I didn't. What did being Swedish mean, anyway? "Is that where they make cuckoo clocks?" they asked me. "What dances do they do there?" I said we didn't have any Swedish dances I could show them. "Strange," they said. We danced, regardless.

I began to gravitate towards the Woodses' residence. Larry flirted, told me how fine I was. The first kiss happened the first time I passed through the doors of his house. Past the sideboard holding the record player, stacked with albums ready to fall as soon as the previous one had played the last track. Barry White's "I Can't Leave You Alone." In the open-plan kitchen, I leaned against a cupboard. A record drops, Parliament-Funkadelic plays, Larry talks. George Clinton sings about that funky stuff. Larry says something smooth: "You so fine." I don't exactly know if I believed him but, still, the notion tasted like chocolate. He moved in. Closer, closer, nowhere to go and there it was, all the elements melting. The mothership landing—funky stuff—brown corduroy kissed my bare legs. His lips stuck to mine, struck me down. All in, I fell.

The bedrooms were at the back, a red bulb in the lightshade, dark and soft. I ended up there one night: a close call. As the clock struck, I ran. In early summer that same year, I had started bleeding. I had my period that night, so I was wearing a pair of my grandma's huge white cotton underpants up to my belly button. I could not be seen or handled in them. But I was in love, wanting and wanting to be wanted—and I was ready.

When, eventually, I went back into the bedroom, the red light in the ceiling was still burning. My body in the dark gave way. I gave way. I just did it. I don't know if I liked it. Scared but not frightened, my mind was racing, wondering in a self-conscious way if I was doing it right. I was basically still a child—so young, thinking I was old, thinking I knew it all, wanting to know nothing at all. I was so full of myself, so impatient and yearning.

•

Moki and Don were finally joining us in Watts. At LAX they put a dime in the phone booth and called to say they had landed. They would get in a taxi and be with us soon. Eagle-Eye and I took up position at the window looking out at 130th Street, waiting for their cab to appear. Having been away from our parents for over two months, we were so excited, pushing, jostling and wrestling, waiting and listening. Where were they?

Our noses glued to the window, we watched as a long black shiny vehicle, black-glass windows, came crawling up the street, slow and sleek: a limousine! Not an everyday sight in Watts. It inched closer and came to a halt right in front of our gate. This limousine was vast. It seemed bigger than Grandma Daisy's house.

We could just see the driver's starched white shirt gleaming through the windscreen. He stepped out, went to open the rear door, but before he got there, I saw the top of Don's donso ngoni case and his hat as our parents appeared, first Don and then Moki. Those deep familiars, a vivid burst of colour, such a contrast to the hard black limo and its monochrome driver. Moki was wearing her famous Bedouin cape. The whole neighbourhood stopped in its tracks to take in the scene.

"Oh, that must be Mrs. McKee's son and wife," they murmured.

Eagle-Eye and I erupted out into the street in euphoria. Our parents were there at last. Two plus two equals four. They smelled like home.

And the limo? That was courtesy of Lou Reed. A fan of Moki and Don, who he had first seen playing with Ornette Coleman in New York in the early sixties, Lou had introduced himself when they bumped into each other at LAX. After niceties, he had invited Don to play that night at his show at the Roxy in West Hollywood. Then he asked where my parents were staying. "Take one of my limos," he told Don. "The driver will drop you off and pick you up in time for the show."

That night, December 1, 1976, Don joined Lou Reed onstage for the first time, no rehearsal. It was the beginning of a long collaboration and relationship. Don always had his feet in an open space, trying different things, going out beyond his comfort zone—he played with everyone, from Coltrane to Ian Dury and the Blockheads. In the late sixties he had sat in with Jimi Hendrix at Steve Roney's psychedelic club in Stockholm. Later, Steve gave me the recording on an old-school reel-to-reel tape. I kept it safe in a studio lock-up for years, and my stepson Marlon had it in his care for some time. But somewhere in the many moves of our life, it vanished. I wake up some nights in a cold sweat as the tape's loss creeps into my consciousness. My prayer is that it will come back someday.

This was the first time that Moki had been to Don's home, and his folks loved her instantly, especially Grandma Daisy. Moki always said that she didn't really know what love was until she went there. She had a way of carrying herself that meant she could pretty much go anywhere and fit in any place: interested, contained, respectful. When she returned to Watts in 1978, she painted the living room. She planted a small pot of rosemary out the back of Don's father's house, where Aunty Barbara now lives. It has grown into a bush. Her enthusiasm and creative energy came from her heart, so people received it as a gift rather than an interference.

Moki made good in the hood. She took walks down 130th Street to Vons supermarket. Not many—in fact, no—white women walked around there, especially dressed like her, but Moki knew no bounds. Anyway, everybody on the block knew the white lady walking around was Daisy and Nana's kin.

Grandma Daisy talked to Don in a way that no one else did. "Donald. Do this. Do that," she would order, and he would answer her, humble and obedient, like a child once more, "Yes, Mamma." To Eagle-Eye, this change in his dad seemed absurd. He later told me that seeing Don as somebody's son, he realised what it meant to be a child, what it meant to be a parent.

I treasure a photograph from that December in Watts, us filling our plates at the table in the blue kitchen: Eagle-Eye, my cousin Lisa in her curlers, Don wearing a top with a shirt collar and tie printed on the front, and me in braids. I look at it now, try to peer into the serving bowls, wondering what we were eating. Every time I go back to that photo, I hope that the angle has somehow miraculously changed so I can finally see what Grandma Daisy cooked for us that day. I could taste the love in every meal my grandmother prepared. It was in the crispy skin of the fried chicken that Daisy would leave in the cast-iron pan on the stove by the back door. She had done this a thousand times and more, but when I bit into it, it always felt like I was eating it for the first time. I crave that food, I crave togetherness, to have them with me, the ones that are now gone: Moki, Don, Grandma, Nana. Beautiful cravings.

When the visit came to a close, Aunty Barbara and Karen drove us all to LAX. It was one of those steamy, slightly misty LA nights. Yellow streetlight, rising heat, leaving love. My heartbeat in my throat, I left the warmth of that home, the family, the smog, the block. I left Larry, soft lips mixed in with tongues, doing the bump.

From the airport, I rang him one more time. In my bag I had a stack of records that held that small section of life and all those feelings together in songs: Earth, Wind and Fire, our beloved Johnny "Guitar" Watson, Parliament, and the Bible, Stevie Wonder's *Songs in the Key of Life*. This little pile of vinyl was a mountain of truth. I had come of age in LA. An internal shift, an alteration that was meant to be. Adolescence had entered my body.

PART TWO

With my siblings Titiyo and Cherno, Ahmadu, and my Gbinti Jah family • My first braids in Sierra Leone • Taking the subway with Ari, New York • The Rip Rig + Panic crew • Eight months pregnant, eighteen years old • Sean Oliver's send-off, the Tabernacle, West London • One of the test shots that got me the Japan modelling trip with the Buffaloes

LONDON

In November 1978, Moki and I left Tågarp for New York, via London. First, we were getting the 24-hour booze cruise from Gothenburg to Harwich. From Harwich we were bound for London, and from London, next stop, New York. Moki had got us on the cheapest flight. It was the first time in a long while that I was travelling on my own with her. I liked that. And this time we were headed in a new direction, off-piste.

As we pulled away from the docks of Sweden, I had a strange feeling: I wasn't just going—I was leaving. And I was allowing something inside to melt away. I'd been angry at Moki a lot lately, because I didn't know who else to be angry with. Now I felt a little bit more grown up. I had put my hands up and surrendered, abandoning the teenage game I had been playing.

That past year, I had lost my shit for a while. No doubt I have always had a bit of a wild streak, looking for risk. Teenage me was scared, awkward, vulnerable. I tried to be bigger than my fear. I wore a brave face—no cracks. I had been drawn to the kids at school who were exploring the periphery: the bolder, louder ones testing the boundaries. I started hanging out with the local raggare crowd, a weird breed of throwbacks, spawned in the fifties when, thanks to the Marshall Plan, American music and films dominated pop culture. Swedish teenagers fell hard in love with the teen rebels in the movies, and consumed the lifestyle and fashion wholesale. The raggare boys were all Jimmy Dean wannabes with their Wranglers and black leather jackets, driving big American cars, maybe some hooch in the boot. The girls were all back-combed hair or high ponytails, cinched waists and skintight pencil skirts, towering stilettos and bright red lipstick.

In my case, the action took place in Hässleholm's town parking lot. My buddies and I were way too young to drive but, if we were lucky, someone would offer us a ride. After spinning around, burning rubber, the cars would line up and we'd crack open some beers, stretch the denim, and . . . that was it. It seemed very cool at the time, but this "edgy" universe was in fact quite limited and also fundamentally racist. Let's just say they were flying the Confederate flag. I am not sure what in the hell I was doing in that world. I guess it was the most risqué posse I could find.

At school I'd started to frequent the *rokruta*, the "smoking box." If you wanted to be someone, the *rokruta* was where it was at. It was a space to hang out, mark our turf, blow smoke at the weeds, look for wings. It was almost romantic: "Don't mess with the wild ones!"

I became friends with an older girl in ninth grade. She wore a cut-off sleeveless denim jacket with a toothbrush in the top pocket, and her family brewed their own hooch. I was in awe. I cut off the sleeves from my denim jacket, ironed a Harley-Davidson patch on the back, popped a toothbrush in the breast pocket, too. She knew a lot of the Hässleholm raggare crowd. Included in that tribe, I took cover, and felt pretty damn roughneck.

From Hässleholm, the raggare would gravitate to a couple of discos on the lake outside town. It was at one of these that I met Benny. He was my first Swedish boyfriend. In fact, he is the only Swedish boyfriend I have ever had. I knew boys liked me, but my colour was an issue: most guys didn't have the nerve to go out with "that girl" and draw that kind of attention to themselves. But it wasn't a concern for Benny. He had a sweetness about him, a round face, a cheeky smile. He was a catch: a cute, cool, double-denim dude. He gave me a necklace, a bullet on a chain. You could unscrew it and inside he had written our names on a little piece of paper. I was besotted. Then someone passed me a note in class. It was from Benny, writing to say that he was breaking up with me. It hurt.

•

Late-night Hässleholm, waiting in the queue by the hot dog stand on the roundabout, just by the Biografen Park that's gone now, I could feel the man's stare, smell his beery breath. There it is: *neg-erfitta*, "nigger cunt." Had I yet turned thirteen? He could shave twice a day if he wanted to. He had a job, maybe kids at home.

I know I was ashamed, embarrassed, aware of the people behind me in that queue clutching at their own reactions. Did they pity me? A small town, in a country where people have deep issues with confrontation, no one had the courage to speak up. I lacked the nerve to say something back. But I did not bend. I do not bend. I sang through a hole in my belly, made a spike with my spine, stood up straight and looked square at him. I showed him I was not scared. I needed him to be a coward. The other people in the line probably felt a sense of relief, because I had taken the insult in the right way. I had made it OK. But was that my responsibility?

I recognised early other people's discomfort about who I was. This was my daily reality, and so I was always a kind of warrior. I saw it as my job to resolve their unease by being able to deal with it. It was like constantly being tested. Can we tease, pull, steal? Is she one of the ones that breaks? Will she? No, no give. She is all right, let her in.

When I started eighth grade in August 1978, my plan had been to stay for the whole year. I had it in my head that I had to remain in Sweden, be with my friends, not to miss out, do the normal thing for once and see school all the way through to the end of ninth grade. It seemed the most important thing in the world. However, even though Moki worried about how hard it was for my brother and me to keep moving around, she wanted us to be with her and Don in New York. They had found a loft to rent on the corner of Vernon Boulevard in Long Island City. It would be our first long-term "home" in America.

But I was insistent—I was staying.

She was due to leave for New York that November. Don and Eagle-Eye had already gone, so it was just me and Moki in the house. It was a Saturday morning. I had been out the night before. I had slept with Moki in her bed and woken up horribly hungover. I must have made myself drink loads of water before bed because, when I went downstairs, I puked it up all over the floor. I felt awful, empty, hopeless.

Later that morning, I was lying next to Moki, watching TV, when it hit me. I shouldn't stay there after all.

"I want to come to New York with you," I told her. She was mightily relieved.

Even when she thought I wasn't right, there was always space for a dialogue. She always listened. Maybe she had just waited, knowing that this is what the teenage years are all about, figuring things out: fighting it out, on your own terms, for better or for worse. Moki went to my school. When she explained that I was not going to finish the term, the teacher said, "Good. Take her away. Whatever she is on this planet to do, it's not going to happen here."

At the time, I didn't fully understand why I decided to leave. In retrospect, I think that I had realised I was on a path to self-destruction. At home I would listen to Dr. John, Marvin Gaye, Billie Holiday, Alice Coltrane, and Stevie Wonder records with Don, and dream away with the music. But when I went out, I felt I had to prove a point. Listen to what the rest were listening to, be into what everyone else was into—cruising in boys' cars, smoking, dancing to "Miss You" by the Rolling Stones. Sure, that was not all bad. Textbook teenager, I guess. But gradually, as I went deeper into that character, I found I could no longer just go home and hang up the uniform. It was a bit like I had been leading two different lives. And that came at a price. It was hard work to have that duality. I was exhausted . . . But there was also something in the dynamic of those contrasts that, no doubt, was the making of who I am. The exposure to different cultural influences *has* to be a good thing.

Perhaps the break-up with Benny and the incident with the guy at the hot dog stand had also played into that unravelling. Maybe a part of me did not know how to navigate Sweden anymore—to be so much of a place but also a stranger. But I hope it was more than that, too. I hope it was also my backbone asserting itself. That morning, lying in bed beside Moki, I had a very strong instinct to save myself. I knew there was a whole world of possibility out there. So, for now, I cut the cord with Sweden.

•

Although I had never set foot in Britain, I'd dreamed and imagined what this weird island with all the great music was like. My relationship with the country was formed of sonic impressions and quirky, pale images from television. That is where it all started. We got a lot of British TV programmes in Sweden. I loved *Monty Python*. I had become slightly obsessed with "English culture," without knowing exactly what that meant, but through the music, especially, I had imagined what London might look like. I wondered if there were punks.

We must have stayed in London for only two or three days, but I was instantly smitten with the city, fascinated especially by the mundane things: fish and chips, orange cordial, the bottled milk that miraculously appeared on doorsteps each morning, Branston Pickle, pickled eggs, olive oil for medicinal use in doll-sized bottles. These foreign things, so particular to this place called

England, were new discoveries for me. Unremarkable, yet still so beguiling.

On our last day, we went to the King's Road. Public Image Ltd were supposed to be performing on some rooftop, but they didn't turn up. The band was the first thing John Lydon did after he quit the Sex Pistols in January that year and they had just put out their first single, "Public Image." To make up for the no-show, we went back to where we were staying—with our friends Leigh and Lee, who we knew from New York. Leigh had a record player in her bedroom and a stack of 7-inch singles. She put on Public Image, and then we listened to the Clash. Overnight, I became a punk. The next morning Leigh dyed my hair bright red with Crazy Color.

I was too young to know what I wanted to do or where I wanted to end up, but after that first visit, I left London with fire in my hair, knowing that I really wanted to go back. I wanted to be English. I had even tried to pick up an English accent on that short stopover.

What if we had not gone via London, if we had flown straight to New York? Would my life have taken a completely different course? I had got to London just at the tail end of punk's heyday. That worked just fine for me.

I had been trying to be invisible—trying to blend in—when, of course, in Sweden I couldn't. And while being in the States would always be a relief because it was a place of colour, even there I still didn't entirely fit in because of being Swedish and from an unconventional background. I had always been aware of my in-between-ness.

But after that first time in London, I never felt compromised in the same way again. With punk, even though it was a very white phenomenon, I had this door to go through to a place where I wasn't hiding. Yes, I was a Black punk, but I could also be me, Neneh, full stop. It was a chance to carry all the parts of me. I peeled off my horrible raggare denim jacket and turned myself inside out.

THE LOFT

Our loft on the corner of Vernon Boulevard in Long Island City was on the top floor of an empty industrial unit, which until very recently had housed a fake-fur factory, part of which was still in use. It was an enormous hangar of a place, with seventeen windows that looked out on the Queensboro Bridge. The East River was right there, just a stone's throw away. Perfectly delineated against the sky, all of Manhattan stood before us like a toy theatre cut out of paper by a steady hand. From our perspective, the Big Apple looked compact.

We were pioneers in Long Island City. Loft living was still mainly a downtown Manhattan phenomenon, but it was starting to become expensive there. We were only the second people to move into the building, arriving simultaneously with Ernie Brooks, the former bass player of the Modern Lovers, and Winnie, his then partner, and her son Josh. Ernie still lives in the building. He is the last of the original 44th Drive tribe. Together, he and Moki sandblasted all the wooden beams and floors in both our lofts at the height of the New York summer. It was 100 degrees Fahrenheit in the shade.

Long Island City was like some forgotten community. There you were, looking out across the East River at this amazing skyline, but nobody in our neighbourhood ever seemed to go to Manhattan. They just looked at it from a distance: "Yo! That's the city." From the 23rd and Ely subway station, our building was straight down 44th Drive. Under the Queensboro Bridge to the north lay the Queensbridge projects. Up to the right, along Vernon

Boulevard, was an old-school Italian neighbourhood populated by grannies who couldn't speak anything but southern Italian dialect. Back down by the train station was a block of apartments housing the local Latino community. And farther down near the loft, it was more industrial, with a few social clubs, garages, and several limousine companies that were probably run by the Mafia. That whole neighbourhood has since been gentrified but then, in the late seventies, our block was desolate.

When I arrived with Don and Eagle-Eye for the very first time, the loft was entirely empty, apart from Eagle-Eye's bedroom, which Moki had built to look like a truck made of massive metal Meccano pieces. The only other furniture was a rented grand piano. In those early times at the loft, Allen Ginsberg and Don often sat at that piano, working and talking together.

Moki was a genius at bringing environments to life. She quickly acquired a long table and bought some folding chairs, and gradually she filled the space with items purchased at the Volunteers of America thrift store or found and gifted by the streets of New York. I can still see Don coming down Vernon Boulevard from the 7 train with the donso ngoni on his back, his trumpet bag on his shoulder, and a found chair on his head.

The loft was not insulated and, during winter, the vast windows let in blasts of icy air. The heating in the building was still set to factory hours, so in the morning, after another freezing night, when the pipes clanked back into action, someone's voice from under the covers would cry, "The heat's ON!" During the coldest months, sometimes we begged the janitor so hard he would take mercy on us and let the heating stay on; otherwise, we kept the gas burning on high in the oven, all of us sitting around the stove. When people came for dinner, we sat at the table in coats and gloves.

Back in the city, Don once more became a ghost. Not solid anymore, see-through, lost to us. The maybe of his presence. The real

Don was inquisitive, vivid, alive, the kind of person who, without needing to be a leader, was always in a central role. But when he was high, his face changed, his temperament was altered, like in a horror film when someone is possessed by a demon. Once again, he would say, "I'm going to go and take care of some business," then disappear and spend all our cash. Moki started to hide money from him, but then couldn't remember where she'd put it.

I was scared of the what-if, of all the things that could go wrong. I was scared that my dad might not come back, that he might die. One day he went off on his roller skates and didn't come home. We didn't see him until late the following day. He'd been arrested in Tompkins Square Park and held overnight. The next morning, he had to attend court in his socks because the roller skates were all he had. The young judge recognised him and threw out the charge.

"Oh, Mr. Cherry. What are you doing here? Please go home," she said, handing him a subway token from her handbag so he could get back to Long Island City. He told it like a funny story and we laughed, but of course it wasn't funny. Really, we laughed to keep from crying.

Moki sometimes spiralled away in her own panic, under too much pressure. When that happened, I would hold Eagle-Eye close, guarding him with my life. I did not want him to experience my terror. Sometimes I would take him over to Manhattan. We would step out of the subway onto Fifth Avenue, my little brother's hand in mine. There, in Chanel land, the sidewalks bustling with affluent Manhattanites going about their day, the world somehow felt more undemanding, structured, controlled, safe.

We liked to wander around the department stores, stopping at the famous FAO Schwarz toy store to slobber over delights we were never likely to get: a giant plush giraffe the size of an actual baby giraffe, teddies as big as a real-life brown bear. Eagle-Eye had an ongoing dream relationship with a go-kart—he even wrote a song about it. Occasionally we went to the brand-new Citycorp Center. Downstairs a shop sold ruby-red fresh strawberries dipped in thick, shiny, dark chocolate. When I had a dollar, I would buy a couple for us to share, then head up to Central Park.

We were on one of those little trips when we met Muhammad Ali. Up by 57th Street, there stood a figure on the corner, a few people around him. He was wearing a light-blue suit with a white shirt. "Look! Look! That's Muhammad Ali!" I told Eagle-Eye.

I was into boxing. I loved the Motor City Cobra, Muhammad Ali, Joe Frazier, and Sugar Ray. I used to watch the fights on TV, my heart all over the place seeing these powerful great Black men throwing punches. They were fighting for a lot more than just a championship title. In the ring they ruled, no one telling them "You are not allowed to be here." That wasn't their experience in the outside world.

He towered over everybody. He was beautiful, gleaming. We went up close, waiting our turn. He was talking to one of the older ladies, being cute with his arm around her. I stuck out my arm and asked, "Yo! Can you just write on my arm?" Ali said, "Girl, if I write on your arm, it's gonna wash off! And if I'm writing my name, you wanna keep it forever because I'm the King! I'm the King!"

"Oh," I said. "Well, I don't have any paper, so—"

He took me under his arm. "Come with me, girl. I'm the King."

I put my arm around his waist. I will never forget his vastness—his suit was skintight. Pulling me and skinny little Eagle-Eye along with him, we walked out into the street. "Come on! You coming with the King! I'm the King!" he pronounced.

"And I'm the Queen," I replied.

New York was crazy around that time, but Muhammad Ali—that was quite an event.

•

Back at home, to cheer up my mother and expend nervous energy, I'd start cleaning, wash the dishes, put the loft in order, trying to create balance, to pretend the dread wasn't there. It worked, sort of. Moki was appreciative of my efforts to distract and calm us both, but she was also a stickler. After I'd done the washing-up, she would still remind me to wipe the sink down. She couldn't help herself. Her creed: if you're going to do something, do it right.

NEW YORK PUNK

At fourteen I ended my formal education.

My parents valued curiosity and learning above almost anything else. Evidently, though, they were not traditionalists in matters of schooling. Eagle-Eye *had* to go to school—he was still only nine. But there in Long Island City, I begged Moki and Don for some time out before starting a new school. No doubt they didn't take the decision lightly, but in the end they allowed me to take a short break. And well, as it turned out, I'm still on it . . .

Moki fed me a constant stream of books: the works of Isaac Bashevis Singer and James Baldwin, *The Autobiography of Malcolm X*, *One Hundred Years of Solitude*, *Crime and Punishment*. I read them all. And I started to feel like myself again. The words in those books made worlds where everything was possible, opening up little spaces in my teenage brain that wanted to think it had all the answers.

•

In the loft, Don played trumpet, the donso ngoni, and the piano. The dominant sounds, however, came from the rest of the inhabitants in the building playing new wave. When Talking Heads were rehearsing—Chris Frantz and Tina Weymouth lived downstairs—the place shook.

I have always had a love affair with bass, although I wasn't particularly musical as a kid. Eagle-Eye was given a grey drum kit when he was just three years old. He loved it, even though he was so small that his feet didn't touch the floor when he sat down to play. One day, he lost his balance and fell off, knocking out a milk tooth on the side of the snare drum. He also played the piano. I mostly just got frustrated when Don tried to teach me. I would lose my shit when I hit a wrong key. But Tina made me want to play an instrument for myself. She gave me my first bass, a red Fender Mustang. I started a band with my friend Natasha, who had moved into a loft at the other end of our building. Her stepdad, Jerry Harrison, had been in the Modern Lovers and was now guitarist for Talking Heads. Jerry had a rehearsal room below their loft, where Natasha and I practised our tentative bass and drum creations.

New York had its own music scene, of course, but fresh from my London awakening, I still thought that the Clash, the Sex Pistols, and Public Image Ltd were everything. We bought all our clothes from thrift shops. I wore my hair out, big, in that Crazy Color red, and I had a camouflage coat that I still have today. I found a pair of German combat boots that were very narrow at the toe and too small, but I squeezed my feet into them and suffered, walking like Frankenstein's monster to break them in. Those boots were just so perfect I had to own them—blisters and all.

Dressing became experimental. I wasn't doing it to fit in; I was doing it to feel free. We were doing our thing and doing it our way. I blossomed: proud, young, Black, Swedish, wishing I was English. I was immediately cut loose and a little louder. Fire-red hair, the colour of African soil. My attitude solid. I wanted to be seen.

I started going out to clubs with Natasha. She was only twelve—two years younger than I was. Babies in a big city. Moki and I had an understanding. She trusted me to make sensible decisions—and I tried, mostly. There were rules, for sure, lines I could not cross, but I knew that if I toed them correctly, more freedom was to be had. When I went out at night, for example, I had to keep a dime in my pocket for the phone booth, so I could call Moki at a certain time. This I always did, right on the money. She would also give me cash for a cab home—15 bucks—and the rule was no train rides back alone. But many nights I spent that money and took the subway, travelling on those dawn-of-the-dead trains carrying exhausted workers who'd just clocked off at last from a late shift, bodies that had no beds, or just packs of kids like us, needing to get indoors before daylight.

We'd head down to the Mudd Club or Danceteria, first at 252 West 37th Street, then in its later incarnation as a four-floor venue at 30 West 21st Street (where the young Madonna worked as an elevator operator), whining at the doormen until they allowed us in. Natasha would shout, "My dad is in Talking Heads. Let us in!" We had no shame. Standing outside in the cold, feeling the smoky, warm, sweaty air leaking out with the beats as other people were let in, we leaned on the ropes, possessed by the promise held inside. No way were we going to give up.

Some of the doormen *did* want us to come in, I guess because we brought something that they wanted in the house. Tier 3—a small but very cool, friendly post-punk venue run by Hilary Jaeger at 225 West Broadway—became our home away from home.

Compared to the super-hip New York club scene, Tier 3 had a more underground vibe. It was spread over three floors and had once been a bar and grill. Natasha and I mostly hung out downstairs, in what would once have been the dining room, where there was a bar, a low stage (due to the low ceilings), a dance floor, and the DJ booth, on which Jean-Michel Basquiat had painted a mural. On the second floor, they screened films and held art and photography shows. The third storey had a dance floor with a disco ball. Hilary booked an eclectic mix of bands—hard punk rock, free jazz, new wave, ska, and reggae—among them 8 Eyed Spy, Richard Hell and the Voidoids, Bush Tetras, and the Lounge Lizards. The Bad Brains, the legendary Black group from DC pioneering hardcore punk with a reggae twist, also used to play there. In 1979 and 1980, this was where it was at—punk had started to cross over with other genres, and reggae was a big part of that evolution.

Soon after the red, I bleached my hair peroxide blond. I didn't really care whether anyone liked how I looked or not. What mattered was that it felt good. In fact, I felt badass. I made friends within the walls of Tier 3. A few of us lived across the bridge in Long Island City; others lived elsewhere in Queens. We all had each other's backs on those ghost trains home, but not before we'd been to Dave's 24-hour diner on Canal Street. We would all squeeze into a booth and order two plates of French fries to soak up the night. I'd slip any leftover packets of Heinz ketchup into my pocket. I loved it and liked to carry spares.

Soon an Irish bar on the Bowery became our meeting spot. It had once been a dance hall, no doubt quite grand, but now they'd serve just about anybody or anything and the drinks were cheap. It had the crumbling feel of somewhere that had once upon a time been full of promise, but where everyone had stayed too long, never gone home, and been trying to drink the place dry for a century.

One night, I was dancing hard in someone's storefront home (a lot of people lived in low-rent, former commercial properties in those days) when a song came on, two girls singing a reggae tune called "Uptown Top Ranking." I begged the young woman in charge of the record player to please, please play it again. It's a sweet tune, but I heard in it something lovingly militant: because they were women singing, and because I was looking for guidance. The imprint that song made on me that night stuck in the collection of things that gave me my voice.

We saw Madness at Hurrah. We went to CBGB before it was known as the legendary New York venue, when it was just another scruffy joint. It had quite an open music policy; it wasn't geared just to punk. There was experimental rock music, B bands who were passing through town—even some arena acts playing unadvertised sets, just for the cred. I saw the rock-chick California band the Runaways there; John Cale, too. The house was full, but it doesn't stick in my memory as a particularly great night out, except that at one point Cale left the stage and disappeared off to the bathroom. He was gone for a while and someone shouted, "He's downstairs somewhere, probably OD-ing on his ego."

On a hot sticky evening during the transit strike in 1980, Natasha and I walked from Long Island City across the 59th Street Bridge to the Lone Star Cafe to see James Brown. At some point after we'd reached Manhattan, we bought over-the-counter asthma meds to speed up the process a little. James Brown was red-hot that night. He'd brought two tour buses full of musicians from the deep south, far too many for the little stage. Some of them were nearly falling off the edges. But with his best man standing in the wings, ready to wrap him in the legendary cape, Mr. Brown found the space to wipe the floor clean with his moves.

Underground clubs had started popping up on the Lower East Side. These were expressive free havens where there was room for different music and sexualities. Of course, people were doing a lot of drugs. Natasha and I couldn't afford any. We were so skint we'd be begging someone to buy us a screwdriver, but almost everyone else on the dance floor had these little glass vials around their necks and the toilets were full of people snorting cocaine. And yet there was something oddly innocent about the culture. People started bands without being able to play instruments properly, but they had a lot to say. It was fun and spontaneous. Others launched small record labels and fanzines. Anybody who wanted to do something could. A lot of music was born out of this world.

It was only when I started listening to punk, and to the singer Poly Styrene in particular, that I began to sing. At home a day didn't go by without music, and often Eagle-Eye and I would be onstage with our parents during performances, singing and dancing alongside them. But other than my bass meanderings at the loft with Natasha, I was a listener.

I loved listening to singers like Roberta Flack, Rose Norwalt of Rose Royce, and Syreeta Wright, and I've always loved Minnie Riperton. These women made me feel and think, but theirs were not the voices that initially led me to find mine. Of course, I sang along with their records, but they were queens, way out of my league. With punk, other things felt possible. Singing along with Poly Styrene, I felt I could. There were so few Black people on the punk scene. She was a woman, so I felt a natural connection. Her spirit was inspiring. I was proud of her and she made me proud of myself. I took refuge in our likeness, making our way in a world that offered so few paths for us. For forging that road, chanting your verse, making my heartbeat stronger, I thank you, Poly, my brown sister.

It was Don who gave me the prompt to sing. After I had blasted out "The Day the World Turned Day Glo" yet another time in Tågarp, he said, "Try this." He liked to buy sheet music for old standards and play them on the piano. This time, for some reason, he chose "Put Another Nickel in the Nickelodeon"—I'm sure he had an instinct. He played the piano, and I sang. In fact, I kind of belted it. It was as if I'd been released. That's when I first dared to stretch out. That's what you have to do when you sing. Singing is a practice that requires freedom and discipline. It's both internal and expansive. I listen to the music, go in, feel the truth of the words, trust—and let go.

AFRICA

In January 1979, just two months shy of my fifteenth birthday, I met my family in Sierra Leone for the first time. My father, Ahmadu, had long dreamed of making this trip. He was constantly homesick and he missed his mother, his family, but he also wanted his wife, Maylen, and his children—me, Titiyo, and Cherno—to know where he, and we, came from, and for our family there to know us.

But a couple of days before I was meant to leave, I had a full-blown panic attack.

Moki knew me better than anyone. I hardly recognised her quiet perseverance when I tried to argue with her, screaming, "I don't want to go!"

"Neneh, you must go. You have to."

She listened, but she didn't take any of my shit. It was not up for discussion. I thank God for her wisdom. By our kitchen table she held me in her arms where it was safe and warm and smelled of that deep familiar. We sat wrapped up like that for a long time, not speaking, just looking out the window at the Queensboro Bridge, until I started to breathe again and then had hiccups. "*Det kommer att bli bra, Neneh*. Everything is going to be fine." She didn't lie.

Before I left, Moki bought me a Canon camera and a bag of film. "Take lots of pictures, Neneh."

We started our trip in Nigeria, where we stayed with a friend of my father's. I arrived in Lagos as I'd left New York—wearing a Clash T-shirt, cut off at the sleeves, a pair of army trousers, and my prized German combat boots. We walked down the aeroplane steps into a hot, humid night, the air pungent with the scent of engine fuel, palm trees, and spice, mixed with something slightly putrid. Arriving in the airport terminal, we were hit by a chaos and noise like I'd never experienced before. New York is loud, but this was another type of force. You might have thought that everyone was shouting at one another, but it was just all these people talking animatedly at the same time.

Ahmadu bribed his way through the airport, which brought us seamlessly through passport control. There was no such thing as a baggage carousel—all the luggage was just dumped in a heap. As we were searching for our cases, three men approached us. Ahmadu spoke in low tones, more money passed hands, and in the blink of an eye we'd passed through customs. Outside, the three guys loaded us and the bags into a white van with sliding doors. I was in the back, with Titiyo and Maylen squished in between me and one of the men. My feet hurt.

The road from the airport felt very quiet. We were a long way out of town, only the odd streetlamps illuminating the route. I saw people walking in the dim light: men in white robes carrying things on their heads, bodies moving softly. There was a smell of burning wood mixed in with something sweet where someone sat on the roadside selling dark brown freshly roasted peanuts in their shells, wrapped in newspaper (this became one of my favourite things).

The man sitting next to me was touching my left breast under my T-shirt. I said nothing, but in that moment I deeply missed Moki, wondering whether I'd ever see her again. I was in Africa. I was terrified that this unknown place, one I also belonged to, was going to eat me up. Eventually the guys in the white van dropped us off at a motel where a handful of people mingled in the lobby, mostly men in suits having drinks, a few dressed in finely starched *qdobas*.

That first night in Lagos, the technicolour dreams started, and they would continue throughout the rest of the trip. I dreamed about Moki a lot. At the back of my mind the image of my mother was always there, strong and definite. Of course, we had been apart before, but I'd never felt so far away from her. I ached for her.

Wherever we went, people noticed us. In Sweden, people would ask, "Where in Africa are you from?" Here we were Europeans. Everyone wanted to talk to us. We drove to a market. As we approached, I could see a vast corrugated-iron roof and, drawing closer, thousands more layers of smaller iron roofs that went on and on into the distance, until the air wobbled. Under this metal patchwork lay a universe of stalls, selling anything and everything. At the edge of the market were the meat sellers, the air thick with the sour reek of iron—blood.

We went farther and farther into the market until we found ourselves in a section with stalls selling women's underwear. Women called to Titiyo, Maylen, and me, "Come, come, come!" My eyes fell on some black-and-white polka-dot bras hanging up at the back. The women surrounded me, commenting on the bras and suggesting what cup size I should take. They were appraising me, not aggressively, but enthusiastically sizing me up, physically fearless, touching my breasts and telling me, "Sister, you need this one. My God! You are ready for babies! What is your age? Yes, you are ready for babies now!" I was shy and embarrassed by their attention, but I also loved these women for their unfiltered blatancy.

After ten days in Lagos, we spent a fortnight in Accra, Ghana, mostly at Labadi Beach, where we stayed with a doctor friend of Ahmadu's. Finally, we made our way to Sierra Leone. A ferry carried us from Lungi Airport across the Sierra Leone River to Freetown. When it reached the other side, some of our vast extended family were there to meet us—perhaps thirty aunts, uncles, and cousins waiting at the bottom of the gangway. The others were preparing to greet us in Gbinti.

Ahmadu was clever in his planning of the trip: he knew Gbinti was going to be overwhelming, but by the time we arrived we had at least acclimatised to being in Africa. I had shed most of my punk gear in favour of a *lappa*, a loose wrapper skirt of printed cotton fabric. It's usually worn with a matching short blouse top and head tie, but I wore mine with a T-shirt, with or without my head tie.

Ahmadu had bought a Range Rover and arranged for it to be shipped to the harbour in advance, ostensibly because he knew that there would be lots of off-roading on the way to his village and he could drive us and his relatives about in style. But it was also a symbol of his success. There was an expectation for him to show that he had made good in the West. I sensed that being back in Africa was emotionally complex for Ahmadu. It often is when you long for something as much as he had.

We drove along the deep-red dirt roads through the bush to Gbinti, more than fifty miles north-east of Freetown. The roads got narrower and rougher as we travelled farther into the countryside. We passed through villages with small houses and huts where everybody stopped to look as we passed, voices shouting, "*Opputo, opputo, eh!*" ("Europeans!") When we reached Gbinti, children started chasing the car, jumping, yelling, and waving. It seemed as if every child in the village had come to greet us.

It has changed quite a lot since that first visit, but back then Gbinti was a big rural village with low single-storey houses, a whitewashed mosque, a primary school, a secondary school, and a police station, with chickens and goats roaming freely along dirt roads leading to small fields and, beyond them, the bush. We pulled up outside an earth-coloured house with three big steps up to a veranda on which a crowd of people had gathered. In the middle of the throng stood a beautiful older woman. She was tall and slim, and I saw my father's face in hers: this was the woman after whom I was named—Haja Neneh, my grandmother. Her skin looked soft, and she was wearing a long dress with slits at the sides so I could see her *lappa* underneath, and a head tie on top, which was another piece of fabric, to signify that she was a *haja*—she had been to Mecca. We had arrived. Ahmadu started to cry.

The compound belonged to my grandmother. The main house had three double bedrooms: one for my grandmother; one for Ahmadu's brother, Uncle Kotebra; and one for Uncle Kotebra's primary wife, Aunty Hawa. Haja Neneh gave up her room to Titiyo and me. She kept her belongings in suitcases and a locked trunk, the keys tied around her waist under bundles of fabric. Sometimes I could hear them rattle as she walked.

At the back of the house was another veranda. Beyond, small shack-like houses were built around the backyard. The space in the middle was the kitchen, where they cooked on an open fire. In anticipation of our arrival, a goat and chickens had been slaughtered. Our cousins were rinsing rice in enamel bowls, and peeling and washing yams, which they then pounded to a paste for fufu. The goat was stewing in a giant pot, along with dried *fidh* (cassava leaf greens) and okra, which made the dish gooey. The women fried the chicken, then cooked it with a red sauce.

Stepping inside the front door of the house, we entered a wide, open space with a couple of wooden chairs and some low stools. At night, the children and some aunties slept on mats at one end of this room. This was where we sat to eat that first meal. It was served on a huge enamel tray covered in rice. Normally the men eat first, then the women, lastly the kids, but that day we, the family of Ahmadu Jah from far, far away, were honoured with first helpings. We didn't have plates or bowls or cutlery. Instead, we all ate together directly from the tray, using our hands to scoop up the food.

"Watch me," Ahmadu said. I watched his right hand find the rice, his fingers gently and effortlessly wrapping up the stew to lift it to his mouth, then how he sucked the juices off his thumb. I'd never seen him eat with his hands before.

As the rice and the goat and the chicken in its sauce was gobbled up, I could see a pattern of flowers appearing on the tray. The bars in the windows were packed tight with the faces of village children squeezed up against them, laughing at us trying to sweep up the food like Ahmadu. We were so clumsy. The children seemed hungry, and we were too. Everything tasted so good.

Spending time alone is not a thing in village culture. In Gbinti, there were people around us constantly, voices speaking in Temne, and it was hard to work out which part of our family they belonged to. But it didn't matter; we were all related in some way, so it seemed simplest to just call all the younger ones my cousins, and all the elders my uncles and aunties. And Haja Neneh—well, I knew who she was. I felt especially close to Aunty Mari, my grandmother's daughter from her second marriage. Everyone said we looked similar. She was pleased that we had a likeness, and so was I: she had attitude and walked real slow, with a determined swagger. I liked it when she spoke to me in Creole: "Neneh, I go take you tailor in Freetown to make nice, nice dress."

And, of course, there were all the other stepsiblings, the children of Ahmadu's stepfather's other wives, as well as his uncle Lamin Sadiki, to whom Ahmadu had been close as a child. Lamin was also well educated, and obviously still held a special place in my father's heart. When we left, Ahmadu gave the Range Rover to him.

At ground level in this society, everything was run by women: not just the day-to-day organisation of family but also most of the wheeling and dealing in the marketplaces. There was such a sense of cooperation and sisterhood, especially in Gbinti, and it became an important inspiration for me. After I'd been to Africa, I felt *complete*. I found myself filled up inside my body. I started to live differently, move differently, and, most important, I knew I wanted to be a mother. I felt proud to be a woman.

•

As our time in Africa neared its end, Ahmadu took us on one last pilgrimage, to Labé in Guinea, an important religious and cultural centre for the Fulani people in West Africa. Driving up through the mountains, we were in the wild, the landscape bathed in a thick, low mist. It was the only time in that three-month journey when the sun hadn't been beating down on us. We eventually arrived in Labé and pulled up outside a community hall, where we would spend the night. We had all been asleep in the car, and when we opened our eyes and looked outside, everything was in complete darkness—there was no electricity in that town. Two white faces were looking in at us, twin albinos standing motionless at the car window. It was the strangest sight, those two expressionless white-black faces staring back at us in the dark.

Everywhere we'd travelled on that journey, people shouted "*Fula mussas*," "Fulani women," at my sister and me. Now, arriving in Labé, I understood why. In the mountains and at the market we sometimes saw nomadic herdsmen. They were fair-skinned, tall and thin with fine angular features and very long hair. Looking at Titiyo, I recognised those same features. Then, in the market the next day, as we were on the hunt for some of the earrings I had seen the tribespeople wearing, I came face to face with my double. Titiyo and Maylen saw her first, walking on the other side of the marketplace. They grabbed my arm and said, "Oh my God, Neneh. She looks just like you." I could see it, too: it was as if I had just found a long-lost identical twin. The woman returned my gaze and smiled, revealing a big gold tooth, then walked away.

Just before we left the village, we sat down with the local griot, who sang us everything he knew of our family's history, accompanied by a kora player. Griots are poets, musicians, and storytellers, the custodians of a community's history, found across many West African societies. They have traditionally been advisors to royalty and leaders, repositories of knowledge. They also operate as mediators in the community. They tell detailed family histories of lineage and children, success and failure, triumph and misfortune. You still find them today at important occasions such as weddings, where they sing the bride's and groom's ancestral stories. They're passing on memory and creating culture using only their voice and, perhaps, an instrument such as the kora or the ngoni.

Ahmadu recorded the whole performance on his new Japanese sound recorder, of which he was very proud, and which Titiyo and I had previously teased him about. Now we were so glad he'd bought it. Priceless connection with our Jah family roots. A haunting sense of tapping into our living heritage through musical storytelling.

The journey to Africa and meeting my family was a profound awakening for me to my Africanness. I had finally found a whole other vital piece of my being that I had not fully known. I was so proud. I left Sierra Leone with my hair in forty-two braids and with a bag full of tailor-made outfits.

SIMPLY WHAT'S HAPPENING

In September 1979, the Slits invited Don to join their Simply What's Happening UK tour. Bruce Smith, genius drummer of Bristol post-punk band the Pop Group, and their lead guitarist, Gareth Sager, had introduced them to Don's music. Here was the kind of experimental tradition-busting union that Don loved. He was in. I went along, too. Moki and Don thought it would be an inspiring journey: I would hear some mind-altering music and meet great people. They were right.

I was fifteen, no longer in school, already a punk, in love with London, and I had heard the Slits' music. I couldn't think of anything more exciting than going on tour with the band, introducing their first album, *Cut*.

It was an extraordinary line-up with a nutbag mix of musicians: as well as the Slits, there was Don, playing with Lou Reed's Happy House band; the Jamaican singer Prince Hammer; and the dub band Creation Rebel. This eclectic approach was not an accident. The Slits—singer Ari Up, guitarist Viv Albertine, and bass player Tessa Pollitt—were stretching out, exploring new dimensions. Their sound has been called "punky reggae." Personally, I think it was more than that. The Slits were monumental. They wanted to bring punk, dub reggae, and jazz musicians together, opening the ears and minds of the audiences to different forms of sound. They had also decided that the three acts would take it in turns to headline.

The Slits and the Pop Group were practically a family collective by this point. They had met while both were recording at Ridge

Farm Studio in Surrey. The Slits were making *Cut* with the almighty record producer and sonic grandfather of UK reggae, Dennis Bovell. The Pop Group were also working with him, on their first album, *Y*. Before long, the Slits' Viv Albertine was going out with Gareth, and then Bruce joined the Slits as drummer for the tour.

We were all travelling on the same tour bus. On the first leg, I sat at the front with Don and his band. Creation Rebel and Prince Hammer sat in the middle with Adrian Sherwood, who at just twenty-one was their producer, manager, and sound guy. He also sold their records out of a bag after the gigs. The Slits sat at the back. John Waddington, the Pop Group's other guitarist, was on the bus too, with Gareth Sager and the DJ and film-maker Don Letts. After the Liverpool gig, Paul Rutherford, later of Frankie Goes to Hollywood, came on board and stayed for the duration. This is how I met my people. All of them would become important to me musically and personally. We became kin. I ended up working with Gareth and Adrian, who would become a legendary dub producer. Bruce Smith and I would marry and have a daughter together, Naima. But first it was Ari Up, the Slits' singer.

I remember Ari sitting at the back of the bus in a green miniskirt and matching box jacket, like a marching-band uniform: short socks, flat stepper shoes, her hair piled up high on her head, her bare legs splayed, her knickers in full view—cotton, big-style; my grandmother would have approved. Her pose wasn't sexual, more unapologetic, uncompromising. Here was a different kind of girl: untamed, unfiltered, female. She was not demonstrating. She was just fighting to be herself.

The first gig was in Leicester. Their music was playful, oddly pop and, at the same time, so experimental. I was hooked. I'd been around amazing women all my life, but I'd never met girls like Tessa, Viv, and Ari. I thought they were beyond cool. That night onstage, Ari had locks tied up, this huge pillar on her head, and she wore a tutu and ballet *pointe* shoes. It was instant love. She spoke English and sometimes a kind of patois with a German accent. She seemed otherworldly, way beyond her years. And yet, really, she was still so childlike. She wasn't much older than me: seventeen turning eighteen; I was fifteen turning sixteen. I was equally in awe of Tessa, entranced by her bass playing. She was brilliant and beautiful, like a punk Liz Taylor, in her little cut-up charity-shop frilly skirt, baggy sweatshirt, white tights, and chunky Doc Martens.

After a few tentative days, I started to talk a little bit with Viv, Tessa, and John Waddington. Ari and I were still sizing each other up, looking for a way in. I felt as if I was checking the boundaries to see if I could edge closer, holding out a hand to see if she would bite.

Don was in good shape during the tour. It was inspiring for him to be in a new environment, and I know it meant a lot to him to have another generation of music-makers interested in his work. In Birmingham, as the show was about to begin, I heard Ari shouting at the backstage door: "These are my bredren, just let them in." It was three guys from the reggae band Steel Pulse. Ari hustled them past the bouncers, who, confronted with the full force of her willpower, didn't know what had hit them. After the gig, the bus carried us to the hotel for the usual after-party drinks in another bar smelling of old carpet, stale beer, and cigarette smoke. I lingered until the bartender called it a night and then took the lift up to the room I was sharing with Don.

Sharing a room with two single beds in strange-to-us towns all over the country, I still felt like his little girl in many ways. We'd get dressed, brush our teeth, comb our hair, grease our skin, side by side. As I grew more confident, I started doing my own thing. Don was cool with it. After all, he'd brought me along so I could do just that.

HIP-HOP BEFORE THE HIP

After the tour ended in the late autumn, we returned to New York. Something had been brewing out in the boroughs. Hip-hop culture was gathering momentum uptown, in the Bronx and Harlem, in Brooklyn and Queensbridge, and on the Lower East Side. Hip-hop was a burst of creativity that grew out of poverty, out of deprivation, from the roots up. Like punk, the posses that were creating the music and the graffiti art had no access to studios, or even musical instruments—hence the decks, the human beatbox. My New York friend Baby Bam of the Jungle Brothers talked about discovering hip-hop one summer in the mid-seventies, when DJs and artists like Kool Herc, Grandmaster Flash, and Afrika Bambaataa were bringing together their crews in the Bronx. His parents had grounded him for a month over the holidays. Stuck in his bedroom with a radio, a record player, and a double cassette recorder, he started making his own mixes and beats, capturing snippets off the radio and cutting things up between tape deck and record decks. By the time he got out of there he was ready to make music. He joined forces with his Brooklyn friends Mike Gee and DJ Sammy B, and that's when the Jungle Brothers were formed.

Although it was an explosion of expression straight from the streets, hip-hop didn't come from nowhere. DJ Herc had arrived in New York in 1967 from Kingston, Jamaica, bringing his experience of DJs "toasting" or chatting over the records they played. Afrika Bambaataa had been a gang leader before he and his people turned to the expressive power of music and rap to transform their frustration and anger into poetry and rhythm. The Black Power movement had always had an artistic wing, with writers like Don and Moki's friend Leroi Jones championing the politics through their work. Now all these strands were being woven together by the kids from the ghettos into a new civil rights movement rooted in pride, creativity, and self-determination.

Hip-hop was unapologetic, a revolution that any of us could claim. It had its birthplace in Black and Latino culture, and spread like wildfire. Everybody who had been marked by urban poverty, discrimination, and disenfranchisement from mainstream culture had ownership of it. Hip-hop became the storytelling of our time, recording history as it played out, forcing us to listen—not that we needed any persuasion to pay attention to these voices that needed to be heard: this is us, this is now.

Hip-hop culture was happening wherever people happened to be: in motion, out on the stoop, at house parties, or on the street. The kids didn't have access to venues, or the money to pay for them. And because, at first, the music and the rap were emerging unscripted, you would never hear the same thing twice. These outdoor events were like old-school sixties happenings. You never quite knew where things were going to go, with the rhythmic trip of the DJs and the MCs playfully improvising, telling their stories, creating seamless collages with the music, scratching and mixing tracks, all to a constant beat—suddenly the DJ might mix in a bit of Fleetwood Mac over this hardcore beat. You could almost see them thinking, *Wait for this. I'm going to really kill 'em with this now.* And they did, because no rules applied, except: be good, do it right, give it everything you got.

Everywhere there were kids rolling out bits of lino so that you could breakdance. Riding the subway and in the stations, kids were rapping. This was an opportunity to listen to what was really going on. This was mouth-to-mouth truth-telling, oral culture with bite. People started to come in from Brooklyn, the Bronx, the Lower

East Side, and gather in Union Square and Washington Square Park. They'd set up the boombox, form the ciphers, and freestyle. It was an unfolding, ever-evolving scene and I wanted to be a part of it. Walking down the street I would hear the inimitable sounds and gravitate to where the action was. I watched these kids who were so masterful—geniuses. What they were doing was artistic. It was poetic, it was graceful, it was peaceful, it was playful, and it was rough, raw, telling it like it was. It was a no-brainer. I got it.

It didn't take long for hip-hop's bass notes to pulse right through contemporary culture. The single "Rapper's Delight" had been released between my departure for London and my return to New York and hit the top of the charts all over the world. Hip-hop was making its way from the streets to the record studios, morphing from a DIY collective art form into the multibillion-dollar juggernaut of popular culture it is today. But for those few months I spent in New York in early 1980, chasing its rhythm from block to block, club to club, it felt like a revelation and a gift.

TEENAGERS OFF ON A TANGENT

By early spring 1980, I was back in London. I stayed with family friends for one night, but the next day I asked if I could use their phone to call Ari. She and I had finally bonded with each other one night on a dance floor, towards the end of the Slits tour. We were like sisters, like children, like young women, so inseparable we all but grew into one. She called me "Nana."

When the tour ended and I left for New York, Ari had given me her phone number, which I kept safe. I felt nervous as I dialled. Luckily, she answered. I went to visit her and that visit became a very long stay. Soon, I was living with Ari and her mum, Nora, in a terraced house in Battersea. I wasn't planning a long-term move to London. I was sixteen and just following my instincts. When I discussed the idea with Moki and Don, they had some concerns about how I would manage but they also trusted that I would find my way. They were pleased that I had found my people and was stepping out to explore the world through music. Their faith emboldened me, but I wouldn't have stayed if it hadn't been for Ari.

We were like two old souls reunited. We sometimes wondered if we had known each other in another life: "Yeah, Nana, maybe we were man and wife, or woman warriors." I told her about my trip to Africa and, because of the way she listened, my time there came back to life, so I could feel how beautiful and important it had been. We shared my tailor-made outfits from Sierra Leone, and I felt so free in Ari's company. Some people are born into the world unable to filter, driven by such a powerful sense of themselves that they can only be who they are. Moki carried that kind of relentless spirit, and so did Ari.

Strong-willed, focused, funny, confident, Ari was utterly uninhibited—an irrepressible and unapologetic force of nature. She was just a spectacular individual, a one-off. She was born Ariane Daniela Forster in Munich in 1962. Her grandfather was a newspaper mogul; her mother, Nora Maier, heiress to the family fortune, married Frank Forster, Ari's father, a popular "schlager" singer. After they divorced, Nora became a music promoter and a manager and was friends with everyone, from Jimi Hendrix to Barry Gibb of the Bee Gees (who was Ari's "stepdad" for about a minute). A great beauty, Nora was an "It girl," a regular feature in German gossip pages. Then, in the early seventies, when Ari was about eight, Nora met the guitarist Chris Spedding and moved with Ari to London.

Returning from boarding school at weekends, Ari found that their Shepherd's Bush home had become a magnet for the city's young punks, including John Lydon and Joe Strummer, who gave Ari her first guitar lessons. At school, Ari, a naturally gifted musician, was classically trained on piano.

In May 1976, Palmolive, drummer with the Flowers of Romance, was at a Clash concert at the Roundhouse in Camden when she laid eyes on Ari. Palmolive wanted to start a band of her own and, struck by the fourteen-year-old's "attitude," she approached her. Ari was immediately taken with Palmolive—she liked her earrings in the shape of pigs. That's how Ari became the lead singer of the Slits.

Ari was an only child, and even though I came from a close family and community, I was also lonely. When you grow up moving around, you get good at adapting to situations and places quickly. But when you are young, identity is rooted in place—where you're from, your tribe. Ari and I did everything together. We slept in the same bed, got ready together, shared *everything*: our clothes, our music, our family histories. Although we were from very different backgrounds, neither of us had a conventional family. We made joint photo albums in which we combined our life stories, filling in the gaps where friends, boyfriends, and family were missing.

Maybe, I thought, Ari inherited some of her free spirit from her grandmother, a burlesque performer in thirties Berlin. We had one of her dresses in our shared wardrobe. It was black with tassels, and we named it the "Sex" dress, or the "Plopp Plopp" dress. Although our bodies were so different, that magic dress fitted us both like a glove.

Ari lived for music. Listening to tunes from her massive collection of cassette tapes kept in a blue old-school laundry bag, some days she would go into deep meditation for hours on end, rocking back and forth, sitting on the couch with a comb to work at the top of her locks and scratch her scalp. She always had a notebook at hand to keep a record of her conversations, ideas, and observations.

•

I managed quite quickly to blag my way into a job at Better Badges on Portobello Road. The company produced badges for bands as well as mixtapes and fanzines, one of which was *i-D*, which then consisted entirely of photographs of people on the street, with captions about what they were wearing. My job, along with two punks called Sarah and Scrubber, was to staple the issues together and to put the pins on the badges. Every morning I'd take the 137 bus from Battersea to Sloane Square, where I'd get the Tube to Notting Hill. All these new names sat oddly in my mouth.

Ari and I didn't discuss when or where we were going to go. We just collided and did it, our meeting places often the streets around Portobello Road. Anywhere with music. London at that time was in a state of flux. Diverse cultures were constantly clashing and harmonising, and it was from that collision that a lot of the music was born. After the initial outburst of rage and wildness, many punk groups had started to branch out. Things have to go somewhere. The rebellion against the norm had opened doors: no rules also meant you could do anything. It wasn't just about people being more receptive to new forms of music or listening to music in a different way—they also felt inspired to use these influences to make something unique of their own. People were freely experimenting.

Ari and I joined the dots quickly. When I arrived in London I had, of course, some punk vibes, and I also brought with me something of the essence of hip-hop, and the influence of jazz in my spirit and soul—an energy that was much of New York, and that city was part of my DNA. It was organic, a natural fuel. But it was almost as if I had to be in London to put those pieces together, to really claim them as my own.

Like many of the punk groups, the Slits were influenced by reggae music and culture, which was why they worked with the producer Dennis Bovell on *Cut*. Dennis had produced and written Janet Kay's 1979 number one hit "Silly Games" and laid foundations in UK Black culture upon which the generations ahead would continue to build. In those days he had his own studio near Southwark Bridge. I used to go there with Ari. It was a trip to watch him working at the mixing board, conducting the dials up and down in a dance. Dennis pretty much invented lovers rock. I mean, who doesn't drop everything to dance and sing along when "Silly Games" comes on? It's impossible not to—everybody reaching for the high notes, the whole room breaking together.

Ari and I spent many nights in Weasel's shebeen on Acklam Road, right on the corner of Portobello Road: a pound on the door to the guy with the gold tooth, pile everyone in, low light from a red bulb in the ceiling, old wallpaper, one record deck, speakers, nowhere to sit. At weekends, we'd sometimes go to a blues—not-so-legal house parties—in other parts of the city. One night, we'd heard about a blues in a flat on the Battersea Park Estate. When we got there, we could hear the music, the bass bouncing between the tower blocks, but we just couldn't figure out where it was coming from. Soon we were a small gang, led by Ari, all on the hunt for the party, up in one lift, down in another. Eventually we asked someone for directions and at last we made our way to the sixth floor. As we walked along the balcony outside the flats, the bass got solid, telling us we'd arrived.

By then, Don Letts was mainly making Super 8 mm films, but, back in 1977, before my time in London, he had been a DJ at the Roxy Club, the pioneering punk nightclub in Neal Street, Covent Garden. The scene was in its infancy and no punk bands had released any records yet, so, in between the live punk sets, Don started playing some serious tunes by artists like King Tubby, Big Youth, Tapper Zukie, and U-Roy. He was instrumental in bringing reggae music into the punk environment. Ari and I went religiously to Don's flat in Stockwell, at least once a week, mainly because he used to get mixtapes for Ari of all the new dubplates, red-hot sound-system tunes, sometimes a live mix with someone toasting. Ari would leave his flat with an exciting new stash for the big blue laundry bag, and we'd play those tapes over and over until they needed a rest.

Don had already introduced Ari, Viv, and Tessa to London sound-system culture. The first time Ari took me to the Bali Hai Club, next to the ice rink in Streatham, was to hear the King of Dub, Jah Shaka, also known as the Zulu Warrior, the Jamaican sound-system legend operating out of south-east London. We stepped into Bali Hai and, suddenly, England was left behind. Dreads stood all the way up the stairs, handing out flyers, selling a £5 draw: a little bit of weed folded up in newspaper. I could feel the bass vibrating in my bones, pulsating through my body. When

I entered the dance hall, I was blown away; no, not away—rather, I felt like I had arrived, in the deep. Jah Shaka was over in the corner like the Wizard of Oz, a slight man, but oh so mighty, a magician on one single deck generating a huge, mind-altering sound. The way he mixed the records—played with them, bringing all the bass out and then the treble, then dropping the bass—was high-energy, spiritual, and so powerful. When he picked up tempo, everyone stood facing him, lost and found in the rhythm, nodding. It was like hearing the horns of victory.

There were the "yout men": feisty young kids in stepper shoes, drainpipe trousers, maybe a flannel in the back pocket, a neat cardigan or jacket, and a crown. Then there was the more militant look, featuring top-to-toe khaki and a high-crown hat. Finally, the look favoured by some of the slightly older dreads was dressed-up-to-the-nines: a three-piece suit and a jacket with a real beaver-fur crown, their locks tucked into the side.

Ari and I dressed in a lot of pleated skirts, fitted shirts, suede-fronted cardigans, and head ties, always with a good pair of flat stepper shoes, all the better for dancing, kicking down doors, or running away from the police or skinheads. Militant footwear to see us through Babylon.

On the dance floor there would be an inner circle of dancers, usually all boys, wild, doing fierce moves. Ari was the only white person in the thick of it. She just stepped right in there and let rip, skanking, freestyling her kung-fu-like moves. She was a wicked dancer. Now she would probably be accused of cultural appropriation, but that wasn't Ari—she could go *anywhere* because she always entered with respect and she was always herself.

We didn't listen to music passively. For Ari and me, listening to reggae and dub was about tuning in to a certain kind of consciousness. The power of the bass was like a meditation. I found it grounding. For me, music has always been like praying: once I'm into it, I just don't hear or feel anything else. To be in those dance halls, away from the reality of the world, was a feeling of relief and release—I was just there, in the sound. It reignited the sense of empowerment I'd experienced in Africa with Ahmadu.

Reggae was the backbone of British music. It was purposeful, political. It was about looking for something meaningful. It was about survival, self-determination, pride. When you consider how Britain was at that time, and what it was to be a young person of colour in this country, people were drawing a fundamental strength from the resonance of that sound. All over London and in other big cities like Bristol and Birmingham, young Black British kids were holding their heads up high.

Like hip-hop in America, sound-system culture was a kind of uprising, and was equally relevant to how and where I was in life. I'd landed in the middle of these contemporaneous yet diverse art forms, all of them going way back to the source in Africa and the enslaved people who had been uprooted from their homeland.

This was a new world that Ari took me into. Those nights we spent together at Bali Hai will remain lodged in my heart forever.

PART-TIME SLIT

It was Ari who brought me in as a part-time member of the Slits, albeit right at the tail end of their story. I wasn't sure what I could offer, but she was very matter-of-fact, saying, "You are part of this." At first, I mainly danced and played some of the simple percussion parts on the bongos and maracas; then gradually I joined in more often on vocals.

I appeared with the Slits onstage for the first time in June 1980 at the Beat the Blues Festival at Alexandra Palace, dancing, playing percussion, and singing on some of the songs. Don Letts made a film of us that day. In it, I'm wearing an old pale green dress from Portobello Market with a pink mohair cardigan, pink ankle socks in schoolgirl sandals, and a bright red beret on top of my dyed red hair. Now I see something so sweet and pure and committed in those captured moments, something we were completely oblivious to back then.

Being onstage next to a performer like Ari—feeling how she controlled the space with such dynamic freedom—that confidence entered my cells. She was my teacher, my guru. I found a clarity in performing. I think I knew that I belonged there. There was an inevitability to it. Maybe there was also a part of me that was longing to let loose, to get up there and embody my spirit. No doubt I had music in my DNA, but it was Ari who got me into a recording studio and in front of a mic for the first time. She was working with Adrian Sherwood on a project that became the dub collective the New Age Steppers. We were in a minicab on our way to Berry Street Studio and she managed to convince me that I should sing on a track called "My Love" that they were recording that day. Ari had a little cassette player in her lap, and we played the backing track over and over as we crossed the city, Ari teaching me the harmony and then singing the lead, until finally it started to gel and we were harmonising. The cab driver must have been losing his shit. When we walked into the studio, Ari announced to Adrian, "Nana is going to be on this record. She is going to sing."

Simultaneously, the Slits were working on their second album, *Return of the Giant Slits*. The new songs were a departure from their first album, *Cut*. They were headed in a more melodic direction, tapping into musical influences from all over the world. Once again, Ari insisted that I join them in the studio to sing backing vocals on "Earthbeat."

That was the beginning. Making music was creeping into my being.

AFTER THE RITZY

On a Sunday night in July 1980, when I was sixteen, I was raped on the street near Nora and Ari's house.

Earlier that night, I'd been at the Ritzy in Brixton, where the Slits had performed a gig. I was wearing a blue velour shorts suit that I'd bought in New York. I remember so clearly how the shorts sat on my body, following the curve of my waistline, hugging the roundness of my backside. I remember my sense of completeness, of feeling special in my clothes: secure and confident in myself—I felt good.

When we got back to Nora's house, at about eleven o'clock, I stepped out onto Lavender Hill to buy some cigarette papers. It was a summer's night, the air still and warm. The streets of Battersea felt quiet and safe by comparison with New York. It was late, but I didn't feel vulnerable. I felt strong, I felt beautiful.

I found a corner shop with its doors still open, but they only had big Rizlas and I wanted regular short ones. I saw a Black guy on the other side of the street and thought, *A young brother. Great, I'll ask him.*

I called out, "Have you got any Rizlas?"

He crossed the street to where I was standing. He was probably a couple of years older than me. Something didn't feel right. He was being a bit pushy, and I realised I needed to get rid of him. I said something like, "Listen, boy, just go away. I'm going home." And when he heard the word "boy," he lost his shit.

He said, "Hold on, girl. I need to walk with you because if I read in the paper that someone's been raped around here, I'm going to feel really bad."

What a weird thing to say. My heartbeat faltered. I wanted to stop what had been set in motion, get away, but there was nothing I could do except keep walking up the road towards Nora's house. Halfway there, he attacked me, pulling me into a dark alley. I struggled to get away, tearing at his skin, but he had his hands around my neck and I couldn't fight him off. Finally, I had to accept that, physically, I couldn't beat him. I tried to. I really tried. But he was stronger than me. Out of view, in the darkest dark, my body on the ground, he put his penis in my mouth and in my vagina. It hurt to the core.

When he was on top of me, raping me, hurting me, raiding me—and taking something from me I can never get back—I put myself somewhere else. I recalled something Moki had told me not long before. She had been at her friend's Manhattan loft on a hot summer night when a group of young men slipped in through an open window. They tied the women's hands and feet and robbed the flat. Before they left, hours later, they raped Moki's friend. God knows, those men could have killed her and her friend, but my mother said she had got through the ordeal by putting herself into a meditative state, almost leaving her body, and the attackers left her alone. She refused to allow them to take her soul.

Now, in that darkest place, that knowledge was part of my armour. I found the light inside me, as if someone had shone a flashlight in a tunnel, and I felt that I had a choice: he could tear at my body parts, but I wouldn't let him have my spirit. To defend that part of me, I tried to leave my body. I don't know how long the rape continued, every second dragging for a lifetime, but eventually I managed to say, "My mum's in the house. She's going to wonder where I am." I just had an instinct that it was the only way I could get away from him. Then I ran. I could remember his face for a long time, but I can't really see it anymore.

Sometimes, though, I think about what it would be like if I saw him again today.

When I made it back to Nora's house, I jumped in the bath. I don't remember crying. I was numb, deeply in shock.

The next morning, Ari was leaving to play a series of gigs in Helsinki. I went to stay with Viv Goldman, my sister, my confidante, my anchor here in London. When I told her what that man had done to me, she was outraged that I hadn't been to the police. But I was sixteen, I was in a foreign city on my own, and, somewhere in my head, I thought that if I reported it, I'd have to sit there and be humiliated. For a long, long time, in fact, I felt responsible for what had happened. I had initiated the encounter, because maybe if I hadn't asked him for those Rizlas . . . I blamed myself for not having been scared.

My coping mechanism was to hold it all in, keep it small. I didn't tell Moki for years. I didn't know *how* to tell her and didn't know if I would be able to bear seeing her pain for me. But when my first solo album, *Raw Like Sushi*, was coming out, I talked about the rape in a *Rolling Stone* interview. I knew I had to tell her what had happened before the article ran. And when I did, she knew exactly what to do: she held me tight. The sensation of that ocean of tears you have shored up for so long is scary. I sometimes think that if I start to cry, maybe I will never stop.

All these years later, I sympathise with my sixteen-year-old self and understand why I didn't immediately go to the police. I hope I might handle it differently today. But even thinking about what I would do if something like that happened now fills me with rage. We still lack safe spaces where women can feel we are listened to, believed, and embraced. There are so many levels of hatred, abuse, and violence against us that still go ignored and unpunished. The reality is that it's sometimes easier, less dangerous, to just let the man have what he wants than to try to stop him. Then as women, as victims, we are made to feel that we are somehow responsible. And yet why shouldn't a woman be able to ask a man for something on the street?

I decided that my rapist was not going to strip me of believing in beauty or love. For me, that response was embodied in my love for people; in having my divine children; in my commitment to family and my deep friendships; the expression of my music and dancing; the meals I cook and the clothes I put on my body. A positive resolve to give and receive more love and communion—those were the choices that I made.

RIP RIG + PANIC

In January 1981, I was with my family at the loft in New York when I got a phone call from Gareth Sager and Bruce Smith of the Pop Group. I was in the bath when the phone rang. I could tell from Moki's tone that she didn't know the caller, but her voice was warm. "Yes, of course you can. Neneh is here, just hold on." I got out and went to the phone in my towel.

"Hi, Neneh. It's Gareth." I could hear Bruce talking in the background. Gareth told me about the music they were making in a new group, with Bruce on drums, Sean Oliver on bass, and Mark Springer, an astonishing, classically trained musician, a virtuoso piano player who also played saxophone. They were called Rip Rig + Panic and they all felt that the missing part might be me. My eyes fixed on the bridge outside the window, bathwater dripping on the floorboards. I tried to keep my cool. I felt at once flattered and flattened by a low-key panic. Or was it excitement?

"Wow, that sounds amazing," I said. "But I'm not sure I can sing."

"We think so," Gareth replied.

"Give me your number and I'll call you back."

I put down the phone, my head reeling, stomach somersaulting, trying to process a million contradictory emotions at once. I felt petrified. Maybe they were mad. But then I thought, *Sure. Yes, maybe I can do this. Why not?* I had been starting to wonder what the hell I was doing with my life. Now, with Gareth's phone call, a strange sense of destiny was strumming a very persistent chord in my head. Ronald Reagan had just taken office at the White House, while, back in Britain, his close pal Margaret Thatcher was in Downing Street. That same month, the New Cross Fire and the subsequent Brixton riots had highlighted the systemic racism of London's Metropolitan Police and the crazily high rate of unemployment, particularly among young Black men—but they also showed that young people were standing up and claiming their right to occupy their own space. I, too, could claim some space. *You can't not do it*, I told myself.

Moki, my wise consigliere, reached the same conclusion: "*Neneh, du måste åka*. Neneh, you must go." There they were, those same words again, spoken in almost the exact spot we had been in just before I went to Africa. I dialled the number. The second Gareth answered, I said, "Hi, I'm coming."

•

"Go, Go, Go! (This Is It)" was the first thing I recorded with Rip Rig + Panic, back at Berry Street Studio in Clerkenwell. Gareth was very sweet, kind of tucking me in under his wing, and right from the beginning he felt like a big brother. I remember putting the cans on, thinking, *I don't know what the fuck I'm doing*. But when I heard the music, I was unleashed.

Mark, Sean, Gareth, and Bruce were inspired by the music I'd grown up with: musicians like Sun Ra, Ornette Coleman, Don, Eric Dolphy, and Archie Shepp. Gareth wrote the lyrics for all the songs—he is a very gifted songwriter and has been my best teacher. The funny thing was that sometimes I didn't know what some of the words meant or understand what the hell I was singing about. It didn't matter. When I sang, "You're my kind of climate, a swinging lost paradise, your touch, your smell. Well, you can tell I ain't talking heaven or hell," my body understood, the metaphors and wordplay expanding my horizons, legacies whispering in my blood, a heat rising within.

Not too long after I joined the band, Bruce and I fell in love. I'd got to know him on the Slits tour the previous year, and since then we'd spent a lot more time together. I liked him, but I couldn't tell if he liked me. He called me "kiddo" once. He wasn't wrong—he was twenty and I was sixteen and, according to him, too young (or too *something*)—and it threw me. I turned the heat down a little. It worked, because eventually the stars said "yes."

I spent the rest of 1981 dashing between New York and London, performing with the Slits and Rip Rig + Panic. Besides the touring, there was also my immigration status to keep me on the move. As a Swedish person, I could stay in the UK for only three months at a time. I was constantly travelling back and forth to New York or Sweden to get a stamp in my passport. In early June, I was in the States with the Slits. We were opening for the Clash on one night of their now-legendary seventeen-night stint at Bond International Casino in Times Square. This extended visit at Bond's was epic. Anybody who was anybody performed on that series of gigs. A lot of the cool-cat hip-hop posse were there: Grandmaster Flash, Afrika Bambaataa, the Funky 4 + 1. The list is long. Only three years earlier, I had been converted to punk partly through listening to the Clash's records in Leigh's flat in London. Now, albeit as a very minor figure, I was performing with the Slits on the same bill as them in Times Square.

Later that month, we gave our first performance as Rip Rig + Panic at University College London. Going onstage that night was terrifying, with me thinking, *How am I going to know what to do?* I had no real understanding of my own ability, but maybe it was healthier not to know. This is what I mean when I say we were innocent. We were making music in the moment, just one step ahead of ourselves, before there was time to overanalyse, be judgemental or self-deprecating. And that left a space for the music to have a kind of purity. I held my breath and closed my eyes as if I was on the edge of a very high diving board. When the music started, the force was so great I found that I could plunge into it. Never underestimate the power of being harnessed by the other members of the group. It is a huge thing to know that the people around you believe in you.

We would put together a loose set listing before we went onstage, but it could take us anywhere—vague directions with a built-in escape route. When I sang with the Slits, I joined in with *their* universe. Being onstage with them was wild, but Rip Rig + Panic's live performances were a few removes further out into another realm. No gig was ever the same from one night to the next. We played off one another and improvised, bringing one another to life and going down all kinds of alleys. We would go off into something wild, but then the next minute Mark Springer would play the piano in a way that seemed to encompass the universe, and we would all stop and listen.

It could be hit-and-miss. Sometimes we were amazing. Sometimes we were dreadful. We were never perfect, but that wasn't the point. It was about being spontaneous, being able to take risks, and when we were good it was like we were flying. We were rowdy as hell, committed and full of heart. For me, it was crucial. I got found in making this music with these people. Although I felt a jumble of things—euphoric, scared, strong, timid a lot of the time—what was more important was my overriding sense of being *whole*, being *home*. And that opened me up as a performer in a different way, because everybody could give and take, listen and move in and out of the clusterfuck of jazz-isms and the funk.

All kinds of very accomplished musicians would turn up to play at our gigs, including Don, who joined us on tour to Japan in 1983. For the first album, *God*, Ari sang on a track called "Shadows Only There Because of the Sun," which I think should be an anthem. Gareth, Mark, and I sang on the others that weren't instrumental.

Andrea Oliver, Sean's sister, later performed vocals and a lot of dancing. The one and only Nico of the Velvet Underground joined us on one of the live sessions for John Peel's BBC Radio One show in September 1981. She sang a beautifully morose song on the organ, and was clearly in trouble. I guess I recognised not the symptoms, but the thing: the aura of heroin, the fallout. The band was like a living organism. Together, we became even more passionate. It was about doing it like you meant it, being there and giving it all that you had in that minute, not just falling back on what you did yesterday. It was an incredible place, as a family and a group, for me to gain confidence and to learn about improvised music and performance—to just be blasted out by the music and have the freedom to allow it to come up through the feet and the body.

In July 1981, the Slits and I flew back to the States for a series of gigs in New York, LA, and San Francisco. In LA, I stayed some nights in the neighbourhood with Grandma Daisy and some nights at the Tropicana Motel with the band. Tessa, Viv, and Ari had a dream to go into a studio in the hood. A friend of Don's put me in touch with Joe Blocker, a producer who worked next to a Baptist church in Compton, and we recorded a song called "Coulda, Shoulda, Woulda." Sadly, the track was never released. When Sunday came around, the church was crammed with women filled with the Holy Ghost, the overspill crowding out from the side doors facing the studio. Compton is the deep hood, gangland, where Dr. Dre and Ice Cube came from. Even today, when I go to visit my family there, my cousins warn me, "You can go two blocks that way, one block that way, but you can't cross Imperial Highway." But Ari was fearless; she would just go off and do her thing, completely fine wandering about the neighbourhood on her own.

I saw Larry Woods again, after all those years. He was still living next door to Grandma. I didn't know that he could play the shit out of the bass. He had a drum set and a bass plugged into a big speaker in the garage, and when Larry and his homeboy drummer hit the groove, my jaw hit the floor. In so many other yards around the hoods, the garages served as creative palaces, breeding grounds for important sounds. Aunty Barbara told me that, as a teenager, Don had used their garage in Watts to rehearse with Sonny Rollins. Imagine them blasting it out in there, not even knowing that they were changing the world. The humble environments of Washington, DC, gave us go-go; in Chicago it was house. But in the heat of LA, in 1981, the pace and spirit of the city's street life was still driven by funk, putting the ounce in the bounce of the lowriders and sending Dr. Dre and co. in the right direction. Later in the eighties, when hip-hop finally did come out of Compton, it nearly started a revolution.

The night before we flew back to London, Ari and I slept on the fold-out bed Eagle-Eye and I had once shared. When I woke up in the morning, my great-grandma Nana was standing over the sleeping Ari, staring at her locks.

"Does that girl not comb her hair?" she said.

"Nana, they're dreadlocks. You know, Bob Marley, right?" It was the easiest reference at that hour. She still didn't get it.

EVERSLEIGH ROAD

Nora had had enough of having me and Ari in residence. One day she announced, "Nana, Ari, I was driving back from Soho last night and I saw this house round the corner. I'm pretty sure it's empty. I think you should squat in it." We got the hint.

A few days later, a professional squatter mate of hers quietly forced open the front door, changed the locks, and like proud homeowners we had our own keys. Nora helped us to move in.

In Eversleigh Road, Ari and I made a home and our own kind of family. People might consider elements of my life chaotic, but that so-called chaos was structured by a specific commitment to life and learning, where creativity and family shared the same space. We packed it and unpacked it, took it with us in our bags and hearts to wherever we landed. When I came to London, I brought that same philosophy in my luggage.

By now I thought I was quite grown up. I knew where to put my feet, even if I didn't necessarily know where I was going. Ari had a bit of money coming in from the Slits and I earned just enough at Better Badges, so we got by. We used to budget together, and we had some nifty money-saving ruses. Nora's squatter friend had shown us how to put a very thin wire into the gas meter so that the dial wouldn't move; then, every once in a while, we'd take it out and shift it so we wouldn't get caught. We also cut a hole in the electricity meter so we could just put in the same 50p piece, over and over again.

We bought a massive second-hand bed and painted our bedroom a tangerine colour. We kept our shared wardrobe in a small box room, where we also had a table at which we used to sit and work on our photo albums. We went to Shepherd's Bush Market and bought net curtains for the kitchen. We both had a taste for granny interiors. I had the food shopping down to a fine art.

Sometimes Ari would go back home to sit and meditate with Nora's superior sound system. I met John Lydon there one evening after swinging by on my way home from work, to pick up Ari to go on somewhere else. By then, John and Nora were an item and, with us kids out of Nora's hair, he probably felt more comfortable spending time at the house.

"Hi, Nana," said Nora. "This is John."

It was kind of wild to be in that living room with the guy who used to call himself "Johnny Rotten." I should have felt more gobsmacked, but he was so unintimidating in person, it felt natural and sweet. The cassette on the sound system played "Ring My Bell." Anita Ward was singing to us. Ari turned up the volume and we talked about how much we loved that song.

•

Ari and I were walking home not long after we moved into the squat when I saw the man who raped me, walking ahead of us.

"That's the fucking guy," I told her.

He let himself into a house right across the street from our place, where it turned out he was living with a woman I took to be his God-fearing mum. After that, of course, I kept seeing him doodling around, fixing a car with his brothers.

We told Adrian Sherwood, who arranged for a friend to come live with us: "He'll have your backs." We barely knew Junior when he moved in, and I must admit we were a bit scared of him at first. He had been a deeply religious Twelve Tribes follower, but although he had shorn his locks and was no longer a strict Rastaman, he still had a seriousness about him. He was one of those people who don't say much, and I sometimes worried that he didn't like me, or thought I was silly, but then I'd see the twinkle in his eye. The three of us would sit up all night playing cards, me in a nylon padded robe, Ari and me with our head ties on, like two funny punky Rasta grannies.

Junior was a brilliant, simple yet soulful cook—he would rustle up some mean fried snappers. I loved hearing the seasoned fish crackle in the thin-bottomed, low-budget pan, the hopeless clank of the non-stick bell banging on the wonky rings of our cheap old electric cooker. Quite frankly, it was sexy when he tipped the crispy fish on to a plate with the fried seasoning: onions, black pepper, salt, vinegar, and tomatoes. That's when I got my serious Encona hot pepper sauce habit. It also inspired me in my own relationship with food.

I had always been drawn to the energy of the kitchen, watching and helping Moki as she cooked alone or with her friends at home, hearing the sort of intimate conversations that only happen there in the clatter of pots and the rhythm of chopping knives. But now, in our squat in Eversleigh Road, I started to find my own flavours, connecting me to my roots. Cooking in itself was like having a conversation; a feeling of togetherness, expressing and giving love. Of course, dinner can't always be a creative act—sometimes it's just a grind—sometimes you've just gotta eat.

BRUCE AND A BABY

In late summer 1981, Bruce and I joined Ari, Viv, and Tessa on a writing retreat at Rockfield, a live-in studio in Wales where Queen had recorded "Bohemian Rhapsody." Just a little bit legendary . . . The food was all vegetarian and every single meal tasted of sage. Tessa and Bruce supplemented their diet with what flourished on the sheep shit out in the surrounding fields.

The Slits were working on what was going to be their third album. We also filmed a video with Mick Calvert for "Earthbeat" from *Return of the Giant Slits*. It features Ari and Tessa riding about a damp Welsh hillside on horses in pursuit of Viv, who's running around in some woods, while I dance in an open field in one of my African gowns.

When we got back to London, Ari found out that she was pregnant with twins. She didn't do anything by halves. While I'd been spending more time with Bruce, she had been on her own in the house with Junior. There was an empty space in the big bed—and the rest is history.

After Ari got together with Junior, I moved in with Bruce in a house in Maida Vale. He had taken over the room from a guy called Mario Tavares. Cheap housing in London was all sublets upon sublets. Every time Bruce had to go to the housing office, he had to pretend to be Mario. In his hip-hop leather coat from Orchard Street along with his funny black vinyl Run-DMC hat, he looked like some weird Miami coke-dealer dude whose name was Mario Tavares. We laughed so hard.

Bruce and I started thinking that maybe we should get married. We were very much a couple, but we probably wouldn't have done it if I hadn't needed to sort out my residency status. We went down to Marylebone registry office, naively imagining that we could just get it done there and then, Hollywood style: "Let's get married—*now*!" But no. Because I was only seventeen, it all took a bit of organising, so we settled on a date for late August. First, I had to get consent from my mother. When I phoned to tell her, she was with a great friend of hers, Uncle Curre.

"Woohoo! Neneh is getting married!" she told him, and they stayed up drinking late into the night. Then the papers turned up and she signed them. Later, Moki said, "What was I thinking? I didn't know Bruce or his parents and I didn't ask any questions: I just signed and figured that everything would be fine."

Ari was my best woman and Sean Oliver, our bass player, was the best man. Bruce's brother Stephan had made me a very cute white dress and Ari was wearing one of the Chinese silk shirts that we were into. We had them in several different colours and that day she was in blue, with a clashing head tie.

When we came out of the registry office, Mark and Gareth were outside playing their saxophones. Afterwards, Donna and Hassel, Bruce's parents, took us all to a Greek restaurant in Shepherd's Bush.

•

Our first Rip Rig + Panic album, *God*, came out with Virgin Records in September 1981. "Beware! This is not a record for people with a heart condition," warned Ian Pye in *Melody Maker*, concluding, "Well beyond categories but never form, this is great, raw, rough, sophisticated music to be embraced and loved." The reception was encouraging—the sales were just OK. But then, making hit records and loads of dosh wasn't really our *raison d'être*.

The following January, the Slits decided to disband. There was no big bust-up, but while Ari was pregnant there had been a gradual drifting towards what would become the next stage of their lives. Things had also changed between Ari and me. We had been passionately close and that couldn't continue in the same way once I was involved with Bruce. Her life moved on as well: first with Junior, then with her twin boys, Pedro and Pablo. Our bond would endure until Ari died in 2010, but our connection began to lose its intensity. I visited her and the babies in the flat they moved into on the Battersea Park Estate, and Ari still came out with us on our missions to dance, not as often as before but as often as she could. But a year after Pedro and Pablo were born, she and Junior took them to live with his family in Jamaica. The relationship with Junior didn't work out, but Ari fell in love with Kingston. She had another son with a different father, and she and her boys ended up dividing their time between Brooklyn and Jamaica. In the Kingston nightclubs, Ari became well known as a dance-hall queen under various names including Ari Up, Baby Whitey, and Madussa. From that point on, our meetings were more sporadic, but quite often she would be in Brooklyn while I was at the loft and sometimes she'd come to London. We missed each other, but we always knew where the other was. The thread that tied us never snapped.

•

Six months after Bruce and I married, I was pregnant. With a baby on the way, we needed our own place, so we went to the housing association. After a series of swaps, we eventually moved into a top-floor flat in Iverson Road, just off Kilburn High Road.

In our bed, I felt the first early flutterings of Naima in my stomach. In my dreams I felt the butterfly in my belly and it woke me up. The sensation was so faint, so unfamiliar, I couldn't immediately identify it. Could it be gas? What had I been eating? But within days, her kicks grew stronger, more insistent, and I thought,

This is my baby. In the middle of the night, I'd lie there, looking out at the rail tracks, thinking of this little person turning somersaults inside me, listening to the eerie rumble of the nuclear-waste trains passing just outside the window.

When I called around various hospitals in London trying to get some information on natural childbirth, I was met with cynicism. In Sweden, the midwives seemed to be more forward-thinking, so I decided that was where I would have my baby. I didn't suffer too badly with morning sickness, but by early spring 1982, my senses heightened, everything smelled nauseating. We had damp in the flat, the kitchen cupboards stank, and I couldn't deal with garlic. Just walking down Kilburn High Road was an ordeal: the stale fishy-grease stench of the chip shops, the raw-meat smell of the butcher's, and the sweet stink of the spices emanating from the Asian shops—all mixed together in a turgid funk.

Rip Rig + Panic's second album, *I Am Cold*, was released in June 1982 to mixed reviews but most of them appreciated Don's contribution on trumpet on six of the tracks: "Cherry plays beautifully throughout," wrote Lynden Barber in *Melody Maker*. I think it was a great record.

On July 18, Rip Rig + Panic played at the first ever World of Music, Arts and Dance (WOMAD) Festival in Somerset. Don joined us for our performance. He had formed a new group called Codona, creating beautiful, improvised music out of free jazz and musical traditions from Brazil, India, and Africa. They played before us in the morning, just after the Chieftains.

It was one of those unforgettable days that still resonates in my memory. Moki was in the audience, as were Bruce's parents and his brother Mark. I was six months pregnant by then, wearing a white lace dress. From the stage, I could see Moki in her grey Mickey Mouse sweatshirt with its sleeves cut off, her dark maroon hair piled into a bun that sat just a little to the side of her head.

That was the first time the Cherrys and the Smiths met. Earlier in the morning, we posed for a family photo outside Donna and Hassel's old rectory in Rode. We all look ridiculously happy, the grandparents-to-be with their arms around each other, embracing new life. Another family circle tied.

At the end of July, Bruce and I left London for Tågarp. In our absence, Rip Rig + Panic kept going, with the mighty South African drummer Louis Moholo taking Bruce's place and Sean's younger sister, Andrea Oliver, on vocals for the songs I would have sung. The group performed in an episode of *The Young Ones*, but I wasn't there. I was having a baby in Sweden.

Those months in the schoolhouse before the birth were sweet like honey. All of us were there: Moki, Don, Eagle-Eye, who was now thirteen. Donna and Hassel came to visit. We spent the long summer days at the house, swam in the lake, took walks in the forest. Every summer for about six years, Eagle-Eye and the other kids in our little community ran a children's theatre group called Octopuss. Moki and Anita Roney made the sets and co-directed with the "yout." That year, Don and Bruce were in the band, performing Ian Dury's unforgettable lullaby, "Sex & Drugs & Rock & Roll," and Nunu Roney did a Billie Holiday song. The first performances took place in the big schoolroom, which was full to the brim with an audience of all ages. The sketches were hip, almost disturbingly sharp, witty and political, and very funny. Everyone roared with laughter, especially the grown-ups. I played an angel in one scene—a heavily pregnant heavenly messenger in a brown dress with puffy sleeves and a sash that Ari had made in Jamaica. Later that summer, Octopuss performed the show in Lund near Malmö and at the Moderna Museet in Stockholm.

When we moved into the schoolhouse in 1970, the old dining table—a half-tonne turn-of-the-century mahogany piece that's seen it all—was already living there. Extended to its full length, it is the size of a small bedsit. On summer nights especially, there might be up to twenty people sitting around it, but that summer in Tågarp, after Donna and Hassel went home, it was mostly the inner circle. With just the five of us at the table, we pushed it near the windows overlooking the kitchen garden. In the farthest corner stood the compost heap with a great big hole in it. What was living in there? Every dinner was a long, delicious, boisterous affair. One night Moki served a lamb stew with anchovies—a meal I will never forget. We were obsessed with our new game: Name the Baby. Don was deadly at this game, nearly killing us. "Padmasambhava," he'd suggest or, looking out at the mystery compost hole, "How about Yard Rat?" We laughed until we cried.

A week after my due date, the night before I was supposed to go back to the antenatal clinic, I got up just after midnight to have a pee and noticed a spot of blood. It was happening! The baby was on its way. Everybody got up to wait with me for the taxi (paid for by the Swedish state). It had to drive up from Hässleholm, so Moki made everyone tea and Bruce put on a tie. Don hugged me and laid those long, beautiful fingers on my cheek.

"Look at you, baby," he said.

I was conscious of our lives changing course. It felt monumental. And then the taxi's headlights appeared in the bend down the road. I got into the back seat, Bruce sat in the front, and, as we pulled out of the yard, I could see Moki, Don, and Eagle-Eye waving from the porch.

During the forty-five-minute journey to the big hospital in Kristianstad, my contractions were gaining strength. When we arrived, despite my dreams of a natural birth, I was swiftly whisked away to a cold grey bathroom where a nurse shaved me with a blunt Bic disposable razor. At 2 a.m., the midwife left Bruce and me mostly alone to journey through the night, waiting for my cervix to be sufficiently dilated. At some point, Bruce fell asleep on the birthing bed, and I laboured on, Moki's voice humming through my thoughts, *When a contraction is done, let it go. Don't anticipate the next one. Try to rest*. For the minutes of respite, I would drift off to a place somewhere between conscious thought and dreaming. Floating, flying, breathing, trying, pushing, sighing, laughing, crying; my divine daughter Naima Jade was born at 8:55 a.m. on October 6, 1982. As she entered the world, I noticed the smell of the sea. Inside women's bodies is an ocean that creates miracles. Bruce and I were reborn as parents.

Motherhood came naturally. Naima and I were together all the time. I breast-fed and kept her close. Bruce and I watched her sleep and stared in amazement at her fingers, her toes. When she was awake, we marvelled at her every movement, whimper, and grimace. I spoke with Ahmadu on the phone, but there wasn't time for him to visit. He would meet his first grandchild in London a few months later.

When Naima was three weeks old, we returned to the UK. Moki joined us on the notorious cruise from Gothenburg, and Donna and Hassel met us at Victoria Station. One night I dressed Naima in her prettiest blue baby-grow, carefully slipped her into a sling with my South American poncho to cover her ears, and we went to see Sun Ra at the Venue. When she was six weeks old, Bruce and I took her on tour with Rip Rig + Panic, in a carry cot in our rented Transit van. She was the funniest, sweetest baby. When we were driving, she would just feed and sleep. And once she went to sleep, she would stay asleep. Our tour manager, Phil, had kids of his own and he would wear her in the sling while we were onstage.

This was the way I had seen women in Africa deal with motherhood and life, and how my mum had approached the need to combine parenting and creativity. The child goes along with you, tied close to your body, riding out the rhythm of your movements. The hope is that when they stand on their own feet, ready to take their first independent steps, there is a confidence bred by intimacy, which equals security. For me, the commitment of becoming a mother was about knowing that, wherever I was, I would try to be emotionally present for my child. I wanted them to know that we would always be here, but that they could expand over there, safe in the arms of others. That is the most important thing anyone can do as a parent. I told myself, *If it doesn't work, if I start freaking out, or if they start freaking out, I will just have to stop, reset. But this is our life, so let's just try it.* And so we did. We just got on with it. Those times on the road with Naima as a baby, and, later, with Tyson and Mabel, were special. Just as Moki had done with me in Stockholm, I always packed some extra baby-grows, some extra nappies, so that if I did stay out longer than expected, I'd be prepared. I'm not going to say that I haven't made mistakes—I know I have, and, unfortunately, my kids have known stress. But I would try to give them a bath at the same time every night, to make my arms a home for them, wherever we might be. As I look back at that time now, I know I did my best, but photographs of me from then also tell the truth: I was so young.

ANDREA

I've been lucky. I have found the loves of my life—or maybe they found me. My friendship with Andrea Oliver spans decades. It has sustained me for a lifetime. Andi is of my soul: it's love, it's friendship, it's sisterhood. We are family—our children are cousins. I was sixteen and Andi was seventeen when we met. It was 1981. Her brother Sean and I had become firm friends. We would go wandering around the West End, flitting into pubs, chatting with the people he knew. Before he was in Rip Rig + Panic, he had been a busker, so he had a whole other life from that street scene.

When I found out that Sean had a younger sister, I immediately wanted to know her. She was still living at home with her mother in Bury St. Edmunds, working in a hairdresser's, and I asked him if she knew how to braid. I was missing her before I even got to know her.

One Thursday night, after we'd all been out at Gaz's Rockin' Blues, Sean and another friend got a lift home. They had only gone as far as Cambridge Circus when the driver wrapped the car around a lamp post at the top of Shaftesbury Avenue. The other passengers were unhurt, but Sean's leg was shattered. He was taken to the since-demolished Middlesex Hospital, where they operated on him to fix the fractures. But the accident and his subsequent surgery triggered a sickle cell attack and he spent weeks in the hospital, flat on his back, his right leg suspended in the air with a metal pin inside. I visited him every day, brought food and read to him.

The moment Andi walked into the ward, I felt an immediate, unspoken bond. It felt as if we had always known each other.

Within minutes, we were outside in the corridor sharing a smoke. By the time we got back to Sean's bedside, we'd decided to make a record. Everyone said, "Yeah, right," but six months later, Andi and I were on the road together. She had become part of Rip Rig + Panic.

We were both soul-starved. We came from very different backgrounds, but we were both battling, breaking out and finding ourselves. In Bury St. Edmunds, Andi had been the only Black kid at her school. When I saw her, it was like hearing a lost voice, that sister I needed to be with. We made each other strong.

As with Ari, Andi and I shared everything. We'd play Earth, Wind and Fire and work out incredibly complex dance routines that we'd forget by the end of the evening. We'd try to sew clothes for Bruce, though neither of us knew what the hell we were doing. We cooked together, sometimes feeding a few, but often many. Once, in preparation for a party, we filled my bathtub with mackerel to wash them. Then we boned and filleted them and roasted them all in my tiny little oven along with a small mountain of chicken. I dread to think how many chickens she and I cooked over the years. We were creating a sense of home, security, and continuity; somewhere good, safe, and kind where people could be.

We cooked like we danced—together, with heart and soul. And we drank as we danced, with heart and soul. We were finding our voices as young Black women: like our music, cooking gave us a means to explore and celebrate where we came from and who we were. Needing nurture and comfort, we were discovering our version of soul food—curried goat, cornbread and big pots of greens, meat loaf, mashed potato and gravy; whatever we could get our hands on, or, rather, could afford. In the heat of the kitchen, sweet-smelling of spice, now here we were, saying all the things that words can't hold. Pots, pans, stages, songs, music, steam rising, Dinah Washington pouring her heart out.

We loved the Black American poet Nikki Giovanni. Sometimes we would sit late into the night, listening to her 1973 album *Like a Ripple on a Pond*, recorded with the New York Community Choir, playing the title track over and over again, drinking up her words. Other nights we would stay up listening to Richard Pryor, which would leave us dying of laughter, creased up on the floor.

We devoured the same books—Alice Walker's *The Color Purple*; *The Joys of Motherhood* by Buchi Emecheta; *The Bluest Eye* by Toni Morrison; *Woman at Point Zero* by Nawal El Saadawi. Moki sent me *The Color Purple* from New York. She had wrapped it in brown paper cut from a grocery bag and slipped a note inside the covers: "My darling Neneh, you have to read this book. I did not want to wait until we saw you, but wanted you to have it now. Miss you and long to see you. Hug Naima. I love you, Mamma."

The day Moki's brown-bag package arrived, Naima was behind me in her high chair, singing and eating porridge out of her yellow stick-to-the-surface Mothercare bowl. The postman passed my window, the letterbox opened. When I read Moki's note, seeing her writing, familiar in a way that no words can explain, it made my heart ache. I looked at my daughter, caught in a moment of wonder. I was nineteen and missed my own mother like a child. But I was a mother, too.

It took me a while to settle into the language of the book, but soon I was transported to a dusty front yard with a little girl with braids on a porch. Once I had the rhythm, the words held me, turned me inside out, and didn't let go. I didn't go very far that weekend. Alice Walker took me hostage.

It was also Moki who sent me *Sassafrass, Cypress & Indigo* by Ntozake Shange. Ntozake was married at the time to David Murray, a jazz saxophonist my dad used to play with. Set in the jazz world of sixties and seventies New York and among the Gullah people of Charleston, South Carolina, the book is about three sisters and their mother, with poetry, letters, and recipes incorporated throughout the story.

Andi and I needed these women to help us see the stories that are not told in history books. We were hungry for them. Those books were a vital part of our education, of our growing up and finding ourselves and taking pride in who we were. We were proud of our connection to these tales, that they were about us. They changed us, fed us, gave us form—those books are our anthems. We found that we belong here, that our story is profound and that it matters. These are the books that we have passed on to our daughters.

When I read the books or listen to the music of women artists who have affected me, I feel that they know me. Writers like Nawal El Saadawi, Isabel Allende, Maya Angelou, Toni Morrison, and Angela Davis do that to me. Or the singing of Patti Smith and Poly Styrene, Chrissie Hynde (who Don adored too), Lauryn Hill, Dinah Washington, Aretha Franklin, Dusty Springfield, and Minnie Riperton; and the hip-hop women—Queen Latifah, Roxanne Shante, MC Lyte, Tanya "Sweet Tee" Winley—bossing it in what was considered the exclusive territory of the boys. They have something that can't help itself.

I don't want to use the word "strong" to describe these artists. Does "strong" include tender, longing, missing, empty, tired, lovesick? Or does *too much* emotion, too many feelings, imply intemperance? These women's voices became a part of me. I shared the intentions within and behind their words. When Chaka Khan sang "I'm Every Woman," it was as if she was singing it directly to me. They passed the baton. And nothing, in theory, was going to stop me. Except sometimes myself.

•

Ari, Tessa, Viv, and Bruce, Andi, Sean, Gareth, and I: we moved as a group and the family ties kept evolving. Ari, who seemed the most unlikely candidate, had dropped the first babies. I had Naima next. Then came Miquita, Andi's daughter with Robin, a Scotsman, in April 1984. Next Tessa got together with Andi's brother Sean (keeping it in the family) and their daughter, Phoebe, was born in 1984, about eighteen months after I had Naima. I was honoured to be present at both Miquita's and Phoebe's births. (Tessa and I were hanging out together at the flat Bruce and I later moved to in Fulham Court when she went into labour. As we waited for the ambulance, I whispered calming words in her ear, between rushing to finish the food I was making to bring to the hospital—a batch of fried chicken wings and a potato salad.)

I wouldn't change these times for anything in the world. But they were also tough. Andi and I were teenage mothers living in a city where neither of us had our parents, realising that motherhood can feel lonely as well as glorious. We didn't have much money. We weren't always sure how to be ourselves—young women of colour—and also be everything we aspired to be for our daughters. We were strong and capable, but also vulnerable. So we propped each other up through some joyful, beautiful moments and some intensely painful ones. Non-judgemental, forgiving, we carry each other through by honouring who we are as individuals.

The promises of love are manifold, but nothing is as abundant as the hands of sisterhood. With Andi and Ari (and my other beloveds: you know who you are), I am blessed. The closeness I shared with those two women is something else. With them I became more.

DJ BATTLES AT THE HOT STY

Andi and I would be out dancing in clubs maybe three nights a week. We would peel off our boots or trainers, tuck our skirts into our knickers, and just dance. We danced so fucking hard. We went dancing like some people go to church. I don't know if we necessarily cleansed our souls, but for sure it strengthened our spirits. We found freedom together.

Deep within the pulsating riot of the dance floor I would reunite with my body—before babies, during babies, after babies—the endorphins washing away stress and pain. My feet pumping to the beat, legs aching, body sweating, swaying in its rhythmic joy. I would let myself sink into a sea of bodies. This was hard-concrete, dopamine-making sport. Living politics.

We were still regulars in the dance halls of west and south-west London, but there was something happening over in the centre of town that drew our attention. The late-night scene in Soho, Covent Garden, as far north as Camden, was becoming much more mixed. The queer culture was already there, but now new club nights were cropping up in odd little venues all over the West End.

The Rip Rig boys were great friends with Rose Boyt, who was renting in a friend's house in Notting Hill—a handy stop-off on their road in from Bristol, where they were based. Andi and I became friends with Rose and her bunch and we started going out as a posse. Everyone we knew wanted to go to the same clubs, but sometimes Rose would babysit Naima and Miquita. Other friends wanted to have a go at looking after them too, to imagine themselves as a parent, perhaps, the idea of babies dwelling not too far in their psyche. Sometimes we would just have to bribe people. Truth be told, sometimes we nagged so hard that they caved in, just said "yes" to get rid of us.

Sometimes we'd congregate at Rose's place, have some drinks, and then head to Soho; or we'd just meet specifically at the French House on Dean Street. We used the place like a clubhouse, to find one another. On Thursdays we would go on to Gaz's Rockin' Blues at Gossip's, also on Dean Street, where DJ Gaz Mayall played a selection of old blues records, mostly 45s—Fats Waller, Nina Simone, ska, rocksteady, some old-school reggae—and where we danced until we dropped. And, of course, the Wag Club on Wardour Street for rowdy nights, many of them run by Chris Sullivan and Ollie O'Donnell. There were so many DJs going in and out with bulging record bags, I couldn't possibly tell you who they all were, but you could always find Fat Tony in there. I can picture him now, leaning on a wall in a pink fake fur, spitting out the sharpest banter in town and spinning the decks: Prince, and of course some pretty intense disco. The Wag action was overseen by the bouncer Winston, a tall West Indian gentleman built like a barn door, in his black suit and bow tie—for any dodgy antics in the toilets or involving Rizlas, he would rap you sharply on the knuckles with a drumstick.

Dave Dorrell was resident DJ at a club called Raw under the YMCA in Tottenham Court Road. The Electric Ballroom in Camden had a weekly hip-hop night in the main room and a jazz-funk room upstairs. I was also a regular at Language Lab, upstairs from Gossip's. Run by James Lebon, it was one of London's first open-mic hip-hop nights, so kids rolled in from all corners of town. Anyone who took to the stage earned a fiver. I improvised with the raps from the records I was listening to, so when I took the mic, I just threw a bunch of things together, collaging them and twisting and turning them and making them my own.

In late 1982, Bruce and Sean started their own club night called the Hot Sty, first in Cass's, one of those classic dank West End basement bars in Leicester Square; then upstairs in Fouberts Club, off Carnaby Street in Soho; and, finally, at 52 Piccadilly. They asked Rose to run it with them, partly because, compared to everyone else, she appeared to be reasonably organised, and because she had a legendary record collection. They paid her £20 a week. All she had to do was bring her records and man the door. We would set up the decks against the back wall and somebody made a banner that we draped behind them. Sean and Bruce DJ'd, playing a mixture of classic funk tunes: the Fatback Band, Parliament, Michael Jackson, James Brown, the Last Poets, and Def Jam records. One night at Fouberts, we'd just come back from New York with the latest hip-hop vinyls in hand; they played like wildfire, red-hot on the turntables. Graffiti artist, hip-hop pioneer, and one of the coolest in NYC, Fab 5 Freddy was in the house, spinning on his head in the middle of the dance floor. On another night, later in Piccadilly, Rose sat in the relative quiet of the door, Miquita sleeping soundly in her Moses basket at her feet.

When Rip Rig + Panic went on tour to Japan, Sean and Bruce didn't want to miss a week of the Hot Sty, so Rose agreed to keep it open and Sean arranged for a friend to DJ. But on the night, Sean's mysterious DJ friend was a no-show. Rose went over to the decks and thought, *Right, this doesn't look that complicated. I'm sure I can do it.* She put a record on, and then another and another. By the end of the night, Rose realised that she had DJ'd the whole Hot Sty night on her own.

After Rose's first impromptu set at the Hot Sty, our friend Jeannette Lee, who was blessed with a sharp eye for an opportunity, suggested she start her own night with just girls. This led to us starting the Midden on Tuesdays at the Wag. I'd already been presenting a rather chaotic radio show on DBC (Dread Broadcasting

Corporation), a west London pirate station, alone or sometimes with Bruce. I guess that, along with the Midden, was my intro to spinning records. Rose had all these old Studio One 45s that she used to play, and then, at some point, a girl called Bionic Rhona started toasting on the B-sides, and I started to do a bit of rapping. Our tenancy at the Wag was short-lived, but Andi, Jeannette, Viv Goldman, and I started another all-ladies one-nighter, the Bite Night, at Legends in Mayfair.

Later Rose and Sean started weekly Saturday night warehouse parties in a disused school hall in Battle Bridge Road, roughly where Pancras Square is now. We put army camouflage netting all over the ceiling and the walls. The only lights were some candles above the decks and bar.

Sean, Bruce, and the Northern Irish brothers Noel and Maurice Watson (ex-punks, former tailors, and now brilliant DJs) alternated on the decks on one side of the stage, their records soon covered in great dollops of candle wax. On the other, Rose ran a bar out of an old bathtub filled with ice, with me as an occasional extra barmaid. I have a vision of her behind the bathtub, barricaded in by a wall of beer boxes, in lace-up Victorian shoes, an Adidas bag full of cash strapped to her ankle. She'd taken so much money on the bar that when she needed to pee, she had to carry the bag of cash across the club and literally keep it underfoot.

Battle Bridge Road was quite a scene. Everyone went there—not just young clubbers, but also all the sex workers and the pimps from King's Cross. We started selling brandy, because that's what they all drank. But things started to get heavy. The Millwall F-Troop came down and tried to put a protection tax on Sean and Rose. They wanted 10 percent of their takings every week and Rose ended up having to physically shove one of them to get him to back off. They had to bring some other guys in, also a bunch of gangsters, to protect them on the club nights. Finally, about six months after it started, we turned up one night and found the whole place barricaded behind giant metal fences. And that was the end of that.

When Battle Bridge Road closed, Rose was headhunted to run the guest list at the Café de Paris, near Leicester Square. Poor Rose. She was supposed to give admittance only to celebrities—Prince, Michael Jackson, you name it, were on the guest list—but she was the most kind and friendly door person, more like a night nurse or agony aunt, handing out free tickets to everybody. Obviously, that meant all us lot could get freebies every week. Around the same time, she also started working at Fred's, the first young people's private club in Soho. Rose was the membership secretary and soon it became the cool place to go for the music, media, and fashion set. She was also the music consultant, booking DJs for the small disco in the basement every night.

Somewhere in all of this, Andi and I started to DJ out and about, at private parties or at the Castle, a pub we all used to go to on Portobello Road. I remember a mad night playing under the Westway just off Portobello Road, watching a seething mass of bodies moving as one to "ABC" by the Jackson 5. We played the tunes that we loved—"Ain't Nothin' Goin' On but the Rent" by Gwen Guthrie; "Sleng Teng" (the first electronic "riddim" to come out of Jamaica); we were obsessed with "La Di Da Di" by Doug E. Fresh and Slick Rick; Joyce Sims; "Somebody Else's Guy" by Jocelyn Brown. Her acapella intro lasts 58 seconds (enough time to walk a long block). As she belted out her tale of jilted love, we'd all sing along—because we all knew how that felt. We would drop it in on top of the end of the previous track, not exactly seamless mixing, but *our* version. We played hard, like we were at a house party. The winning ticket was the flawless "Vicious Rap" by Tanya "Sweet Tee" Winley. I blindly bought it in a store on 34th Street in New York because it was the only record by a female rapper. And it just happened to be one of the toughest, most unapologetic songs I'd ever heard.

One night, Andi and I were in a DJ battle with the guys from Funkapolitan—Tom Dixon, Toby Anderson, and the others—at their club night, Titanic, in Berkeley Square. They had a whole super-slick set-up with scaffolding on the stage and musicians positioned on different levels of the structure, playing along to the records. They had given us a smaller, weaker sound system up towards the bar at the back. Next thing we knew, someone had unplugged us. Now it was all-out war. Sean found the lead and plugged it back in and we came right back at them with "Get Up" by James Brown. Everyone went apeshit. We won.

The pubs closed at 11 p.m. and, except for Fridays and Saturdays, there weren't many places to choose from. Anyway, you would always end up at the Wag, or there was Heaven. But the "one-nighter" culture in London was constantly evolving. There were the now-fabled Blitz and Mud clubs. Blitz was all about how outrageous and original your outfits could be, and Mud Club had some of that same fashion vibe, mixed with a smattering of current pop stars, the always-fun gay crowd, all to the soundtrack of a beautiful mishmash of current dance mixes, pop classics, and old-school Motown hits, with the odd torch song thrown in for good measure. And, later on, at Leigh Bowery's club Taboo, where they had a big screen above the dance floor, Jeffrey Hinton had carte blanche, controlling the sound, visuals, and lighting. Under Leigh's scrutiny, the dress code, strictly enforced, was "Dress as if your life depends on it or don't bother."

Everyone went to one another's nights. We'd all bump into each other at one club or another and move on to the next one and the next and the next. I would step into these spaces and know I was in a safe zone. I was able to leave a lot of my defence mechanisms at the door. Everybody who wanted to be part of creating the experience, rather than it being sold to them, was gathering there. It was somewhere in the dark where people could be together and get lost, make things happen, where there was room for all of us. In our day, we felt allied. We were a community. That mattered.

When I wrote the song "Synchronised Devotion," I was reaching for the memory of those sounds, smells, and emotions from the days when we would go into those places, leave our shit at the door, and be all right for a while. Those were our battlefields. I can almost taste them still.

FLIGHT TO TOKYO

In the first week of October 1984, when I was twenty, I went on a modelling trip to Japan with Ray Petri's Buffalo posse, a radical, diverse collective of artists, photographers, designers, musicians, models, and students in his orbit who were setting the tempo for a creative explosion in fashion. The term "Buffalo" had a number of different influences: American Indian male dress and the culture of reverence for the almighty buffalo, which fed, clothed, and sustained them, and which they worshipped; the chain tags worn by Jack Negrit's Buffalo Security lads; as well as Bob Marley's song "Buffalo Soldier," which had been inspired by the name given to the African American cavalry regiments of the US army by the American Indians who fought them during the American Indian Wars. The Black soldiers were judged to be so fierce that they fought like buffaloes. The name stuck, and continued to be used of Black regiments in the American Civil War, the two world wars, and the Korean War. A Buffalo was a warrior, a rebel, but also, perhaps, an underdog, and Marley's song was an anthem of resistance. That was all summed up in Ray's anti-establishment outlook and his work in fashion. This was the heyday of *i-D* and *The Face* magazines, and Ray was their visionary, a subversive stylist (before "styling" was a profession) marrying high fashion, classic style, sportswear, and streetwear, putting a beautiful Black man in Lycra cycling shorts, a designer bomber jacket, a Native Indian feather headdress, and jewellery.

The Japan trip happened in a roundabout way: a friend, Ralph Shandilya, who was a talent scout for the Japanese designer Takeo

Kikuchi, asked Ray to put together a group of young British models to show his collection in Japan. At the same time, Ralph rang to see if I might be interested, so I had some photos taken, skanking around in one of my Clare Thom outfits and a head tie, and I was chosen as one of only two women models in the entourage: the other was the photographer Ari Ashley.

Bruce was on tour, so I left Naima with Donna at our home in Fulham Court on a grey morning and took the Tube to Heathrow. I was conflicted about the trip. I really didn't want to leave my baby. Naima would have her second birthday while I was away. But then—Japan, planes, new people, being a model, walking a catwalk, albeit a slightly absurd concept—another part of me couldn't wait to go.

When I got to the check-in desk, all the guys from those now-legendary spreads in *i-D* and *The Face* were already there: Nick and Barry Kamen, Mark and James Lebon, Howard Napper, Jack Negril, Jamie Morgan, Ari Ashley, Ray Petri (of course), and the photographers Brett Walker and Roger Charity. And among the assembled Buffaloes was Cameron McVey, sitting on a baggage trolley in a cowboy hat. Piercing blue eyes, big turn-ups on his dark-wash jeans: cool as a summer night's breeze.

I walked up to him and said, "Hi, how you doing? I'm Neneh." Cam was, like me, also there to model but, again like me, his profession was not modelling. I soon discovered that he already had a successful career as a fashion photographer, video and commercials director, and television maker, as well as a record producer and songwriter. He told me his name but was not otherwise particularly forthcoming. In fact, he played it so cool that I thought, *Let me just remove myself.*

Not long after take-off, things turned a bit kooky. Cam had brought a banana cake in his hand luggage and offered everyone a slice. I took one and it was delicious, with a good crunch. I thought the walnuts were a nice touch. Of course, as I found out soon enough, they weren't nuts but substantial chunks of hash. Ari Ashley said we might as well sleep as it was a twelve-hour flight, so I had a couple of wines from the drinks trolley and then took a sleeping pill.

As I waited for the pill to take effect, the hash kicked in. I was trying to watch the Gene Wilder movie *The Woman in Red*, but I couldn't understand what the hell was going on and I couldn't stop laughing. And sleep—what was that? Everyone who'd gobbled a piece of Cam's banana cake was either falling about in hysterics or falling apart. At one point, Nick Kamen had a panic attack and started flailing about at the cabin door, trying to get off the plane. By the time we got to the stopover in Anchorage, we all had the most insane munchies and were scrabbling to get into the terminal. We descended on the noodle bar, throwing bowl after bowl of noodles down our throats. Was it breakfast, lunch, or dinner? Who cared—nothing had ever tasted so good. Most of us were still stoned. Somebody (who shall remain nameless) was off in the duty-free area, shoplifting. It was mayhem. The wild times continued once we arrived in Tokyo, where we were all staying in the same hotel. After work and what felt like endless fittings, we would hit the town, dancing hard in bars and clubs all night, every night.

Following my non-starter of a conversation with Cameron at Heathrow, I had gravitated towards other people while we were in Tokyo, but on about the fourth day, we found each other. I danced with him that night. He was wearing a tartan shorts suit and, yes, I felt something like a small tremor.

The next day we were doing a fitting. I was standing with my top off when Cam walked past and said something like, "Yes, girl."

Oh, OK, I thought. *Interesting*. Not rude, a bit cheeky, in a nice way . . .

Afterwards, we took the bullet train to Osaka and from there we took a coach to Kobe to do the first show. It was on that bus, rolling along, black outside the windows, that we connected. Everyone was exhausted from all the sleepless nights, so most of the others had nodded off, but Cam and I talked. He was wearing shades and I was thankful I didn't have to look straight into those blue eyes.

This was my third time in Japan. When I was ten, Eagle-Eye and I had travelled with Moki and Don when they were doing shows there. I'd been back there on tour again, with Rip Rig + Panic and Don, in 1983.

Cam had spent quite a lot of time in Japan, too. His ex-wife, Vonnie, worked for Issey Miyake and had been living there when they first met, so he used to travel to see her. Arriving in the hotel lobby in Kobe, I heard him ask someone, "Where can we eat *okonomiyaki*?" He was given an address, and we set off with Ari Ashley and Brett Walker. We sat on the floor in a booth, Cam and me next to each other, with the hotplate between all of us, cooking our own cabbage pancakes. We also drank a bucket of sake. I remember that I was wearing a white dress by Clare, cut very deep with a single strap across the back, and at one point Cam put a finger on my bare skin.

After we finished eating, we walked outside into a warm night. The street quiet except for the four of us, Cam and I had some kind of a drunken running race on the wide empty sidewalk. I thought, *I'm gonna beat this bitch*, but annoyingly he overtook me. Back in his room, drinking a carton of cold sake from a vending machine, we got even more drunk. At some point, Ari went out to get something and, as soon as she left, my eyes got stuck in the deep blue of Cam's. He stretched out an arm and pulled me gently towards him. When Ari got back, Cam and I were standing close together. Ari's expression did something funny. Slightly twitchy, she said, "I think I need to go to bed."

I slept in Cam's room that night, but I was clear that nothing was going to go down. I've always enjoyed a metaphorical fling on a dance floor. But one-night stands—emotionally, I just wasn't well equipped to deal with all that messiness. Under the covers, fully clothed, I had chewing gum in my mouth and he said, "Give me your gum so that you don't get it in your hair in the night." There was something so tender and sweet in that gesture. He fell asleep with my gum in his hand, and when we woke up in the morning, it was stuck all over his arm. That's where it started.

The catwalk shows that day were epic, complete with gospel singers, a motorcycle gang, lasers, and a snowstorm of white and gold confetti at the finale. Afterwards, Cam and I changed out of our catwalk clothes and went for a walk outside the arena. It was a gargantuan steel-encased structure, dark grey, imposing, like a giant fat mechanical woodlouse from a Studio Ghibli film. We found a patch of grass and lay down, watching eagles circling in the sky.

NENEH CHERRY &
CAMERON McVEY
WOULD LIKE TO INVITE
TO A
PARTY
TO CELEBRATE THEIR
WEDDING
TO BE HELD AT
COBDENS WORKING MENS CLUB
170-172 KENSAL RD NW10
ON FRIDAY 7TH DECEMBER
1990
STARTING AT 10.00 PM
& FINISHING MUCH MUCH LATER
RSVP
c/o ELLIE MILNER THE CHERRY BEAR
TEL: 081 960 6291

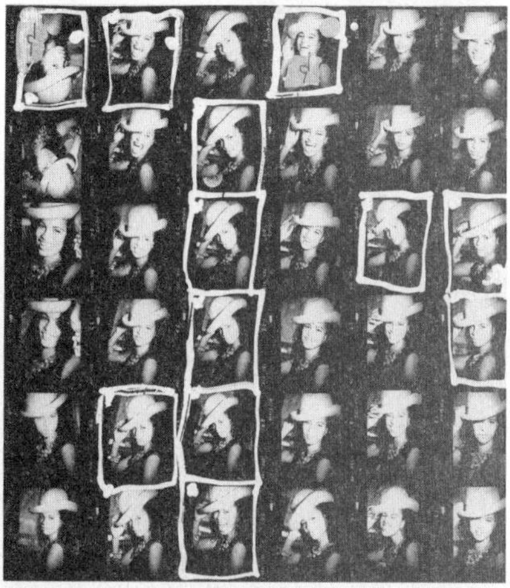

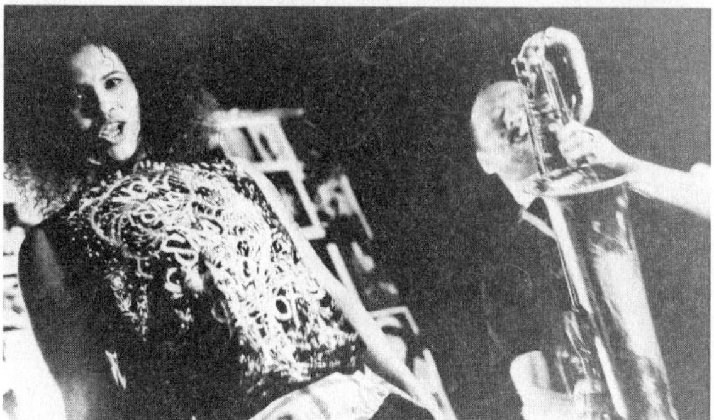

PART THREE

Last vacation with Marlon and Naima before Tyson! • So many wonderful nights out together • With Queen Latifah • On the cover of *Face*, 1989 • The invitation designed by Judy • With Tyson in Spain, 1993 • With Don in those last months in Spain, 1995 • Wearing a nice bit of Noki, with Mats Gustafsson playing to my left

WE WRITE THE SONGS

Cam and I returned to London from Tokyo in love. He lived in a top-floor studio flat in Rupert Street in Soho, up four long flights of stairs. The studio's open windows let in the cries of the barrow boys peddling fruit and veg in the street below, and there was a megaphone on the floor next to the window so Cam could alert the women peddling their bodies when Babylon was closing in.

From the start, I recognised Cam as that person I had known existed out there somewhere. Cameron Andrew McVey was born in Bounds Green on August 11, 1957, where his parents lived with Cam's nan, a seamstress, and his pop, who worked at Billingsgate Fish Market. Cam's dad, Duncan, was Scottish and his Mumma Jean came from old East End stock, near Victoria Park, and they had met when the teenage Jean had been evacuated to Scotland during the war. I never met Duncan, as he passed away when Cam was sixteen, but I loved Mumma Jean dearly. A physiotherapist, Jean had lost her eyesight after an incorrectly treated eye infection when she was five years old. She was a very witty, fiercely independent woman who became a big inspiration to me. Maybe that's why Cam is such an interesting character. I sensed immediately that ours was not just a meeting of minds, nor merely a physical attraction, but a connection in body and soul. You are lucky if you find that with even one person in life.

Before I continue with this love story, though, there was another love story unfinished. Bruce and I were married. How do you leave something that is solid, that is almost everything, that is also *love*? I was terrified of us breaking up, and what it would do to Bruce, to Naima, to me. I knew about family. I understood it. I needed it. But there was also something inside me that was lonely, longing for and needing a harbour. I tried to run away from my feelings for Cameron, but every time I saw him, they sucked me back in. I didn't want to leave one man for another, or to be dishonest; so, panicked by the full-magnitude quake, no mere tremor now, I kept pushing the feelings away.

But even before I met Cam, I don't think Bruce and I had been making each other happy, although we weren't unhappy either. There was a security in our marriage. We were friends, companions, and had a lot of fun doing great things together. But after Naima was born, Bruce was away touring a lot. He was bread-winning for us, taking opportunities when they came. He was also nurturing his immense talent. When Dennis Bovell called and said, "Bruce, we need you! Come play with the Linton Kwesi Johnson Band," of course he had to go. Later, he joined PiL (he still plays with them). But I know well the hollowness that sometimes follows a big tour. It can feel as if you're lost in your own echo chamber. Somewhere in the centre of our relationship, a distance had grown.

I had been just seventeen when we got married. We'd had a child, made a home together, and we wanted to be good parents. From early childhood, stepping up when Don disappeared and Moki broke down—that imperative to be good, to be capable, to get on with it—had been ingrained in me. Bruce and I had taken on all that responsibility, and that meant denying my own needs and desires. I probably didn't know how to handle or articulate those longings, even to myself, because I was so young. I think neither of us had really finished growing up. Bruce and I spoke about this just recently. We see now that we still had so much to experience to become who we are today. Our paths and destinities led us apart, not without some regrets, but, ultimately, things became as they were meant to be.

I had fallen deeply in love with Cameron and kept that relationship a secret for two years, which made me feel horrible. Being in love is a very powerful energy, but I also knew how much pain it would cause Bruce and Naima. Their pain was also my pain, because, of course, change hurts. It bleeds and it leaves its scars. It triggered a trauma hangover from my childhood—the stress I felt in our family back then in the loft. I am very disturbed by conflict. So my being the cause of discord was really hard to reconcile. My divided heart was in turmoil and it held the weight of responsibility and guilt. I'm not a dishonest person. I truly care about behaving well, and not hurting others. At the same time, there was Cameron, waiting. He never ever put any pressure on me, but, justifiably, he must have been thinking, *What the fuck is going on?*

I was so scared of shit hitting the fan, and then finally it did. Bruce was away on tour and couldn't get hold of me, so he called Sean. And Sean just couldn't lie anymore. He told Bruce that I was with Cameron in Rupert Street, and Bruce called there. I am not proud of all the heartache that followed.

We broke up pretty much straightaway. It was done. Bruce moved out of our flat. He and Naima would always have a relationship, however. I was never going to get in the way of them seeing each other. There were a couple of difficult years when Bruce was wounded and angry, but he and I were always civil. Gradually, we became friends again. His family—Donna and Hassel and his brothers, Uncle Mark and Stephan—remained my family in England, and Naima and I continued to see them. I was grateful for their open-hearted acceptance, their unquantified measure of love that never ends.

After the break-up, Naima and I were placed in another housing association flat on Edith Road, between Fulham and Hammersmith. That two-bedroom flat with its tiny kitchen is where I started to write songs. "Manchild" came to life there, as did

"Buffalo Stance." Cameron came to live with us, and my stepson, Marlon, often stayed, too. As our family constellation shifted, it creaked in places that sometimes hurt.

•

It was late 1986 and the Wicked Witch of the West, Margaret Thatcher, was ruling the land with her iron knuckles. As wine bars started appearing in my new neighbourhood, the wallpaper was peeling in the libraries. Miners went out on strike, women set up camp on Greenham Common, and Maggie's emotionless voice harped on in an unceasing loop of destruction. Broke, broken, broker.

Words started to form in my head, spilling out onto the pages of notebooks. In the hours when my daughter was happily playing at nursery, I began to hum and write in a more concentrated way.

Cam is a great encourager, with an eye for talent and a mentor to many. With me he simply said, "You can write. Why are you not writing songs?" One of the first presents he gave me was a Dictaphone, so I could record my thoughts and capture my ideas.

I knew that I could stand on a stage and perform. I felt blessed to have been part of the Slits with Ari, and then with Rip Rig + Panic, where we had so much freedom as individuals to do what we wanted within the group. I had needed the security of that family, as I was not yet ready to stand on my own two feet—or to write songs. But something in me was stirring. Working with Gareth Sager had prepared me for this moment. His songwriting technique and his lyrics were a huge influence when I was taking my first steps as a songwriter. Now, with Cam, I felt safe to expand outwards, take chances. He had confidence in me and he was there, saying, "Write, explore, express. You can do it. So do it now."

The first song I wrote was "Looking Through the Eyes of Love." I wrote it before Cam and I moved in together, without any instruments or music—just made it up, sang it into the Dictaphone, and plonked the tiny cassette through the letterbox of Cam's flat in Rupert Street. He phoned me two hours later. He'd put chords to my words and down the phone line he sang my humble mumblings back to me. I couldn't believe that it sounded like a song—except the middle eight was missing. Thirty minutes later, I called him back.

"Hi, Cam, there's another bit," I said. " 'Can't stay for no vulture love, I'll be back when my heart's above.' " I think I was quite proud of the vulture metaphor for love gone bad.

"Oh, shit. OK, let me look at that," Cam replied.

That call confirmed in his eyes that his instincts were right. "That's when I knew you really were a songwriter," he says now. It's a talent to be able to identify and tap into things about you that perhaps you're aware of but can't access. Thank God. We could both sense the possibilities, like unborn dreams, waiting to happen.

LOOKING GOOD DIVING WITH THE WILD BUNCH

I'm walking to the store in the late afternoon to get some milk and maybe a Red Stripe, my feet wading through the damp autumn leaves on the footpath. It's dark but still early, about 5 p.m., and as I step onto the kerb there is something in my stride. I have a vision of a crocodile shoe, and something a friend called Barnsley shouted to me on a dance floor a week earlier pops into my head: "I'm bad like a gigolo."

A flash of pick-up lines and teenage resolutions, the empty rigmarole, loud, unsure, testosterone overflow and young women overthinking. He wants to be king, or at least somebody. Her body wants to be seen. The street scene unfolds in my head.

As I hit the pavement, the rap fell out. "Who's that gigolo on the street, his hands in his pockets and his crocodile feet." A flimsy plastic carrier bag holding the shopping, my head holding the rhyme, I went back to Cam and Jamie Morgan, who were in the living room of our flat, to continue writing.

"Buffalo Stance" is made up of two stories that became one. The first story goes like this. Cam and Jamie had been making music together as Morgan McVey. Their first and only single, "Looking Good Diving," was to be released in 1987. They wanted the B-side to be the remix, so that's what we were doing in that afternoon writing session in Edith Road when I popped out to the store for milk: we were looking for our sound, pumping hearts, pumping culture, re-creating the song. We had a drum machine and Cam had copied some beats from some hip-hop tracks. We're both addicted to melody, especially when it's hoarding the melancholy, so the

B-side would lead with the melodies, but the rap and the rhymes would lay down the law. That afternoon, sharing space, writing different parts, we put it all together. At the end of the session, in a low melody, Jamie sang, "No money man can win my love, it's sweetness that I'm thinking of." But I heard the melody going up at the end and sang it higher, and we had the chorus. The light changed in the room and time sort of stopped, making way for the birth of something. I think we could all feel it: something plopping out, fully formed, golden like a blessing, made up of composite matter falling in from the universe, dressed in the uniform of coincidence. Who's that gigolo on the street? Bombastic, lost, conniving, hustling, wrapping those girls in the padded bras around his fingers.

Nellee Hooper and the Bristol-based DJ Milo of the Wild Bunch produced the track, which we called "Looking Good Diving with the Wild Bunch." I knew Nellee from when he was playing timbales in a post-punk Bristol band called Maximum Joy, who had supported the Slits at one point.

We recorded the track in an afternoon at Matrix Studios in the West End. The last thing we did was to record the ad libs, influenced by DJ Fat Tony's razor-sharp wit and by Barnsley's habitual verbal diarrhoea, always delivered to me, for some bizarre reason, in a strong American accent. I say bizarre because he is, in fact, from Barnsley. That day I went into the vocal booth with my two buddies infiltrating my thoughts, and it just rolled off my tongue naturally: "What is he like? Yo, the guy's a gigolo, man."

The single came out, and the funny threesome of Jamie, Cam, and I went on a weird little UK tour, doing brief appearances in crummy clubs up and down the country. We were often out in the middle of nowhere, our performance nothing but a disruption to the open-shirted lads on a night out, but on and on we ploughed to the beat. The boys went onstage first, hoping that the backing track would start playing on cue and, fingers crossed, that someone might look up from their pint glass. "Is the mic working?" And then the fishbowl effect of eyes staring at the stage.

After I'd done my turn on what we were now referring to as "Buffalo Stance," we'd jump straight in the car and, if it wasn't too far, drive home fast. Otherwise, we'd have to spend a gloomy night in a budget hotel.

In a small town in Northern Ireland, we checked into what seemed to be a youth hostel. The lounge was full of kids watching TV, smoking fags, and drinking tea and beer. Where were we? At the gig that night, halfway through "Buffalo Stance," in the middle of a chorus, I heard a shout of "Nigger!"

Cameron flew off the stage and into a cluster of male bodies, found the guy that had said it, and head-butted him hard, then got back onstage in time for the next chorus. I stayed put. It hurt in multiple directions, but the resistance was mightier than the fear. I looked them straight in the eyes and carried on with the song: *I am going nowhere; I am going somewhere. Take that and eat it.*

The single did its thing and we all moved on, making new tunes, looking ahead.

One night at Nellee Hooper's house, Bomb the Bass, aka Tim Simenon, a young producer and DJ at the Wag Club, heard the sleeping B-side of "Looking Good Diving" and wondered what it was and how he hadn't heard it before. He loved it. The next day, he called Jamie asking questions. He wanted to cut a new version of the track. Cam and I had been so engrossed in creating and writing that we had no thoughts of going back to the song. To us, it was like done, ready, forgotten. But Tim didn't give in.

His positivity and energy were strong enough to give the song a new lifeline. A couple of weeks later, we met in the studio and re-recorded the whole thing in an afternoon. Tim had a clear idea of what he wanted to do. Thank God he had the vision because

Cam and I never would have reworked the song otherwise. But it became a gateway for us, a golden nugget.

I had recently signed as a solo artist with Circa Records, a boutique label formed in 1987 by the late former Island PR exec Ray Cooper and the A&R man Ashley Newton. There were other offers, some of them for more money, but I knew Ashley, and Cam and I saw eye-to-eye with both him and Ray. Signing to them felt more home-based, and also as if it was going to buy us more freedom. There was no way Cam and I were going to sacrifice the songs we were slowly shaping together.

As soon as Circa heard the new track, they decided to release it on 7-inch, and the date was set: November 28, 1988.

THE BATON IS PASSED

About five months before the single was due to come out, I became pregnant with Tyson. We had just bought a three-bedroom terraced house on Mortimer Road, Kensal Rise, with the money from a publishing deal with EMI—a huge blessing. When my period didn't arrive, after a weekend away with Cam to think it all through, I confided in Ray Petri.

Our trip to Japan had been a bonding experience and by now I'd grown to love and trust Ray. He was an inspired mentor and, in a way, a father figure to the Buffaloes—and to me. He styled the clothes that a staggeringly beautiful teenage Naomi Campbell, Andi, and I wore in the video for "Looking Good Diving." He put me into a super-tight Azzedine Alaïa dress; I'd never worn anything like it before and I felt self-conscious, unsure. But Ray's words were so respectful and supportive, he gently drew me out from the security of the nest. He was saying: "You're ready. Move with it, carry it." I felt elevated to some new level of womanly pizzazz. Ray showed me how to bring a strut to my movement and to bear myself in a different way, with dignity and an understanding of my own grace.

But Ray was sick. What he had thought was a stye on his eye was, in fact, Kaposi's sarcoma. The day he got the diagnosis, Cam went with him to see a Harley Street doctor who delivered his sentence publicly and aggressively in the reception area: "You have HIV." The doctor didn't want him in his consulting room.

Moki was in New York when HIV really started to rip through the city. She told me about a mystery virus that was killing people fast. There was barely any treatment, let alone a cure. In the early days, before the doctors and scientists made incredible advances, there was so much fear and misinformation about how the disease was transmitted, and so much scapegoating and indifference towards its victims. Some gay people thought it was all just a conspiracy to outlaw their sexuality, so they continued defiantly to lead freewheeling lives. The political and health authorities allowed HIV to tear through the gay community and there was little compassion from the public at large.

Cheap heroin was also playing its deadly part in the disaster. In London in the mid-eighties, it was as easy to get hold of heroin as weed. While I was living in Fulham Court with Bruce, drug raids had become a daily occurrence on the estate, where it was teenage kids, not rock stars, chasing the dragon and walking around goggle-eyed. The dominoes fell only in one direction. Addicts were sharing needles. First, heroin addiction, and then AIDS became epidemic.

The winds changed the day Ray was diagnosed. He was the nucleus of our Buffalo unit, and now we were like particles blowing around trying to find a way back to the centre. Before long he was too ill to be on his own, so Cam and I installed his mattress on the floor in our living room. His stomach was bad and he struggled to eat, but he liked it when I made him vegetable mash with melted cheese on top.

In the following months, he developed more sarcomas on his body and he became very weak, but he continued to carry himself with a regal poise, like the don he always was. He went to fashion week in Paris, Buffalo-sharp in a crisp white shirt, baggy trousers, dark blue bomber jacket, polished US police shoes, his signature pork-pie hat and carrying his cane, old-school and proud. Some of the Paris fashion police were upset by his appearance, his diseased skin, the way he wore his illness with such beauty—that he had the audacity to turn up like that and subject them to his reality. But Jean Paul Gaultier seated him in the front row. AIDS was now a battle line in a culture war. I was ready to fight.

On that sunny day, not long after I'd found out I was pregnant, Ray and I met in Soho Square to talk. "What should I do?" I asked him. I was starting to realise that my muddy feelings about the pregnancy were tangled up in the new commitment of being signed to a record label. I now had a legally binding contract with my signature on it, committing me to do certain things at certain times.

"I think you should have the baby, Neneh," he told me. "I'm dying and it feels like it's meant to happen this way."

I wept.

When I found out I was pregnant with Naima, Moki had told me, "Don't separate the life that you're going to make with this child from all the other things that you are and that you want to do." Now, resolved, I put Ray in a cab and then walked straight over to the Circa office on nearby Wardour Street.

"I'm pregnant," I blurted. All the colour washed away from Ashley Newton's face. "Don't worry," I continued. "I've done this before and I can work right up until the end. It will all be fine." Honestly, it felt more dramatic than telling my parents I was knocked up when I was eighteen, but I left the building with a sense of relief and clarity.

One thing I know about life is that it never comes empty-handed. The plates were now in motion. "Buffalo Stance" hadn't started to spin quite yet, but it would. I knew we had a first single. For once, I didn't find myself saying, "Oh, it's not mixed right. Ouch! Watch for that vocal, it's too loud." I liked watching people's faces when they heard it for the first time. It seemed to resonate instantly. Ray was spinning another plate. But his song was a blues for his failing body. He would be the baby's godfather.

Walking through Soho, down Wardour Street, right onto Old Compton Street, my body carrying another inside, all the mental clutter fell into a calm space. "This is what matters," I said to my baby. "We will do this our way."

Once I got home, I went straight to the kitchen. Cam was working with Phil Chill, our collaborator at the time, and I could hear them upstairs mixing a track in the back bedroom. Stuck on a cupboard door in front of me, in Naima's handwriting, was a daily instruction: "Eat your vitamins, sucka." This was us. This was our life, the place where we hatched our homemade strategies. These plates needed to spin for anything to function. I had an overwhelming feeling of all the different aspects of change happening around me, but also the consoling hum of right here, right now. This is where we are and whatever comes after, bring it.

With the November 28 release date looming, we were in crash mode. Ellie Milner, a friend of Bruce's brother Uncle Mark, came to the rescue, running the office from our living room, documenting, filing, and organising our life. She quickly joined the management team, helping us keep our shit together, basically. God bless Ellie.

We needed to think about the visuals: the promotional shots, the record cover, the video. It was only ever going to be Ray who would carry us through all that. One morning I was sitting with him on his mattress. I'd just dropped Naima at school, and I passed him a cup of herbal tea. We sat quietly for a second as he sipped it. I could feel his pain. Then he told me he was too sick and didn't have the strength to carry on with his work. Judy Blame was the one for me, he said. And so the baton was passed.

JUDY BLAME

Without a doubt, Judy Blame, aka Ma, Jude, Mother, was one of the great loves of my life. He had a low baritone voice, a good strong chin, and a splendid nose—features fashioned from Dickensian leftovers. His parents might have christened him Christopher Barnes, but he was always Judy. Legend has it that when he worked as a coat-check girl at the nightclub Heaven, he'd get everyone's coats mixed up. "Don't blame me," he'd say. "And anyway, you look much better in that one!" So that's where the "Blame" came from. The Judy bit, he borrowed from Ms. Garland, perhaps.

When I was out dancing with Andi at the Wag Club, Taboo, or Heaven, anytime Judy and I saw each other, we'd say hello. I just had a feeling for him. We noticed each other.

Judy was a true original—in the outrageous way he dressed, his hairstyles, and his use of junk and recycled items for the jewellery he made and wore. But, above all, he was an artist, a member of his own cult creative fashion and art outlet in Dalston, "The House of Beauty and Culture," a group of designers who shared a post-punk, anti-establishment approach to design and making. They prioritised raw creativity and craftsmanship and used whatever salvaged materials they could lay their hands on—postal sacks, coins, bits of hair and string—turning them into one-off avant-garde riches, as a deliberate counterpoint to mass production. Judy loved going mudlarking along the banks of the Thames, rooting out treasures like bleached old bones and broken clay pipes and fashioning them into something beautiful. His work was radical and exquisite, entirely fearless. He was a genius. I became an instant devotee.

Nellee Hooper, who at that time was in Soul II Soul, wore one of the amazing, stylised jackets that Judy and Chris Nemeth made together: a contemporary take on eighteenth-century peasant dress—at once both archaic and ahead of its time. When I found myself standing at the bar next to Judy one night, I asked, "If I find some postal sacks, would you and Chris make me a jacket?"

The first time he came over to discuss working with me, he had one of his trademark black sketchbooks with him—he always had at least one. He was a few years older than me and both of us were shy: I fought my diffidence, pretending confidence.

"I've had some ideas," he told me, opening his book to a page with a beautiful drawing in simple black ink. It was of me: hair up, some curls falling, big earrings. It moved something in me, I don't know what exactly, but I instantly felt trust. Judy's approach somehow felt soft and tender but also completely direct.

Judy and I gelled instantly. His razor-sharp eye, dry wit, and practical sense of "less is more unless more is needed" made us a perfect match. We kept things pretty ragga—rough and ready, mixing and matching, playing with metaphors—but we also wanted the look and feel to be hard, elegant, defined. Mostly things came together almost instinctively. I felt safe, seen, covered. I couldn't have handled having to manufacture a "version" of myself or spending hours looking at pictures of myself, discussing my image and how someone was going to market "me."

We went together to World, a shop in Covent Garden owned by Michael and Gerlinde Costiff, who were also the force behind Kinky Gerlinky, the West End's wildest monthly club night. World was like a pirate's lair jam-packed full of booty: curios and artefacts; clothes, vintage and new; Brazilian carnival feather headdresses; and the treasured door-knocker earrings along with a dollar-sign necklace straight out of NY, all in fabulous fake gold, which provided just the right weight to add balance to any outfit.

Judy's work was stunning. There is a magnetism, I think, that pulls you towards things you already know. He was very like Moki: they both smoked like chimneys, were pretty good at drinking, were artist activists, had an irreverent sense of humour, and their creativity operated in a similar way. He had that same ingenious magpie eye. Like Moki, he delighted in turning detritus into art. As Moki had dived into dumpsters in search of fabric remnants, Judy collected old keys and buttons, or rifled through the bins of Dalston and Shoreditch to style extras in Duran Duran's video for "Wild Boys." He considered a safety pin as beautiful as a diamond. "Bottle tops could be chic," he said. With him, they were.

Judy's creative energy was always with him: it wasn't as if he could switch it off. He would hear and see things that the rest of us would miss. He might overhear something funny on a bus, for example, and next thing it would be a slogan on a T-shirt. I'm not creative all day every day—sometimes I don't feel the need to make things, I just need to be—but my observations of life somehow filter through into my music. Judy had that same relationship to being alive. He would see things, hear things, and while he didn't always know what to do with them immediately, in the end he would turn them into art.

BUFFALO STANCE

In December 1988, when I performed "Buffalo Stance" on *Top of the Pops* at seven months pregnant, motherhood simply didn't figure in anyone's picture of what a pop star should look like. But I wasn't trying to make a statement. It was just where I was at the time, and why would I hide that? Standing there, yes, I was shitting myself, but at the same time I felt charged, strong—even proud. I thought, *I'm not going to go away. I'm not going to go away.*

Ray and Judy were instrumental in guiding me to that moment of pride in who I was. Along with many other instinctively and exquisitely creative people I'd met on the queer scene, they showed me a freedom of expression, the spirit of extravaganza and flamboyance. It gave me the courage to know my power. That was vital in a world that was often threatened by change, by skin colour, or by anything too different; one in which women, especially Black women, are told, "You are too loud. Too big. You're taking up too much space."

But ain't nothing gonna stop us now. Let go and trust was all I could do.

Andi and other women friends of mine felt the same way. Sharing space with gay men and women, with queer people of every identity, we found freedom in the margins of a big world. We went to Judy's west London flat to do a photoshoot with his flatmate, Eddie Monsoon. Eddie was just starting out as a young photographer and he was going to take some shots for the press and the cover for the single. I had Cam's white beaver crown on my head, my white snakeskin Adidas on my feet, and Judy had wangled a few designer bits, including a pastel-pink Azzedine Alaïa dress.

Boombox blaring, my bum perched on Judy's chunky Frick and Frack table, I tried to just be in my skin, look Eddie in the eye through the camera lens, stay chilled, be in tune. Then Judy said something that me laugh.

When we got the contact sheets, we took turns peering at them through a magnifying glass. Not too drab. I was pleasantly surprised. Cam swiftly ran his eye over them and said right away, "That's the cover!" Judy didn't agree with his selection, and I thought I looked a bit goofy—my hand up, my head back, laughing. But Cam was right and, eventually, the rest of us saw the light. With the image selected, Judy had someone in mind to work on the cover design. He got in touch with the brilliant artist and designer Jamie Reid, who had famously created the groundbreaking découpage cover for the Sex Pistols' *Never Mind the Bollocks*. Jamie took one look at the photograph, and then nicely fucked it up with his magic pen.

Driving down Ladbroke Grove with Cam a few weeks later, I looked up and there I was: that picture on a massive poster, papered to a wall. It was me, for sure, but also not. The photograph could only ever capture that "me," frozen in time in the energy of that fleeting moment. It was static. It didn't define me. A little less than a year later, we were in LA to promote *Raw Like Sushi*, my first album, and at the airport we met up with Don, who was also in town. Cam and I were going to stay in one of the bungalows at the Chateau Marmont hotel, very fancy. On our way there, as we drove past the Tower Records store, I looked up and saw a giant billboard—of me—looming over Sunset Boulevard. Don got out of the car and stood beneath it. There was Don, seeming tiny, craning his neck and smiling up at gigantic me-but-not-me. He was delighted, a little amused and totally unfazed by that outsize snapshot of his daughter's success.

"Buffalo Stance" was in motion. If you were shooting for hit records in the late eighties, everything hung on getting airtime on

BBC Radio One and—the holy grail of pop success—appearing on *Top of the Pops*. That show, at 7 p.m. on Thursday nights, was a really big deal—a "stay in" event. While this wasn't exactly my first rodeo, I hadn't had many dealings with the commercial end of the music industry. This was all new to me. The "plugger"—employed by the record label or from an independent company—is the person who takes the material to the radio and TV broadcasters, and I soon learned that Nigel Sweeney and Neil Ferris, of Ferret 'N' Spanner Plugging Co. Limited, were like royalty in this industry. If we got them working on "Buffalo Stance," we instantly upped our chances. Starsky & Hutch, Bonnie & Clyde, Ferret 'N' Spanner—even their name had a ring of success to it, like famous outlaws or rock stars. And we got the thumbs-up: lovely Nigel Sweeney, aka Spanner, became our man and remained my "plugger" for many years.

We moved on to think about the video. Judy suggested the artist and film-maker John Maybury as director and Alan MacDonald of Frick and Frack as the set designer. Under John's direction, it was to be vibrant and oozing with colour, overlaid with a floral paper-cut collage. When we came to our shoot day, I was six months pregnant. Judy squeezed me into a black fitted Rifat Ozbek dress, a Junior Gaultier bomber jacket, and, of course, my gold door-knocker earrings from World. Mushroom, of the Bristol graffiti collective and sound system Wild Bunch, was one of the best-looking boys we knew, and we persuaded him to get the train to London and be the B-boy in the video. We also brought in two incredible girls to dance. A few nights before the video shoot, Judy and I were out at the Wag Club. These girls were in their own zone on the dance floor, wearing odd little hats, looking unlike any of the other Mad Hatters around them.

"Judy," I bellowed above the beat. "We have to get them to dance in the video!"

Between songs, we moved in on them, feeling slightly unsavoury, like two creeps with a bag of sweets. "Do you want to be in a music video?" we asked. We were in luck—they said "yes."

In early November 1988, my belly swelling under my clothes, we went on a whistle-stop tour with Bomb the Bass and others. I only performed three songs at these gigs, but as we were making our way around the country, I noticed that people were responding to "Buffalo Stance" because they recognised it. By the time we got up north, it was a vibe. Our song was getting radio airplay.

A beautiful thing about this time was that I was not out there on my own. I was part of a community that was in the throes of a kind of takeover. We were loud and proud of our culture. Hip-hop, R&B, dance, reggae, pure or combined, and then mixed with everything else to make something new and with heart. We were making it, just as we went along, and we couldn't be kept underground any longer. No sell-out. Tell it like it is. We mixed our shine with some of the grime and inner-city grit of the times. Artists like the hip-hop producer Mantronix came along, giving us "Come Into My Life" by Joyce Sims. It killed me every time it dropped. One night, when Nellee was DJing somewhere on Dean Street in Soho and hadn't brought that track in his record bag, I made him take a taxi back to his flat in Camden to fetch it.

I did my best to represent. I think a space was waiting for my skin, my womanhood, my Swedish–New York pregnant self. I tried to fill it—for myself, for all of us.

When "Buffalo Stance" was officially released at the end of November, the first person to play the song on national radio was John Peel. That was everything—to get his approval was huge. He was a taste-maker, a rebel with great influence. (Rip Rig + Panic did several live sessions for him, and so did the Slits—in fact, he was pretty much the only one who would play us on the radio.)

Suddenly I was in demand, the PR machine cranking into top gear. I did interviews for Radio One and Capital FM, features for *Smash Hits*, *NME*, *Melody Maker*, *Sounds*, *Record Mirror*. You name it, I was in it. The following Thursday, when the midweek chart positions came through, Spanner phoned to tell us that our record was at number 15. If it didn't drop its position, he said, we had a chance of appearing on *Top of the Pops*.

As the phone began to ring more and more, and we wrote more songs, I clung to normality. Play good, play hard, school runs, play dates, good mates. A childhood friend from Tågarp came to help with Naima and Marlon. After bonkers days of interviews and photoshoots, I had such a strong desire to retreat back into home life. Often, I'd have spent all day daydreaming about what I would cook that night. I'd go to the supermarket to pick up the ingredients, come home, put the bags down, and be engulfed in the household commotion again—the kids running up and down the stairs, drawing at the kitchen table, the stereo playing, rubbing some spice onto the chicken. After bubble baths, their warm little bodies in PJs, we would read bedtime stories. We loved Astrid Lindgren's Pippi Longstocking books—books I had read as a child—also *The Velveteen Rabbit* by Margery Williams, *Green Eggs and Ham*, and everything else by Dr. Seuss. Their favourite, though, was when Cam improvised his "Jose the Onion Salesman" stories. That was comfort for me—family routines were at the core of a day's recovery.

By the following Sunday, when the official UK chart positions were released, we learned that the single had gone up to number 13. We got it. On Thursday, December 22, seven months pregnant, I performed for the first time on *Top of the Pops*.

The show was recorded at the BBC Television Centre in White City the day before the programme aired. We pulled up in a full car: Ellie and Cam were the management team; Judy was there, naturally; as was a make-up artist, Pearl. We had to smuggle Pearl into the studio—I think we said she was Judy's wardrobe assistant—because, due to union issues, all hair and make-up was supposed to be done by BBC in-house staff. The problem was that, in my experience, most people working in TV at that time were white, and no one had any training in dealing with a non-white person's hair or face. Their make-up kits contained maybe one or two foundations for "darker" skin tones, but that was all.

My make-up having been surreptitiously fixed by Pearl, we made our way to the stage to record our slot. Homeboy Mushroom was the DJ, there were the two young dancers from the Wag Club, and me. I wore high-top trainers, a black Lycra miniskirt, gold bra and gold jacket, with a huge gold medallion draped over my bump.

The truth is, I remember very little about that first *Top of the Pops* experience. After a bunch of run-throughs, when it came to the actual recording—"Up at number 13 this week is Neneh Cherry"—the last thing I recall is the cameras zooming in—"Give me a beat"—then total darkness. And it was over.

The next day, Andi and I were stuck in Sainsbury's on Ladbroke Grove (some things never change), loading a huge trolley full of supplies onto the conveyor belt at the check-out, when some young local Black women with their kids recognised me and waved hello.

"Oh, my God! We have to get home. My friend is on *Top of the Pops* in a minute and we're going to miss it," Andi told them, making us all laugh.

"Well, what are you doing here?" they asked.

I know, right? Even though we were loading heavy bags in a cold sweat, it felt kind of good being with Andi and those women in the supermarket at that moment.

We were having a gathering to celebrate being on *Top of the Pops*, the end of an eventful year, and Christmas being upon us. A minicab plonked us outside the house and we dragged the bags inside just in time to see nearly the whole song. I must admit it felt a trifle crazy watching myself on the small TV in the corner of our living room, everybody crowding around, knowing that right then I was on TV screens in thousands of people's living rooms all around the country. Naima, Marlon, Andi's daughter, Miquita, and Tessa's Phoebe were jumping up and down on the sofa. We were all buzzed, but I felt mostly relieved that it was over. Afterwards, Ray, as always, spoke his truth to me with heart. "That was good, Neneh. But next time look more to the camera."

Thinking about it now, I can see that it was important to be able to appear on the show, pregnant and proud, though at the time I didn't quite know what the media fuss was about. But change comes about partly through our choices being seen. Back then, it was even harder to be both a mother *and* a musician. Just as Moki had done in the sixties, people like Tessa, Andi, Ari, and I were proudly owning and showing our right to be our full-bodied selves *and* make these choices as artists. We were creating a new rhythm where it was all part of the same thing: our life.

•

That Christmas, Naima went to stay with Bruce and her grandparents, and Marlon was with his mum. Cam, Judy, and I flew to Jamaica. That holiday was one of the all-time greats. We stayed in a run-down but still beautiful motel in Oracabessa Bay, not far from Goldeneye, James Bond author Ian Fleming's legendary home. The minute I landed in the Caribbean, my cravings for jerk chicken kicked in. As soon as I caught a scent of the grills, I just had to stop, sit down, and eat. The spices, the sweet jerk sauce, and the white doughy bread sticking to the top of my mouth left me feeling filled up and content. Heaven.

On Old Year's Night, we travelled from Oracabessa to Montego Bay, to spend the last two nights before going back home. There was a power cut in the whole city, the hotel lobby candlelit. We were starving, so once we'd checked in, we hailed a taxi.

"Take us to where you like to eat," I told the driver.

He dropped us at his favourite spot. It had a long wooden counter, a couple of mammas running the kitchen, blue walls, flickering candles, and the best curried goat I've ever eaten. Judy and I were sucking the last traces of meat from the bones when we noticed Cam outside with a young man. I'd barely registered he'd gone. "He's going to take us to dance!" Cam shouted. It was quite a sight, my husband and this sharp-as-knives youth working a baggy white vest, black shorts, white snakeskin cap, and matching glasses—a look. We walked down a passage by the side of a closed chemist's shop. No sound of a dance.

"Really? Is this where the dance is?" I asked, thinking, *Are we about to get mugged?*

"Ye, mon. It's here," said the youth.

Past a little bakery, up some stairs, and then the sound hit me, like I'd swallowed a mouthful of bass: baby kicks. It was mostly dark, but there must have been electricity because the sound system said so. The centre of the dance floor was occupied by a boxing ring full of dance-hall queens, holding court in silver bikinis. We danced and moved with the party for the rest of the night, ringing in the New Year.

The next morning, New Year's Day, sitting on a beach in Montego Bay, I said, "If the record doesn't go up in the charts, let's stay here another week."

Cam went to find a phone to call Spanner in London. Judy and I sat there, kind of hoping the bloody record had, if not sunk down the charts, not exactly shot up. We really didn't want to leave. The baby danced inside me to the bass. We saw Cam walking back, a speck on the beach getting bigger. Was it good news? And what would have been bad, anyway?

"It's gone up!"

Not bad. Not bad at all. It was January 1, 1989, and "Buffalo Stance" was number 3 in the UK charts. Happy New Year, suckers.

When we got back to London, Spanner rang to say that they wanted me to come on the *Pops* again that Thursday. For the second round, I wore my dollar-sign earrings from one of the Jamaican markets. And I remembered what Ray had told me: I looked straight at the camera.

RAW LIKE SUSHI

I heard that Quincy Jones once said that he never recorded with a menstruating woman, which I think is a bit extreme if true, but maybe being pregnant *can* affect your pitch. Everything is squished, so your diaphragm is battling for space with some part of a baby jammed in there. We recorded my first album all the way through my pregnancy—I sang the vocals to "Outré Risqué Locomotive" ten days before my due date. I was having Braxton Hicks contractions and had to stand with one leg resting on a chair. It's quite a hedonistic track, so there I was singing, "My body's clean but my mind is so bad," trying not to get thrown off-key by the twinges in my belly.

When we weren't recording, we were writing. I wrote so many songs at our kitchen table, or at the stove, a pen in one hand, trying to catch the words before I lost them; the other hand turning chicken in the pan, kids and people coming in and out, organised chaos, finding something quiet in that space. My comfort zone.

Sometimes I wrote in bed. It was there, when Tyson was just big enough to stroke my insides with an elbow, that I wrote a song called "Inna City Mamma," as my bed flew me to a rooftop in New York. Sounds, smells, sweet and putrid, sophisticated and coarse, a block of clocking clouds, marking time. What time is it, inna city mamma? A love song for a city.

My songs are an accumulation of impressions that have built up inside me. Eventually, they become stories. I'll grab a bit of melody and start singing some words that don't necessarily mean anything. I tend to blurt things out, then I listen back and see what sticks.

Quite often, snippets of conversation or experiences gleaned from everyday life find their place as references and metaphors. Sometimes I might have a few words or a snatch of melody, but I can't get beyond them. I'm stuck. I begin to build a visual environment in blocks: an impression here, another there. I can often see the lines and verses in my head like a series of rooms, or like scenes in a film, each evoking a different atmosphere. There are characters within these pictures. It's only when I ask myself—who are these people, where are they, what are they doing—that I can feel the stories start to unfold and the song free itself.

When I'm writing songs, it's as if I access some part of my being where language doesn't exist, but where I can tap into whatever it is I can't put words to. I think some people understand art as coming from a place of exclusivity that is somehow apart from us. But I believe we all have that creative potential. It's part of us, an almost meditative space we can visit to release what needs to be released.

There are resources we all hold in common that we can draw on to be creative. The structure of a pop song, for example. That's in our DNA. There's a built-in expectation so we instinctively feel when the chorus should come. But that's all the more reason to try to change it up. Within that formula, I like to think you can stretch it any which way you want—make a pop song that's nine minutes long, for example. Or, when we made "Manchild," we had the idea of using the contrast of strings alongside the hip-hop beat, and put quite a long rap in the middle. Why break the code if it works? Just crush it a little. Maybe that's what we've always done in our sound, and I say "we" because the writing of the songs has been so much a collaboration between Cam and me.

I still write sometimes on Cam's tiny old Casio keyboard, which has an auto-chord accompaniment system. Its sound is cutting and distinct and oddly beautiful, although nowadays the keyboard is held together with gaffer tape. "Manchild" was the first thing I wrote on it. I was on the bus, and the words came into my head: "Is it the pain of the drinking or the Sunday sinking feeling?" When I got home, all was quiet. A little reluctantly, I picked up the keyboard and sang the melody I'd heard in my head, using my ear to lead me to the chords, and then to others. I went off-piste and found the rest of the verse:

> The car never seems to work
> When it's late, your girlfriend's on a date
> And the hero with her in your dream
> In your sleep it seemed like you.

When I sent the finished song to Don, he said, "Damn, there's seven chords in the verse. That's kind of jazz!"

I can still see the rooms where "Manchild" plays itself out. The second verse takes me into a dark bar, the radio playing, a young guy, clean and neatly dressed, leaning in at the bar with a glass in his hand, washing away the creeping uncertainty. At the top of the song, this same young guy is always there. He's fixing cars in a garage day in, day out. He has dreams and hopes and fears that he can't ever show. There's oil on his hands: "Manchild, will you ever win?"

•

Our baby was due on March 10. We would share a birthday—a cute present—but, really, did I want to spend my special day blowing balloons and making up party bags for the next ten years? On March 7, just as we were putting the finishing touches to the album tracks, Cam and I went to a party at Judy's flat around the corner in Elgin Avenue. At the end of the night, I told Judy that Cam and I needed to go home to have some good hard sex in the hope of bringing on my labour. As we left, Judy handed us a black plastic-wrapped cube—a heavy-duty bin bag of a condom.

The next morning, I awoke with an urgent need to comb out all the knots in my hair. Sitting on the back step in my bathrobe in the weak spring sun, I knew the sex had done the trick. I was in labour. I kept Naima home from school and got into the bath. This baby would have to wait until I'd got my hair washed, conditioned, and combed smooth. The warm water soothed me, and then Naima took my hand and helped me to stand up. That's when my body shifted into full-on labour, my contractions coming strong and fast. Even with all the booklets and clinic visits, and the midwife's instructions telling me to have a bag packed and ready, I was not prepared for this baby's imminent arrival. Naima, my beautiful, clever seven-year-old girl, bless her, quickly helped me to organise my things before Ellie took me to the hospital.

"I love you, Naima. What would I do without you?" I told her. "Next time I see you, you'll be a big sister."

An hour later, on March 8, 1989, my second daughter, Tyson, was born at Queen Charlotte's Maternity Unit in London. Cam had made it to the birthing room just in time and he immediately called his mother, Mumma Jean, to tell her that her second grandchild was here. "Are her eyes OK?" she asked anxiously. But Tyson was perfect: 8 lbs. 8 oz. and with a head full of black hair. Judy was her godmother.

Two weeks later, Cam went to pick up the photographer Jean-Baptiste Mondino, who'd come from Paris to hang out with us in search of a plot for the video of "Manchild." The front door slammed hard, but Cam was alone. He'd left J-B sitting outside in the Fiat Panda listening to the track—eight bars in, the beat drops and then in come the strings, forty hand-picked players, playing in perfect synchronicity. As he rewound the tape, listening to the song for a second time, and again, his ideas fizzing out and chasing each other down the street, unable to connect, my next-door neighbour stepped out of her house in her slippers with a broom and started to sweep in time with the song. She was the picture of Raggy-O glam with her layers of gold chains from which hung a tiny bottle of Opium perfume: "Well, Neneh, you never know when you might meet a man and need a quick refresh!" Watching her, a dime had dropped and J-B was on to something. He ran inside where I was sitting on the stairs in the hall, Tyson on one shoulder, a towel on my head, gold door-knockers in my lobes. "Hugs and *bisous*," Mondino cried. "Oh, darling, this is perfect. Just like this, as you are: the towel, the baby. I love the way you carry this child. What if we make the video imagery rock like a cradle?"

We shot it in Paris in early May. The whole tribe was there—Marlon, Naima, Barry Kamen, Andi, Judy, and six-week-old Tyson were taking part in the shoot, with Ellie, Cam, Ray, and Dick Jewell making up the all-important support crew. I believe it was Ray's last trip before he made his journey to forever. Too weak to venture far from our hotel, he held court in his bed. But on the first night, he made it out for dinner with us all around the corner at La Coupole—a great favourite of his.

First thing the next morning, Judy and I went next door to a lingerie shop, not quite sure what we were looking for, but we bought a pair of black cycling-style shorts and a black lace-edged top cut low in the neck and with sleeves to the elbow. At the video set, Judy added a light blue wetsuit-like Gaultier jacket and a pair of snakeskin high-tops, then pulled out a black towel for my head. We were filmed in front of a huge blue screen and the floor was coated in plastic waterproof with an inch of water on top. There was also a child's swing, a washing line, and a tree. Inspired by my sweeping neighbour in Mortimer Road, Andi's role was to hang the washing. The swing was for Naima. All good so far. But for nearly the entire first day, the camera, which was housed in a structure specially built for the occasion, didn't work. To achieve the visual effect J-B had in mind, the camera had to swing but the mechanism wouldn't function. Every second we were in the studio, we were burning through cash. Thankfully, though, before the day ended some genius got the thing to operate and the wondrous "Manchild" universe came to life. J-B and I would go on to make a video together for every album except *Broken Politics*. I treasure this relationship.

In the video, I'm holding Tyson for the first part of the song. Then, when I start rapping, Barry Kamen's hands come into shot as I pass the baby and let rip. By the eighth take, my breasts began to leak. As I passed Tyson to him, I pulled up my top and a jet of breast milk shot all over his face. A pack of disposable nursing pads was now an essential part of Judy's styling kit, but it wasn't uncommon for him to send back to the designers various borrowed outfits encrusted in my breast milk.

The resulting video for "Manchild" unfolded in a dreamlike sequence. The baby, the children, our family, Andi at the washing line; the camera in its cradle took all of us in.

It was the first and only time Cam and I allowed our kids to be involved in this way. I wanted to create the best world for my children, but just as my parents had done with me and Eagle-Eye as kids, I didn't want to separate them from my life and work as a musician. I wanted to bring them with Cam and me out into the world. Yet, while we've always moved as a family unit, we have done our best to keep our children out of the public eye. We tried to approach any showbiz razzmatazz in a matter-of-fact way, wanting our kids to be aware of their privilege and also to know that it would never make them better than anyone else. Keeping it real. No matter, at school Marlon still got into trouble with some jealous kids who'd seen him on TV and decided to punish him for "showing off."

Raw Like Sushi was released a month later in early June. The album struck a chord and sold more than 100,000 copies in its first week, going platinum four months later. I was nominated for Best New Artist at both the Brits and the Grammy Awards. Overwhelming and utterly strange.

Thank goodness for family. Now, more than ever, I needed Don and Moki and my little brother. I loved picking up the phone and speaking to each of them at least once a week. We would just ease back into the conversation from where we'd left off. They were pleased, proud, excited, and supportive, but they were also undazzled. They absolutely believed in me while also being very good at talking to me about other things. Not because they weren't interested, but because they knew from experience that the creative life is about so much more than how many records you've sold. The release of the album and its success brought huge changes for all of us, not least financially. For the first time I had a plastic credit card and the record sales allowed us a life of luxury we could never have imagined, but I didn't ever truly trust or count on it. I somehow felt it was all fake, like a Fabergé egg, something precious that could shatter in an instant. I still went to the shops in my house shoes. It's almost as if I wanted to spurn the business we now firmly had our feet in. It's not that I didn't like success and all that came with it. Who wouldn't? Being on a roll tastes good. But it did affect us. How could it not? So, like warriors, we—the family and all of the good people around us—stood at attention, protecting our . . . *us*. In we went to the fabricated new glassy spaces, determined to own them before they owned us. Inquisitive, with our eyes wide open, we tried to keep sight of ourselves and reality, who we really were. We would not allow ourselves to be blinded by any transitory bullshit.

•

Ongoing promotion was a contractual obligation, and so the whole circus needed to get back on the road again. I had to be away a lot and I decided that it would be good for Naima to have continuity at home and at school, in Kensal Rise. Ditte, the daughter of some close friends of the family, came to be our nanny. Bruce, meanwhile, was also away on tour a lot, so there were stretches of time when neither of us could be with Naima. And it was hard for her, because all she saw was that I was taking the new baby with me and leaving her alone at home. In retrospect, I see that it was a mistake, but at the time I was just trying to do what I thought was best. Everything that Cam and I did revolved around our family. That's how we've always operated. I would be in the studio in the spare room all day, friends and whoever was working with us would come and go, but every night we still sat down to eat together at the kitchen table. Within that hubbub of community, our children—Naima, Marlon, and baby Tyson—were at the core.

Throughout 1989, we had to cross the Atlantic several times for promo tours and other record-related business in the States. "Buffalo Stance" was making waves in the *Billboard* charts and so the bigwigs in the US Virgin head office, Geoff Ayeroff and Jordan Harris, had summoned us to a promo meeting. The first time we travelled en masse: me, Cam, Tyson, Judy, our artist and film-maker friend Dick Jewell, and Tessa Pollitt, who offered to help out with babysitting. On landing, a chauffeur greeted us in arrivals. Outside, he put on a pair of aviator shades and led us to an enormous black limo that was way shinier than his hair. He opened the passenger door.

"Miss Cherry, please get in."

We had arrived in La La Land. I went with the whole crew to meet the Virgin bosses, baby Tyson on my hip. Cameron and I always had some crusty residue of her puke and snot on our shoulders. "Let's break some balls." This is how we rolled. As we walked through the Virgin offices, I felt a vibe sounding like a buzz.

On another trip, both Tyson and Naima came with us. The flight crew gave Tyson a blow-up dolphin that she quietly toddled up and down the first-class aisles with, and we drank champagne as we flew thousands of feet above the waves. Moki used to call the Atlantic Ocean "the restless sea," because of all the blood and tears spilled from bodies carried over it against their will. This particular trip had a weird undertone. We were going to make a video for a song called "Heart" that none of us believed should be a single. The United States was the only country that didn't release "Manchild" as the second single after "Buffalo Stance." "Too avant-garde," they told us—no one will get it. We were not convinced this was true, but we were exhausted, after a year and a half of writing, recording, releasing, and promoting the record, not to mention having a new baby in the middle of it all, so we just said, "OK." I understand why and how that happened, but as far as I'm concerned, that decision threw the whole project off kilter. The yin and yang of "Buffalo Stance" and "Manchild" were equally important. Without "Manchild," the way the album was heard did not work as well.

You can't always follow your intuition—sometimes the circumstances just don't allow it; sometimes, maybe, you have to learn from a mistake. When it came to making images for the record, though, Judy, Cam, and I were prepared to stand our ground. Judy had my back on all those never-ending photoshoots, always. We ran our thing. Judy would go through the rails of designer clothes that a publicity person wanted us to use, saying, "Nope, nope, nope. Not that. OK, maybe that, and we can do something with that." We would never go for the designer look wholesale. Judy would always fuck it up and make it better.

We did a *Vogue* magazine shoot in New York. When the hair and make-up guy wanted to straighten my hair and re-curl it, highlight my nose to make it look straight, before I could speak up, Judy did. He wasn't having it. He said, "What are you doing? Are you having a laugh? Look at her. Over my dead body."

We weren't trying to be obnoxious. We knew there were different points of view over how to do the job. We understood we were there to sell records. But we wanted to sell them in a way that was true to our ideas about identity, politics, self-expression, freedom, everything. We wanted to *like* the images we were producing—for them to be beautiful, stylish, and to promote the ideas about sensuality or womanhood or strength that we were exploring in the music.

Some indigenous peoples believe that a part of your spirit is stolen every time you have your picture taken. I think there is some truth in that. When people are poring over photos of you, assessing them, it's hard to stay centred, be professional, and be yourself. The way I have chosen to express myself, physically and verbally, has been very much "take me as I am," but of course I've struggled with my body. I've had meltdowns, especially when I've been getting dressed to go onstage and haven't felt right in my clothes, not felt right in myself. At that time, I was the thinnest I've ever been, and when I returned to my normal size people were like, "She's got fat!" Mostly, I think I held it pretty good, did my job, tried to stay level. Of course, sometimes I have felt totally disconnected from my body. It hurts and it is so easy to focus on the negative—I wouldn't have been able to bear it without Judy.

We also had a lot of fun. In LA we would divert a limo to Ralph's Superstore to buy Mickey Mouse baby bottles and dummies for Tyson, and other stuff we didn't need. In NY, we'd go to 14th and Orchard streets, where I bought bonkers church dresses for the girls and stocked up on more fake jewels. We both loved a bargain. We'd eat a slice of pizza and just walk, just *be* together. There were many photoshoots where the champagne flowed as fast as the jokes. Judy was seriously good at drinking. He loved a Red

Stripe for breakfast, lunch, and dinner, and wasn't shy of a glass of bubbly or a lug of voddy. Once, on a shoot at the height of Judy's headier days, Cam noticed that he was knocking back an extraordinary number of cans of Coca-Cola. Cam and I conferred. Why was the residue of liquid that was clinging to the groove around the can's rim transparent, and not blackish brown? Simple: Judy was taking a can of Coke into the loo, emptying almost all of it down the toilet, and replacing it with vodka.

Having the baby on the road ended up maintaining our sanity. Finishing a day's promo and lying in bed, breastfeeding Tyson—no doubt this stopped me from being swept up in any drama or the strange whirlwind of the album's success. I was determined to make it work within everyday life as I knew it. But sometimes it seemed I was exhaling more air than I could take in. In New York, if Moki was in town, we'd hang out with her at the loft, spend time with Eagle-Eye. To be with them was something we all really craved and being able to go home felt so good. Once we stepped inside, we could put this crazy new existence of interviews, radio appearances, pictures, flashing lights on hold. With my mother's arms around me, we'd spend whatever time we had together figuring out what we were going to cook, then we'd wander along to the store, talking about nothing, or something.

Towards the end of our US promo tour we decided that, rather than going to Sweden as usual, we would spend the summer in upstate New York. We rented a rambling house in a place called Brewster, with an undulating lawn leading to a kidney-shaped pool, a nice big drive—all-American. We even rented a wood-panelled station wagon. At the beginning of September 1989, we were going to do a two-month tour in America with the Fine Young Cannibals.

Moki had left New York for Sweden earlier in May that year. She and Don had recently separated for good. In the end, heroin won. There had been previous splits, and Don had moved out a couple of times, but they had always been reconciled. Back in the early eighties, when I was living in London, Eagle-Eye had told me that Don and Moki were going through some very heavy shit, arguing, deeply unhappy, Moki completely desperate. There were some awful fights. My brother and I have never properly talked about it, but I can understand how traumatic that must have been to witness as a barely adolescent boy. Now Don was living downtown with a new partner. Moki continued to love him and worry about him, but she just had to let him go.

Moki and I talked a lot on the phone about Don, and how it had all ended. I found it difficult to hear because I guess a part of me thought that they'd figure it out, as they had before. It was hard to accept that this was it. We had been such a close family and now we were splintered, scattered to different corners of the globe. Moki was heartbroken by Don's choices. He was the love of her life, and she never had another partner after him, but I sensed that she was also relieved. She had dragged Don out of death's oblivion many times. Now she could rest from that state of hyper-vigilance in which she had lived for more than twenty years. She was able to focus on herself.

In 1979, she had her first solo show outside Sweden, *Moki Cherry—Tapestries*, at the Los Angeles gallery LAX 814. That year she also went back to the Pompidou and ran another *atelier des enfants*. Throughout the eighties she had solo and group shows in New York and Stockholm, worked as a set builder at the Apollo Theater in Harlem, and made costumes and sets for a Swedish children's TV show.

Moki's creativity was like breathing. She sold many pieces over the years, though mostly privately, because her art was not considered an obvious fit in commercial galleries. Their self-important owners perceived it as naive. Let's also not underestimate the age-old disdain for women's artistic production, especially if it is craft-based. And Moki wasn't the kind of person who went out of her way to work the hoity-toity cocktail-party gallery-opening circuit. I don't think she felt included, but she did have powerful perseverance, establishing herself in the self-funded New York underground art scene.

•

One night that summer, I went into the city to a Young MC release party in the East Village. I arrived on my own. I was wearing a mustard-yellow stretch WilliWear dress, a favourite of mine and Judy's. Its designer, the fabulous Willi Smith, was a pioneer—a Black gay man, as sharp as nails. Sometimes I wore it with a red, gold, and green tube of fabric as a head tie, but that night I had my hair out. Mustard skin over mine, holding me in place; on my feet, Air Jordans, white and red. It felt good rolling in there on my own.

All the crème de la crème of the hip-hop community were in the house: the Dust Brothers—producers of Tone Lōc and the Beastie Boys, among others—were DJing and, of course, Young MC himself grabbed the mic. The place was jumping. I had a heated discussion with the X Clan crew from Brooklyn. We talked about Marcus Garvey in Harlem, Malcolm X, and the fact that I was with a white man.

"Girl, if all of our sisters run off with white men, that's it—over," went their argument.

"Yeah, I hear you," I replied. "Believe me, there was a time when I thought my destiny was having Black kids with a man of colour. Love came and changed that path. It hasn't made me any less Black." I stood my ground. They pressed, I pressed back. I know my history. We banged heads, found respect, and laughed.

Chuck D turned up. We were talking at the bar when he said, "We're watching you." There was something very serious in his tone, but I think he meant well. I must admit that talking to this unapologetic founder, leader, and frontman of the mighty Public Enemy, I was starstruck.

That year, *3 Feet High and Rising*, the first album by De La Soul, came out. Proud, poetic, free, fun, uplifting—that record was in its own dimension. Playing the tracks over and over, we wore the vinyl out. They were at that party. We found each other, danced hard. I liked them straight away and I think they liked me back. They introduced me to Q-Tip, who featured on their album.

He said, "We're making a record. We're called A Tribe Called Quest. There's a track you should sing on. Can you do it?"

"Yeah, I can do it," I answered.

One afternoon, weeks later, the phone rang. When I picked it up, I heard that voice: it was the inimitable Q-Tip. He told me about the track. I had Tyson on my hip, pulling my hair; heard Naima and Marlon messing around outside. I was touched that they wanted me to sing, but I was a little nervous and my hands felt full. I was exhausted, and we were about to start rehearsals for the Fine Young Cannibals' US tour. In the end, I declined Q-Tip's offer.

This is one of my biggest regrets. A Tribe Called Quest's first album, *People's Instinctive Travels and the Paths of Rhythm*, came out in April 1990 and became one of my favourite records of all time. Some of the tracks on what became a classic carried me and the tribe through that era: "Can I Kick It?" "I Left My Wallet in El Segundo," and "Bonita Applebum." I can hear the song we might have made together in my head, how it could have been.

•

At the end of August, I was in the kitchen fixing something to eat when we got a call to tell us that Ray had died. He was just shy of his forty-second birthday. We were getting ready to come back to London that day, because I was recording *Top of the Pops* the following afternoon. I had also realised, after just one show, that I was going to have to jump ship from the Fine Young Cannibals' tour. I was absolutely spent after a year of travelling, promoting, and caring for a baby and a seven-year-old. I was in pieces. Overcome with grief. We were losing so many people, either to drugs or AIDS, and it was another layer to all this unfathomable pain and loss. But also, it was Ray.

We said goodbye to Marlon and Naima, who were staying in America with Nunu Roney, who had joined us to help with the kids. We chucked our bags into the back of the car and drove to a Holiday Inn at JFK, where I sat down on the edge of the bed holding Tyson and looked out at the airport. Everything felt desolate.

Ray's funeral at Kensal Green Cemetery was a massive affair with all Buffaloes present, dressed to the nines, like good soldiers standing at arms. But I couldn't be there because, after *Top of the Pops*, I had to fly straight back to the States to be with the kids. AIDS was a pandemic, a catastrophe, and a blow to our people. I was heartbroken that I couldn't pay my respects to this hero of a man. Cam did attend, and all I could do was try to find solace in what he told me about the solidarity of the occasion.

•

It was autumn in London, 1989. There was a part of me that felt wrung out like a sponge. Talking about the same things over and over again on the promo tour, I was tired. Perhaps I was even a bit allergic to the sound of myself, myself, myself. I've always had an impulse to keep moving. My biggest nightmare was to get stuck in

"What is he loike?" and just churn out "Buffalo Stance" forever. I didn't want to be that girl with the quirky ad libs for the rest of my life. After the *Raw Like Sushi* campaign, I was healed of the desire to play the fame game. It was good to be home: the smell of rice and peas cooking in coconut milk and thyme, and the sound of West Indian tunes on a Sunday coming from our ever-sweet neighbours on both sides.

Ahmadu visited, bearing gifts. He always insisted on taking the kids out to buy them new shoes. Having grown up mostly barefoot, he loved to buy shoes. He also loved going to the butcher's and buying cuts of meat that were hard to find in Sweden. When he came home one evening with an entire beef tongue that filled our biggest pot, Naima and Marlon were as if possessed, and wanted to keep looking at the dinosaur licking thing that he'd left to soak in cold water. Obligingly, he'd lift the lid slowly for them to have a peek and then they'd run shrieking up the stairs. The stew he made with that tongue was unforgettable.

I needed to rest, but Cam was full of energy. He was working with Massive Attack. The Bristol posse had by this point evolved out of the Wild Bunch, and so started finessing their incredible music, collaging together all the post-punk, roots-reggae, dub, ska, and hip-hop influences they'd absorbed from years of DJing on the Bristol scene. They were on the brink of recording their era-defining sounds, but although they undoubtedly had the talent, they needed some pushing to harness it, to go to the next place. With the gains and experience we had from *Raw Like Sushi*, it was a natural reflex for us to nurture something new, so we kicked their asses into the studio in our spare room to demo some tunes. They kind of took over the space and ended up recording a lot of their first album, *Blue Lines*, there. They also used to eat all the cereal and drink all the milk in the wee hours before I got the kids up for school.

Lying on my bed nursing Tyson, listening to what Massive Attack and Shara Nelson, who was working with them, were doing in the next room, I could hear the tracks come to life. Hearing their song "Lately" float around upstairs, I remembered who I was. It was medicinal for me to be around this music. It helped me recover from the churning repetitive pop bubble I had been stuck in that whole year.

NIGHTS I'LL NEVER FORGET

On February 11, 1990, Nelson Mandela was released from prison in South Africa. I had heard his name my whole life. My family had boycotted South African produce and we'd joined the demonstrations at the South African Embassy. The day he walked out of the jailhouse, where he'd been held for almost thirty years, was monumental. His release was televised live worldwide, and everyone was watching. I was captivated. Finally, South Africa was going to come out of apartheid. It was more than monumental—it was history. A remarkable, triumphant change was unfolding in front of our eyes.

Two months later, on April 16, I was standing in front of Mr. Mandela himself at Wembley Stadium. I was going to perform at a gig in his honour. I was very proud to have been asked, and we suggested I do a performance with the Jungle Brothers—aka Afrika Baby Bam and Mike Gee. I was a big fan of their music, which was playful and conscious and part of the family of De La Soul, A Tribe Called Quest, and Queen Latifah. Long before I met them, I'd bought a copy of their album *Done by the Forces of Nature*, and when I was looking through the sleeve notes, reading all the credits, I was amazed to see that they'd thanked me. I was gobsmacked. It meant so much.

Their manager, Steve Finan, brought them along to our house with Monie Love. Baby Bam told me he'd been in a hotel room watching MTV when the video for "Buffalo Stance" came on. MTV was still so white in those days, and he said he was really excited that we were pushing through colour boundaries. There, hanging out in our living room, we decided that for the Nelson Mandela concert, we'd perform "There Ain't No Peace, 'Til Mama is Free." I would do Monie Love's verse, and Baby Bam and Mike Gee would do a verse each.

Backstage at Wembley Stadium, we all met Nelson and Winnie Mandela. Shaking his hand, I looked into his face, my overwhelming thought that, after so many years held captive, there was so much freedom and hope shining in his kind eyes.

That afternoon there were 75,000 people in the stadium. The show would be broadcast in more than sixty countries. It was a bright spring day. Nelson and Winnie were sitting right at the front, so we could see them from the side of the stage. We had rehearsed our song that morning. About forty-five minutes before we were due to go on, Steve and Mike suddenly said, "Where's Baby Bam?" Nobody knew where he was.

The other acts were going on, doing their one or two songs, and the clock was ticking. We hadn't prepared any other tunes and we were in a flat panic. Cameron said, "OK, Stetsasonic are here. Let's go find Daddy-O." We frantically tracked him down, explained that one half of the Jungle Brothers was AWOL, and asked him if they had a human beatbox. One of the young men in his posse said, "I can be your guy." He and I stood outside their trailer, rehearsed for a couple of minutes, then got up on stage—and we did it. It was an entirely acoustic performance, just the five of us. I looked down and saw Winnie and Nelson, and beyond them a sea of people.

It was one of life's great moments. The fact that we didn't have a big backing track, just me, Mike Gee, and our homeboy human beatbox, felt exactly right. Our time on that vast stage became very intimate. It was as if the whole of Wembley drew close. So, in the end, it was what it was meant to be.

•

When Tyson was around eighteen months old, Cam was so deep into finishing work on *Blue Lines* at Coach House Studios in Massive Attack's hometown, Bristol, we decided to rent a house in a village called the Shoe, outside Chippenham. We got Naima into a local primary school and Tyson made friends with a donkey, Doddy, who lived in the field beyond our garden. At the weekends, the Bristol brotherhood would come out and play football on the lawn. The legendary Jamaican roots-reggae singer-songwriter Horace Andy came and stayed to work on a new track. One morning I woke to hear him practising "One Love," which he had written with Massive Attack the day before. He and Cam were about to leave to record the final vocal, and he was walking back and forth inside the house, the music playing from a cassette. There was warm morning sun and Horace's voice echoing off the walls. I still have goose bumps.

A few months later, I heard about Red Hot Org, one of the first AIDS charity projects. The organisation was putting out an album featuring covers of Cole Porter's great songs, called *Red Hot + Blue*, to raise money for the AIDS activist group Act Up. Sinéad O'Connor sang "You Do Something to Me," Salif Keita did his version of "Begin the Beguine," and Debbie Harry and Iggy Pop did a version of "Well Did You Evah!" So many of our tribe had fallen with the virus, and when they asked me to take part, I felt great personal relief. In our grief and anger, we had been searching for a way to do something useful, to raise our voices and shout out for change. This was it. Looking at the song list, it was a no-brainer: it had to be "I've Got You Under My Skin." The title said everything, right there. We devoted the rest of the year to what became our own goodbye to Ray.

This was also the perfect opportunity to collaborate once more with the Jungle Brothers. But when Afrika Baby Bam came to stay with us in the Shoe, where we had set up a small studio in an outbuilding, we spent a whole day fiddling and just couldn't find a way in. I was trying to lock in to the original, but it all sounded a bit wack. If you're going to do a version of somebody else's song, you have to make it your own. We needed to make something honest and beautiful because of the ugly stigma around AIDS. And because it meant so much, and we felt so strongly about getting it right, we were all a bit overwhelmed, overthinking everything. At the end of the day, Baby Bam finally hit that bass line and it just fell out. I started singing the chorus: "I've got you under my skin." We found our ownership with the bass line. It's always the bass.

We told a story about a girl called Mary Jane, who was sharing needles. We felt that to fully own the song, the storytelling needed to be raw and direct, communicating plain facts in our language. This was no time for anything less. "Share your love, but don't share your needles . . . and wear a condom." Our version of the song was renamed, simply, "Under My Skin," and we dedicated it "with every ounce of our love to the memory of Ray Petri." When the album came out at the end of September 1990, the track was chosen as the lead single, and we made a video with Jean-Baptiste Mondino. Judy did the styling. The voguer, my friend Roy (Anthony Brown), wore a shiny PVC bodysuit and a beaded mask, which Leigh Bowery had made specially for the shoot. Unfortunately, Judy and I managed to lose it one night after performing the track at Kinky Gerlinky. What idiots we were.

Of all the projects we worked on together, I think this video was the one that made us most proud.

A SECOND WEDDING

In 1990, on a Friday night in Fat Tony's DJ box at the Wag Club, I proposed. "Will you marry me?"

Cam grabbed me, sweating, and shouted, "Yes!" We'd had a big row earlier that afternoon, but the storm had passed and we'd decided to head into town, stopping by the house of a friend who was paying the rent by selling these little pills that were now all the rage. In the clubs, people had gone from hard dancing to lying on top of each other, all madly "in love." The music of that era just didn't hit me in the right spot, so I was slightly suspicious of this new rave culture and these tiny tablets. But that night, I succumbed. I guess the time had come to see what the hell everybody was going on about.

Cam and I dropped the E and, the streetlights winking at us, we walked over to the Wag. Then, a couple of songs in, overwhelmed by love, we became engaged.

We began to plan a wedding. It had been a big year, and we'd also just lost two of our nearest and dearest. Ray had died in August 1989, and then, late one night the following March, the phone rang at the farmhouse in the Shoe. It was Andi, telling me her brother, Sean, was gone.

Sean was only twenty-seven, just two years older than me. He was my dear friend, my brother. How could his time be now, already? Cam and I crawled back to bed, holding on to each other. It wasn't supposed to be like this: in this little bit of our lives where we could still feel like immortals, angels kept falling. (Sean left way too early, but thank God he left behind two wonderful children, Phoebe and Theo.)

Moki was visiting us, and the next morning I told her about Sean. It felt like a dream. But she said something I've never forgotten: "Neneh, you can't defuse energy."

The most remarkable thing is that in all the darkness, the resonance of life is still there, like a contradiction, even when you can't bear to see or hear it. All the little things, like a snowdrop pushing through the cold, wet soil; a baby's hand reaching out for a sibling's fingers on a bus; the juice of a ripe peach dripping down your chin. All this is the sweetness of life calling out, "Know how precious I am. Don't squander me, bitch."

The loss of Sean and Ray put a sharp line of urgency into our lives. We couldn't take anything for granted anymore. So we decided to celebrate the fact that we'd come this far—with our wedding. It was a way of giving thanks for everything we had—the album's success, each other, our family, our kids—and of commemorating what we'd lost.

We set the date for December 7, 1990. Judy and Cam had been scheming, and one evening after work the three of us (Judy carrying the can of Red Stripe we were sharing) went gold shopping on Queensway. My magpie eye fell on a beautiful ring in a shop window, with a big knot, but then I spied another one: two entwined snakes. I loved them both. I tried them on: the chunky knot blessing my index finger, the snakes on the ring finger. I couldn't make up my mind. Typical Judy, he said, "Well, you'll have to get her both!" I wore them always, until they were gone. Another story.

In November, Judy and I decided to go to Azzedine Alaïa's studio in Paris, where we knew we'd find something amazing for me to get married in. Azzedine was one of the most gorgeous souls, his creativity articulate and familiar, like home. As usual, he was dressed in his black kung fu uniform and shoes, his little dogs around his feet.

"I'm getting married," I told him.

"Oh la la!" came his response.

Judy said, "We're hoping to find something here."

But Azzedine replied, "Oh, no, no, no, Neneh. I have to make the dress! Come back tomorrow and I'll get started."

So we booked into a hotel, bought toothbrushes, had dinner, and the next day we went back to Azzedine, who took my measurements and showed us some sketches. While we were in his studio, he made a call to order the beadwork embroidery from a place that Judy knew all about. He couldn't believe his ears. "Oh, my God, Neneh! He's calling up Monsieur Lesage!" he exclaimed.

I was like, "Who?!"

Our wedding was a crazy day. Everyone I loved was able to come, apart from Don, who was by then living in San Francisco with his new partner, Pat. I was still carrying some sadness that he and Moki were no longer together, but there was no bitterness. In fact, I felt some relief that Don had moved with Pat to California, where he had great musician friends. He and I had spoken on the phone. He wanted to come but he just couldn't. That was fine. I knew his love for me was there in the room.

That day, I cried from the moment I woke up. Azzedine arrived at my house at 8 a.m. having flown from Paris to London on a propeller plane with two of his assistants, the couture dress carefully wrapped in silk paper. It was short and sleeveless in a light blue ribbed silk with cream polka dots and matching shorts. There was also a deep blue jacket made from a divine sheer net material, weighed down by Monsieur Lesage's silver polka-dot beadwork. My eyes filled again at the sight of it. When Moki saw me there with Azzedine on his knees making tiny final adjustments, she had tears too. He stood up and reached for the jacket, tied the belt around my waist just so, and gave it a little tug.

Andi was my best woman, Judy my best queen. My nieces, Miquita and Phoebe, and Marlon, Tyson, and Naima were bridesmaids. The girls designed their own dresses and Bruce's brother Uncle Stephan made their frilly pink fantasy-princess dreams come true. Marlon chose to wear a tracksuit, white with red, gold, and green hearts, which he wore with a big chain—hip-hop! Moki had made herself a pinafore dress—red velvet with a dog print.

Dressed and ready to go, we all piled into an old Rolls-Royce to make the short journey to Willesden registry office, just two minutes around the corner from the house. We were waiting on the front steps when, finally, Cam turned up late from the hotel—his peaky face said it all. I could see a Solpadeine painkiller overflowing from a plastic cup on the car floor. His excuse? He'd been accosted by some familiar faces in the hotel bar the night before. An impromptu stag invasion. He looked beautiful, nonetheless. This was the man I was about to marry.

Seeing virtually all the people I loved the most gathered in that small space, looking up at me, smiling, was overwhelming. I cried all the way down the aisle. When the celebrant said, "If any person here present knows of any lawful impediment to this marriage, they should declare it now," Ahmadu, in traditional dress, stood up and asked, "Where are my fifteen pregnant cows?"

We hired the old Cobden Working Men's Social Club for a wedding lunch with more than a hundred of our friends and family. Cam and I went back to the hotel after the ceremony to rest and change outfits. I put on my second Azzedine piece of the day. This one was a shortish black lace number that I wore with trainers, ready for the grind. As we walked back into the Cobden club, the joint was already heaving, the Massive boys and Nellee Hooper on the decks, Noel and Maurice Watson from our

Battle Bridge days; Goldie, too. Judy had changed into a lemon-yellow suit with an orb of net covering his entire head, made especially for the occasion by his great friend Philip Treacy. Years later, Philip and I laughed when we remembered how Judy had to drink his beer through this headpiece all night, leaving great rings of froth on the fine netting, because Philip had forgotten to make a watering hole at the mouth.

Jean Paul Gaultier sent me a gift—a collection of small, very detailed Victorian objects, all packed inside a vast wooden crate about the size of a dumpster. At some point in the evening, a forklift arrived and deposited this onto the pavement outside the club, and I had to be lifted inside to discover all the little items secreted in a ton of wood shavings.

We danced till our feet bled. We didn't want it to stop. But as morning started to close in on us, time was running out. Nellee tried to bribe the staff to let us keep partying—£100, £200, £400. No one wanted to leave. Dancing with Andi, Ahmadu said, "You remind me of home." My Muslim father didn't normally drink alcohol but, that night, after raising a few glasses, he ended up taking a nap in our doorway at Mortimer Road. Inside, their heads heavy with champagne bubbles, the rest of my sleeping family didn't hear him ringing the bell.

The day felt sublime, richer than a bag of precious stones. After a couple of nights at the Halcyon Hotel in Holland Park, we packed up the tribe—all the kids and a few friends—and took them with us on our honeymoon to the Seychelles.

Cam and I are still here, still married, and we try not to take our life and our good luck for granted. Although I love him always, over the years we have got better at creating breathing space, then finding each other again and pushing through. Sometimes we make it by the skin of our teeth.

We see each other for who we are. I don't have to try to be anyone but myself: I can be both weak and strong. We've seen the best sides, but also the depths of the ugliest and most ridiculous aspects of each other, and yet we have still managed to keep a separate, private part of ourselves. Between us there is a playful, unknown space that retains some mystery. I love this. We travel our own paths and can still discover new things about each other.

HOMEBREW

Listening to Massive Attack's sounds and that beat—raw and slow, mellow and sensual, as Daddy G said, "dance music for the head rather than the feet"—helped me to pass through into what became my second album. In that sense, *Homebrew* was the digestion of *Raw Like Sushi*. The tunes in *Homebrew* came out of the most focused period of my songwriting life. They allowed me to heal and grow.

We decided to buy a new, bigger house just up the road in Willesden. We had room to put in a real studio, and Sharlene, our cherished Kiwi nanny, moved in. I had my own space in which to work and write, supposedly away from the family noise—not just one but two adjoining rooms on the first floor. In the first room I kept my records and record deck, hundreds of cassette tapes, and a long wooden table covered with scraps of paper, where I could jot down thought sequences, stories, and song fragments.

The first track, "Move with Me," was commissioned for the soundtrack of a 1991 Wim Wenders movie called *Until the End of the World*. That was how we got inside making another album. One of my favourite songs, "Somedays," came to life almost fully formed. Cam and I met Geoff Barrow when Massive were working on *Blue Lines* at Coach House Studios, where he was working as the tea boy. He was already making music and would soon form Portishead with Beth Gibbons and Adrian Utley. Cam asked him if he had any tunes up his sleeve, and Geoff passed us a backing track sampling Beethoven's "Moonlight" Sonata. I've always been fascinated by the quiet of Sundays—the day begging for rest, and how even in a place that's either very loud or always peaceful, you still get that muted sense of life in standstill. The pressure of Monday impending—"Tomorrow, girl, it's back to the grind"—memories from school days, that empty-belly lethargy, still lingering. As soon as I heard Geoff's backing track, it took me to that place. That was "Somedays."

Me, Cam, and Jonny Dollar, our then collaborator, did some tracks with the NYC homeboy heroes Gang Starr—genius hip-hop producer DJ Premier and jazz rapper Guru—who were leading the way in nineties hip-hop. One of the joys of having success is that people don't take you for a stalker when you call. When Gang Starr travelled to London, we got in touch, and they came over to the house. I fed them some chicken and, once we'd sized one another up, they were in. Later, they came into the studio and we wrote "Sassy" and "I Ain't Gone Under Yet," which they co-produced. DJ Premier is one of the best producers I've ever worked with. His style is refined, uncompromising, and oddly understated. We also worked with Michael Stipe on a song called "Trout." We remain really close friends.

Sometimes a random conversation turned into a song. I called Moki one evening, needing to hear her voice, and she told me about an experience she'd had going to the Korean supermarket in Long Island City. As she walked up the block, she could see people standing outside the store, and a young man sitting by the door spilling blood. Someone had put a hole in him with a knife. Sirens in the distance, blue lights flashing—an ambulance was on the way. Moki stood there for a while, wondering about this young man, his life ebbing away. Other people stepped over him and walked in, leaving bloody footprints through the supermarket. His life on their shoes, like red emulsion. I was learning how to use a drum machine. I made a beat, found some chords on the Casio, and wrote "Red Paint."

We recorded most of the songs at home in London with Jonny but decided to put the final touches to the album back at the schoolhouse in Sweden. In spring 1992, we gathered the tribe, packed two cars with the kids, Sharlene, and Mr. Eric—Cam's Jamaican assistant, man about the house, and night-time DJ—and got on that dreaded overnight ferry to Gothenburg. Moki was in New York when we rolled up at Tågarp, but my grandparents Mormar and Morfar had been there to ready things for our arrival. They'd bought a couple of electric radiators to heat up the bedrooms, but it was still freezing, until we managed to get the fires going properly.

There were never fewer than ten for dinner. My cousin Pa Jah, from Sierra Leone, was there and he made a wicked groundnut stew and fried chicken; Eric made shepherd's pie infused with West Indian memories. Sharlene and I made Swedish summer food—new potatoes boiled with dill and dripping with butter and loads of salt and black pepper, herring fillets stuffed with garlic, fresh thyme, and curry butter, gently rolled in flour before frying, and dished up with sour cream and chives. The kids drank milk straight from the farm while we got through a fair bit of wine. Making music all day, cooking in the evening: these were sweet times. Often ending with a bit of a party.

Music was always another nutrient essential for everyone in the house. The record collection was still there from when I was a kid, and we'd also brought a pile of new sounds with us. After Moki arrived, in May, she was often the one to initiate the after-dinner dancing. The Atlanta hip-hop duo Kriss Kross made us jump, the kids all putting their clothes on back to front like they did on the cover. "Hip Hop Hooray," said Naughty by Nature, the streets of the city paving the dirt roads of Skåne County. We drove to Dr. Dre, passing green fields filled with black-and-white cows. I turned from the front to see Tyson sitting in her baby seat in the back, singing along, including the swear words. Whoops!

We more or less took over the schoolhouse. We'd filled it with our whole team and installed the studio in the larger classroom.

But this was what my parents had always intended for Tågarp: the continuing creative life, the next generation.

Moki had a show of new work opening later that summer and had a crazy deadline. At that time she was making light sculptures with plywood. She set up camp in the workshop at the back of the house, sawing and painting at a table in the grass. With her show just weeks away, it became a collaborative endeavour. She'd get anyone with a pair of spare, steady hands to help to meticulously paint the pieces of wood, and under her beady-eyed supervision they became otherworldly characters that yet belonged in this world. That summer, a neighbour gave Moki two roosters and she made a coop for them alongside her in the workshop. They'd keep her company, rootling around at her feet in the sawdust on the lawn. One of the birds was very black with a little bit of red around the beak. Moki thought him especially splendid and, much to my disapproval, she sometimes brought him to the dinner table, where he would sit in her lap and peck at her plate.

Moki and Judy would potter about in her studio, Judy sifting through materials she'd gathered over the years, exploring what this environment had to offer. They didn't chat a lot about their creative practice but they shared insights and outlook, and those added up to a deep understanding between them.

In early summer, Eagle-Eye arrived, as did the usual suspects who pass through in the season that seldom sees the dark. We were lucky. That summer was a hot one, nearly every day sunny, a sweet journey that took us into the early stages of autumn. Geoff Barrow arrived to work on the album then. When we took him around the local second-hand shops, going through bins of old records, he couldn't believe his luck at repeatedly striking pure gold.

We took most of the pictures for the campaign right there in Tågarp. Hair, make-up, music journalists: everybody came to the schoolhouse. Maybe after everything we'd passed through, we just needed to bring it back home. Eddie Monsoon, Juergen Teller, and Mondino shot me at the bus shed in the front yard, standing with an empty old pram. It was one of Moki's flea-market finds. A bit rusty now but sturdy as a Cadillac, it had carried all the kids over the years, navigating the bumpy roads on its elongated springs. The empty pram, no baby in my belly; the kids, not in the picture: that photograph became the cover.

Nearly there. We mixed the album in Copenhagen, and DJ Premier and Guru joined us to finish "Sassy." The single "Money Love" was released in September 1992. Many critics seemed to like the mix of rock riffs and hip-hop beats. *Homebrew* followed a month later. But the album didn't really hit in the UK. In America, though, it got a great response, so in early spring 1993, we decided to move to Brooklyn, to work it stateside.

SEVEN SECONDS AND A HOLD-UP IN BROOKLYN

From the bedroom window of our house, a three-storey brownstone in Fort Greene, we could see the clock tower in downtown Brooklyn.

In those days, Fort Greene was a slightly arty Black neighbourhood that was just starting to be gentrified. Spike Lee and Cecil Taylor lived there, for example. But Bed-Stuy was just around the corner, neighbourhood of Mike Tyson and the Notorious B.I.G.

In the early nineties, New York's districts were still very segregated by class, colour, religion, and ethnicity. It was as if some neighbourhoods were surrounded by a magnetic field. Closed in, there was so little outside support to help you to find your wings. But inside there was so much, each community like its own living universe.

As a mixed-race couple with light-skinned kids, Cam and I attracted some attention, predominantly from Black men in the community. I understood it, although the history is cold and long, toxic and complicated and racist. "Salt and peppa, hey, what you doing with him?" Mostly it was just comments made under the breath, but sometimes the tone burned with aggression and stung me hard. Cameron found it difficult to be himself or to feel comfortable with being there for us. He was also very conscious that if he responded to the comments, the situation could quite easily escalate.

•

We had released "Buddy X" as a single in 1992. Now the Swedish duo Falcon and Fabian Torsson, who I'd known since childhood, wanted to remix it. Alex Strehl, another young Swede who had become part of the family wallpaper, was doing an internship at Bad Boy Records, Puff Daddy's label. He suggested that we get one of the new young buck rappers from the label on it: Biggie Smalls, aka the Notorious B.I.G.

We picked up the teenage Biggie in Bed-Stuy, where he was waiting on his stoop, dressed in full camouflage, with his homeboy. Homeboy got in the back with me, and Biggie sat in the front next to Cam, evidently confused by this weird white guy and his London accent. It was one of those cold, sunny New York days, the sky a clean crisp blue colour that made all the skyscrapers look extra sharp around the edges. Biggie lit a blunt that filled the car with smoke. Cam pressed play on the cassette player. It was some new Massive Attack backing tracks and, as we went over the Manhattan Bridge, Biggie started freestyling, the words flowing eloquently as we drove up the island to 38th Street.

The recording studio was on the fourth floor of the building, but Biggie hesitated at the elevator door. "Nah," he said. "I'm not getting in, we're way over the limit." I insisted he'd be fine to squeeze in next to me, Cam, Homeboy, and an Asian man delivering food. The elevator slowly started its ascent, but one storey up, we got stuck. A jolt, then the lift started slipping. *Boom boom*; we bounced, then it stopped dead. Was this the end?

Thank God, it righted itself and we started moving upwards once more. When the doors finally opened, standing there behind the desk in reception was Q-Tip from A Tribe Called Quest. I have never been so happy to see anybody in my life. Busta Rhymes was there too, spreading an infectious energy in his light-up sneakers. Q-Tip introduced us, and when Busta said hello to Cam, he did it with a fearless hug. It melted some ice. Biggie and Homeboy started to breathe easier. We relaxed, and when we went into the studio and put our track on, Biggie, notoriously on his way to becoming B.I.G., recorded his verse in one take.

•

Collaborating with other people is a huge part of what I love about what I do. You never know exactly how it is going to fall together and that can be a real buzz. It can also make me nervous. Will we find the ingredients that make it real? Will we be able to connect and join the disparate elements?

We'd been living in Brooklyn for a few months when Verna Gillis—a musician, manager, and old family friend, part of the jazz tribe in New York—tracked us down and told us that Youssou N'Dour was going to be in town, that we needed to get together, maybe work on a tune. Youssou and I had spent some time together at a big Amnesty International event at Wembley Stadium not many years before, and he'd told me about staying in Tågarp with his band Super Étoile de Dakar (the Star Band) when he was eighteen. My family, with friends, had formed a community organisation to put on exhibitions and events. They showed films in our house and held concerts in our friends' barn, up the lane. I wasn't there at the time—I was in London—but I heard all about the Star Band's stay, not least because, according to Eagle-Eye, they ate all our hot sauce. Youssou told me that being with my family had been like being back home in Senegal, so he knew all about where I came from.

Ever since our meeting in London, Verna and Cam had been brainstorming, determined that this thing with Youssou, whatever it might be, should happen. Suddenly, the time was *now*. Eagle-Eye was living not far from us on the other side of Atlantic Avenue, and we used his studio, which was also his bedroom. Jonny Dollar came over from London and started to create a backing track, a soundscape, the modulation of the strings, and the beat. But Cam and I still hadn't come up with any words to put to the music. Then, just a couple of days before Youssou was due to arrive, Cam went into a store in Fort Greene, a bodega, where he used to get weed. This time, his usual guy wasn't there. Instead, it was a young Black man Cam hadn't met before, and he started to scream at Cam because he was white. Cam just stood there, hearing the man's fury and his pain, unable to say anything to make any difference. It was not his time to speak. All he could do was bow his head, absorb the verbal blows, and leave. Deeply affected, he bought a quart of whiskey and started writing. We were talking about resilience and hope and sustaining, sketching away as we do. Then he wrote, "When a child is born it has no concept of the colour of the skin it's living in." I sat with the idea, and I don't know why or where the notion of using a number of seconds came from, or if I knew exactly what I wanted to say, but somehow to his words I added, "Seven seconds away, I'll still be waiting."

The next day we went back to Eagle-Eye's studio and hammered through what became the chorus. Essentially, we now had the skeleton of a song, and we left spaces for Youssou because we wanted to combine our languages: the French and the Wolof of Youssou with my English.

I remember thinking that the chorus sounded too square, too uniform, too structured. But when Youssou arrived at Eagle-Eye's place and started singing, his voice brought the magic to the song. He took it into another dimension. With the addition of his scales, the variations of notes in his melodic range, he made it soar, sending us out through Eagle-Eye's bedroom window, past the crackheads on the street, past the clean washing-powder smell of the nearby laundromat, to lands free and untarnished by man or woman. It was a special moment. Each time we did a take, he sang it slightly differently. We spent the whole day perfecting it, Cam honing the vocals. By the time we finished, we knew we had hit on something very beautiful.

Youssou brought with him a whole history of emotions. There is so much power and resonance in his voice. It recalls the journey of humanity. He is descended from a long line of griots, his mother among them, those gifted improvisers who have elephant memories for the twists and turns of both story and melody. I hear their legacy woven through Don's improvised music and in the rap battles of the teenage MCs I used to hear dishing out their truths on the street corners of New York City, with urgency and sly wit. Supreme storytellers of our times.

"Seven Seconds" came out as a single in 1994 and sat at the very top of the charts in France for seventeen weeks straight. As Black artists in a non-inclusive society, we seemed to touch a chord all over the world. Youssou and I won the first prize of the night at the first European MTV Awards in Berlin. When Youssou arrived back in Dakar, the capital of Senegal, five thousand people greeted him at the airport and ran alongside the car all the way to his house as if he'd won the World Cup.

The most precious collaborations have typically developed over time and evolved organically. Sometimes the chemistry is in place from the beginning. Sometimes you get there by spending time together until you find one idea that clicks. And sometimes you simply don't find it. Not a beef . . . a thing, a problem with anybody—it's just that it doesn't happen. We are all just making things up as we go along, figuring it out, bumbling through. If everything was amazing all of the time, I think we'd all be speechless, and if you make that your starting point for creativity, you're going nowhere.

•

One Sunday night in late spring 1993, Cam and I were having a bit of an argument driving home from dinner. He said he didn't feel as if he could protect our family in New York. I'd lived in the city for large parts of my life, so I thought I knew how to handle it. I was telling him that he just had to ride it through, not be scared, and own it. It was all going to be fine. We pulled up at the house, took the tape machine out of the car—as everyone had told us we must, so nobody would smash the window and steal it. As we crossed the street, two figures dressed in black came running from behind and held us at gunpoint.

It was dark and the street was silent—nobody else in sight, not a single car, which was so unusual. As if the world had stopped and gone to sleep. The first thing they grabbed was the portable tape machine. Cameron pulled out all the cash he had in his pocket and handed it to them. They told me to take off both of my beloved gold engagement rings. I was also wearing a big brass necklace, but when I started to remove it, one of them said, "Leave it." Even in the dark, they could tell it was worthless. I was trying to take off my wedding ring, but it didn't want to leave my finger, then one of them barked, "No! We don't want that. It's bad luck." I thought, *OK, so there's time for superstition—amazing.*

All the possibilities of everything that could go wrong flashed through my mind. I remember thinking, *Choose your fucking words.*

"Look, he's the father of my kids," I stammered. "They're in the house. Please, just let us go."

Everything slowed right down. I could see them looking at each other, contemplating. It was probably just seconds, but it felt much longer. Finally, they told us to turn around and start walking.

We turned around and . . . just stood there. I couldn't move, the panic causing havoc in my mind and body. The bullets so close, so easy, so smooth. My blood, my love's blood. My breath was gone and my knees gave way. Cameron took my arm, and hissed, "Walk!

Just walk." But I didn't know how. He practically carried me to our stoop as the two men disappeared into the night. We went to bed but the dark kept us awake, freaking out. What if they came back? We called the police and the next day a cop came to the house with a pile of folders full of mugshots, but it was overwhelming. The police officer had a look of resignation about him. He was nice enough, but we could just tell it was hopeless.

That's the thing with a place like New York. I love the effect it has on my swagger. You start thinking you're a bit bad, feeling like you own the city, like it's in your blood. But just when you think you're holding it, it comes for you and smacks you in the face. That was one of those moments. It smacked us hard. New York, New York, so bad they named it twice.

IT IS NOW THAT MATTERS

A week later, we left Fort Greene, moved back to the loft, and then, briefly, back to London. London is at the core of who we are. Many of the people we work with will always be here, as well as a family of friendships made of the kind of love that sustains a lifetime. It was the obvious place for us to return to, but we were looking for a different quality of life. We knew that we were lucky. It's a privilege when you have a choice over where you live.

But Spain was one place that was pulling us. Using a Lonely Planet travel guide, a map and our noses, we took a road trip through Andalusia with Naima, Tyson, and Uncle Mark, driving around, scoping potential towns. We stayed in random hotels, the only must being a swimming pool. Tyson had a pink snail float strapped around her waist. She named it "High Low" and wore it throughout the whole trip. In Tarifa, the nearest tip to the motherland, I could sense all the travels made by people over the centuries. Sitting on a patio eating dinner, I said, "What are those lights?" I thought it was a distant Iberian bay. "It's Africa," said Cam. The proximity had a forceful effect that struck something deep in me. We were in Europe, but my ancestors' continent was right there.

We wound up staying for a while at Finca la Mota, a family-run guesthouse in the campo of Alhaurín el Grande, on the north side of the Sierra de Mijas near Malaga. We felt at home there. When we left, we asked the owners, Arun and Jeanie, to let us know if they heard of a house for rent. In August 1993 we got a call from Arun, packed up two Volvo estates, and off we went, Cam driving one, Eric and Sharlene taking it in turns to drive the other.

I can still feel, arriving in the valley of Urique and getting the keys to our very first Spanish house, the heat, the smell of the nighttime bloom, the shadows of the mountains, hidden in the dark. The house was simple but big enough and we had a pool. Our landlord always had rolls of pesetas in the pockets of his unbuttoned shirt when he tended to the orchard's oranges, tangerines, and avocados. Around Easter time, the orange blossom infused the air like an aphrodisiac. At Christmas, in bliss, I would go out and fill baskets with our garden's offerings: satsumas, clementines, divine Seville and navel oranges. The landlord kept his hens in the garden shed, so we always had fresh eggs. There wasn't a day when the mountains looked the same. When I walked into the open, endless hills of scattered rocks and arid red soil, where even the most beautiful plant is armed with spikes to fight the rough terrain, I'd think, *I am on a planet in space*. Living there made me *feel*. We ended up staying for four years.

When we arrived, none of us spoke Spanish. In the supermarket wanting to buy a non-cow cheese, I pointed at the cheese counter going, "Baaa baaa."

"Aaaah, *queso de cabra*!"

We enrolled the children at the English-speaking international school outside Fuengirola. Later Naima moved to the Swedish school in the same town. Gradually, we all picked up basic Spanish.

Once we were settled, Cam and I took a trip to San Francisco to see Don. I always spoke regularly with my parents, even if often continents kept us apart. If we were out when Don called, he would leave a message on our answering machine: sometimes he would speak, sometimes he would play the flute, sometimes both, blending his love for us in words and sounds.

When Don and Moki split up, it shifted our family dynamic. Change is part of life and it did change us. It was different, but when Don and I were together, we always found each other again. Our meetings were often quite random because we'd find each other in New York or LA at the same time. When he was in London, he'd stay at the house, goofing around with the kids. He'd show them how to play the melodica he kept in his bag, tenderly placing their little fingers correctly and telling them to blow. Then he'd start playing "The March of the Hobbits," get them singing along, their little voices picking up steam. But I hadn't been to see him in San Francisco, where he had lived with Pat, for nearly four years. Pat had died not long before and I didn't know what to expect. When we got there, everything was very tidy and ordered but Don was in pretty bad shape. He was still shooting up. And even though he maintained a grace and a force that were formidable, the years of abuse had taken their toll. He was starting to lose his balance and his teeth were ruined. He had a sense of great shame about losing his teeth, and he could no longer play the trumpet. Heroin was the mistress, sure, but his relationship to and with music was *his life*. Although he still managed to play piano and the donso ngoni, the trumpet was his first instrument. I could tell how bad that hurt him.

It was very hard to see Don like that. Eagle-Eye was always able to be more openly angry with him, but I had never found it possible to confront him. I was silenced by my love for him, but still we had a profound communication. We talked about everything else. Before Cam and I returned to Spain, we spoke with Don's friend Horazio, a Guatemalan jazz musician and a lovely man, who was looking out for him. One of many in the community whose love and respect was sustaining Don through his troubles. If we need to come back, we said, please tell us.

Back in Alhaurín, the locals took us in. Obviously, Spain is not immune to racism, but for some reason I've always felt a lot less judged there than in other parts of Europe, at least in the communities I've lived in. At the weekend everybody would come out to the *campo* to look after their gardens, cook, eat, drink, talk, music blaring from radios. They were so full of life, it didn't take long to fall in love with the culture and spirit of the people. I appreciate humans taking time to live. The love for a party is never wrong.

On weekend nights most of the town was out, all dressed up, and all ages, till the small hours. People were living life on the outside instead of looking out from the inside and it had a good effect on all of us.

We always had friends and family passing through, as per usual. Our entourage occupied the rooms at the finca virtually year-round. Tricky was there a lot with Martina Topley-Bird. Cam was working with the Swedish band Whale, so they were often around. Judy and Andi visited so frequently that they eventually got their own flats in the village. Chrissie Hynde adopted a donkey because she felt so sorry for it.

We started writing again and set up a cluster of little studios and an office. We named the main studio "Paco's Shed," because we rented it from Paco, the farmer up the hill. Tricky and I did a lot of work there. We would set the mic up under the grapevines in the yard. It was always so sweet singing outside under those vines, hanging heavy with fruit, the perfect contrast when we were doing a track like "Crack Baby," which we wrote together, Tricky taking hits on his inhaler for sound effect. Sometimes Paco would crack open a bottle of the muscatel wine he made from those grapes; way too sweet but we drank it anyway.

•

In February 1995, Horazio rang to say that Don wasn't doing well. We booked them both on a flight to Malaga.

When we met them off the plane, it was immediately obvious that Don was very fragile. He had abscesses on his arms, his feet were swollen, and his balance had deteriorated further. Every day, while he was still able, he liked to go to Finca la Mota for a coffee and cognac. Sometimes he still tried to play his trumpet, but it wouldn't respond to his call. He played the keyboard in the living room. His sense of mortality made his life flash around his mind, and he talked a lot about his experiences. This made me restless because I knew why he had this reflex, but I listened carefully despite my muted panic. I wish I'd recorded those conversations. Don, as a teenager, working for a drugstore that delivered opiates in the hills of Hollywood to people like Vincent Price, Doris Day, and Ronald Reagan. And there was a time before that, not long out of Oklahoma, when some children put the small boy in a barrel of water. They didn't know why, but something the big people around them said about colour got inside their thinking, so they sat on the lid until Donald thought he was going to die. Gasping for air, the water over his head, it made him uneasy around water for the rest of his days.

When he spoke about meeting Ornette Coleman for the first time, I saw an expression in his hands on the kitchen table, those hands that had held me for so long that I can still feel them now. They were saying something about truth and love and even though you forget some things, others will never fade away because we carry inside the tears and scars that make something so vigorously alive, it can't die. I know now what I didn't know then, which was that Mabel, my third baby, was there too, teeny tiny, inside me, and she heard.

That summer I had shows, mostly festivals, so we left for a while, taking the kids for some of it. Out there, with the band, I danced so hard I sometimes flew. My period didn't arrive and somewhere after one of those nights, I did a pregnancy test, but by then I knew. I recognised the feeling. My babies were all born seven years apart—I guess it's my lucky number.

The afternoon we arrived back at the house, Don was standing in the kitchen finishing a pot of rice pudding. It was the only thing he could eat by then. Something had changed. He'd always been skinny but now he was alarmingly thin, just skin on bone. He came out to the hallway and held me.

"Hey, sugar."

"Daddy, I'm pregnant," I told him.

He smiled all the way and said, "I'm so happy. It feels right."

After that, things happened quickly. We'd only been back a few days when Cam had to take Don to Malaga Hospital. The emergency doctor noted some shadowing on his liver and said that he needed to see a specialist. A couple of days later, we drove to a rather fancy clinic near the beach where we were greeted with stern patriarchal and racist overtones. The doctors clearly didn't like the look of us. It was a bit like when Ray was told about his illness. They didn't do any tests but they yelled at us outside Don's examination room, saying that he had liver cancer and probably AIDS, because he was a user, and that he only had six weeks to live. Six weeks. The judgement fell like a hammer blow on my head.

We took Don home. There was little the doctors at the clinic could do for him, and in any case, Don wanted to do it in his own way. We found a wonderful local Colombian doctor who is still a friend. He did tests and found that Don had hep C, which was attacking his liver. He said Don wasn't strong enough to deal with withdrawal, so we helped him administer his heroin. We just wanted to do all we could to make him as comfortable and pain-free as possible.

We rented a small house for him right next door, which had a patio covered in wisteria weighed down with fat purple blossoms. This was to be Don's own space with a nurse on duty living upstairs. Moki came with our friend Steve Roney to get the house ready for him. She scrubbed the rooms from top to bottom. Then, overwhelmed with a thing called love, she lit the Tibetan incense as a final touch. Or nearly—there was one more thing she needed to do. Folded into a small rectangle inside a bag was her huge Chenrezig tapestry. Moki and Steve hung it on the wall outside. The wise Buddha Chenrezig watching over them, they pushed Don down the bumpy lane in his wheelchair, just the three of them: Don, the love of his life, and his dearest friend. When they reached the patio, they stopped to look at that familiar piece that had accompanied our family to so many places. In the bottom corner Moki had stitched our house in Tågarp. I like to imagine that when Don looked at it, a memory of woodsmoke and green birch swept through him like a soaring, weightless swallow diving into the nest on the veranda. *I wanna go home, I wanna go home* . . . I picture those three dear old friends sitting outside together, Moki and Steve eating the gravlax and drinking the schnapps Steve had brought from Sweden. Don just watched. No matter—they were in unison.

In those weeks, my family and friends gathered around us. My brothers arrived, Eagle-Eye and Christian. Andi came from London and, towards the end, my sister Jan came from LA. After judgement day, everything dropped. We all nursed him, got him to eat, kept him clean. Don had always been on a mission. But in the last few weeks of his life, he entered a peaceful, still place. For us, his kids, it was amazing to be with him like that: out in the countryside, no interference, and every day felt like a lifetime. He spent a lot of time with his hands on my belly, feeling the life that was Mabel growing inside, but also putting his life force into me.

"Tell people about me," he said. "Don't let them forget."

His voice barely worked anymore, just a faint whisper in my ear. The day before he died, he said to me, "Get me out of here, I want to go home." He said, "I'm seeing white light around all of your heads, like you're becoming spirits."

The day he died, October 19, 1995, I had an appointment for an ultrasound. We sat with his body, the doors open to the patio, surrounded by the blooming wisteria, and listened to a recording of Don talking in a radio interview. As his hands and face grew cold, I had a very powerful sensation of his moving on, and I remembered what Moki said when Sean died: "You can't defuse energy."

After the ambulance came to take Don to the mortuary, everyone piled into the car and we went en masse for the scan. The doctor smeared the cold, wet jelly on my bump and together we watched a new life, in the embryonic form of Mabel, appear on the black-and-white screen; heard her determined, steady heartbeat. As Don always said, it is *now* that matters.

•

During this final period of Don staying with us, for some mad reason Cam and I gathered a group of musicians and went into a live-in studio, just forty minutes away to the north of Marbella. We recorded twelve album tracks—about life and death and love—for a new album, *Man*, in just two weeks.

After Don died, I felt deeply guilty that I'd squandered a portion of the precious time we had left, sometimes spending days at a stretch away from him. But in retrospect, working seemed to make sense when nothing else did. Don got it, I think. He helped me with "Woman" when I was having problems vocalising the track. Back at the house after a tricky session, it was Don who said, "You should sing it a bit more staccato, a little more chopped. Don't draw out the lines so much." I was working it all out, or rather singing it out in these new songs: having a baby, making life, holding on to the ones I have. What else could we do? Like laughing when you're crying the most. Even though we had all this sadness and frustration, we'd also been fuelled by a kind of mad life force. Everything took on this urgency and, through making the music, we shed a lot of things that needed to go. I'd got to a point with my singing where I'd started to be a bit careful, thinking too much before I did it. Making *Man* unleashed something. Perhaps because there was nothing I could do to change what was happening. There was a freedom from responsibility that reminded me of being a little girl again.

•

Mabel was born on February 19, 1996, exactly four months to the day after Don's death. I was making breakfast for the kids when something warm ran down my legs. It was the waters around Mabel leaving my body, but it was hardly a torrent, so I put a pad on and got in the car with Sharlene, Tyson, and Naima. I wanted to drop the kids off at school ceremoniously, before our family constellation changed. After lunch, the contractions were definitely real. Cam drove me to the Malaga clinic, and when we got there, we took a few minutes, sitting in a square, to just be. I drank a glass of cold beer and then, at 3 p.m., we went in. Fifty minutes later, Mabel Alabama Pearl was born with a head full of dark hair. She was perfectly calm, and chubby. Divine instant love.

That summer, when she was about five months old, we held a memorial for Don in Sweden. When he was dying, he had talked so much about going home to Tågarp. The plan was to scatter his ashes in the garden at the schoolhouse. I had a gig in Stockholm, so I travelled ahead with our girls, Mabel, Tyson, and Naima. Cam would join us there, bringing Don in his luggage. This was against all the rules. You can't travel with human remains without authorisation. The night before Cam flew to Sweden he'd gone out and hadn't slept much. He checked in at the airport, still a little out of it, and, at security, he put his bag and the nylon case with the urn in it on the conveyor belt to go through the scanner. We passed through the airport so often that the guys operating the belts knew us. They asked him what it was.

"*Es mi padre,*" he told them.

And they just said, "Whatever, fuck it," and blessed love, they let him go through.

We took the train to Tågarp with Don in the black nylon case. A friend of ours, who is a local journalist, wrote a small piece in the paper about our plans for the memorial and the scattering of Don's ashes. One of our neighbours saw it and came to see us.

"You can't do that," he said. "It's completely illegal."

Oh, shit. OK. So that put an end to it all. We had a beautiful memorial, but Don's ashes remained unscattered, sealed in the golden urn. Every year, when Moki went back to the loft in New York, she would put him somewhere safe in the schoolhouse—sometimes inside the piano, which she covered with a duvet.

•

Man came out in September 1996. I had a tour in Europe. John Tonks joined us as the band's musical director (or, as I like to say, "curator") and he took the live set to another level. That October, just coming up to the first anniversary of Don's death, I went to promote it in Australia and New Zealand, taking baby Mabel with me.

It had been arranged that on the day we arrived in New Zealand, we would be invited to a *pōwhiri*, the traditional Māori welcoming ceremony. I was humbled to receive such an honour. At the airport, I got into one car with Mabel, my tour manager, and a record company guy. Katie, who had been one of Don's nurses and was from New Zealand, had come to help me look after Mabel. Her parents drove to the airport to pick her up and we set off in convoy to the *marae*, the sacred Māori meeting place.

The elders were all on one side of the *marae*, and when the teenagers performed the haka, they looked wild. My hair stood up on end and it sent the fear of God through Mabel. According to the *pōwhiri* tradition, people took turns to speak and sing. When my turn came, I was terrified. I sang a weird rendition of "Manchild" and I spoke about Don and the fact that it was a year since his death, because that was what came into my head. He was there. My ancestors were there. I could feel them. A quiet truth sat in that room, thousands of years old.

Katie, meanwhile, was stuck outside. They'd fallen behind us on the drive and the elders had to close the door to the *marae* before the opening of the ceremony. And so, while I was inside, talking about Don, she and her parents were sitting in the car parked on a cliff edge. And there below in the bay, in the light of the full moon, for the entire duration of the *pōwhiri*, a whale was dancing in the waves with its baby. Don had always attracted a kind of magic.

Don was not the father who made me, but he was my dad. He soothed my tears, kept a cocoa butter stick handy to fix childhood cuts and scrapes. He carried me in his arms and on his shoulders. Lying on his back, he balanced me on his feet and lifted me up to help me fly—through life. He taught me the art of living: the breath, that freedom, that inner creative quest, that driving pursuit of beauty—never-ending. The music, the life force, ran through all of it.

HOME LIFE

After *Man* I didn't release another solo album for sixteen years. Even to my ears that sounds absurd. How can so much time have passed? People have said, "What happened to you? Where did you go?" That's the thing, though: I didn't go anywhere. My kids were growing up fast and I tried to catch those years. I didn't stop making music—it's simply that I made it with other people, in performance and sometimes on their records. I released two records with our family band, CirKus, and we toured a lot, especially in France. But there was no album with my name on it until *The Cherry Thing* in 2012. Sometimes I feel that in the absence of a product to show, it's as if you don't exist. But I think that I wanted to feel I was authentically inhabiting my life. I needed music and home; time with my family; the forest in Tågarp; space to listen and to think. I needed time to digest this world.

In November 1996, when Mabel was about nine months old, we moved back to London, to a small Victorian mews house in Primrose Hill. Cam had been commuting to London for work; and at fourteen, educationally and socially, Naima needed something more than small-town Spanish life could offer.

Landing back in Britain just as winter began to bite sucked. It rained hard. It was difficult. Compared to the open space and light of Alhaurín, we felt hemmed in and on top of one another. We went through some shit in that small, dark house. During our four years in Spain, eight-year-old Tyson had run free. She had barely worn a pair of shoes other than to go to school and, at one point, had a baby chicken living in her bedroom cupboard. Life in London sent her into a state of shock. In retrospect, it must have been a kind of depression.

And Naima, bless her, had suddenly passed into the teen void. Being back in London was a huge transition for her. She started going out to parties in search of her own tribe. We coexisted in a strange hollow silence. Sometimes the distance between us felt like a canyon, where not saying anything at all seemed easier than a fight. And what teenager doesn't glare at you when you ask them, for the hundredth time: "Are you all right?"

Throughout that winter into spring 1997, I was away a lot touring *Man*, so much so that when I did come home to London briefly, I didn't even bother to unpack. I just left my suitcases in the hallway, ready for the next departure. The compact living of the tour bus has a kind of intensity. Sharing that small space unavoidably triggers a muscle memory of tribal life: the rhythm of being on wheels reminiscent of my childhood travels in our various buses. It gives me a feeling of freedom—sometimes I just want to drive and keep going. This bus was a lot more luxurious than our old VW van, though. Kitchen, lounge with a big telly, rows of comfy bunks for rest and recuperation.

I brought Sharlene and the kids around Europe with me and they had a ball. The kids would find their favourite band members, climb on their heads. We travelled with a deluxe Scrabble set, bought them knitting kits and new colouring pens in little stationery shops in random cities. Tyson's favourite thing was helping with the catering.

Of course, while there was always an intention for the bus to be a family environment, it was also a party destination. In the grip of a post-gig adrenaline rush, as we left the dressing room the band and I would scoop up whatever booze or food we could find and bring it back on board. To let off steam, we sometimes played a stupid game where people would collect all the bottles from a minibar, put them in a bag, and then we'd do a lucky dip.

We had to drive overnight to Madrid, across the Pyrenees. Coming down a mountainside in the black of night, Tonks woke up to an odd smell. The brakes were failing. It could have been a disaster. All of us had to squeeze into the crew bus, now carrying twenty-two bodies, to continue to Madrid. There were sleeping people everywhere. I lay comfortably squished in the lounge, awake for most of the night, looking out the panoramic window. As the sun started to rise, the landscape lay empty, quiet and expressive.

•

Back in London, I wish I'd been able to honour everything I had accomplished and say to myself, *It's OK. Just breathe. Maybe take a break*. Eighteen years after starting with Rip Rig + Panic, and with three kids, I deserved one. But I didn't have that insight and I didn't take a break. Instead, Cam and I made another album.

It would have been the fourth, but it was never released. We spent many months on it but we couldn't even find a working title and, listening to it one day, we felt like something else was missing. Oh yeah—it was *me*. I could feel the songs spinning around my head, but I'd lost my intuition and I was constantly overthinking. In that battle I lost all joy in the process. I couldn't catch a ride and just go. I didn't manage to get out of the waiting room and into the space where creativity soars and things start to happen. Some artists can make good music without leading from their hearts. It can be production-led and not be heartless. But I'm not a classically trained singer, and I don't have a massive voice. If I'm not present, it just doesn't resonate. One good thing did come out of that failed album, though. We wrote our first song with Paul Simm, a musician, composer, and producer who's still very much in my life.

Cam and I also began to lose sight of each other. We were partying too much, not seeing things clearly. Finally, after an especially unpleasant row, Cam moved out and stayed away for six long months. All of us had become sad, separate. We all went through changes, each of us in our own lonely dimension. I cried every night.

Eventually Cam and I got our marriage back on track. But the fallout from the failed album left me with a kind of creative anxiety that made it harder to write new songs. So I found comfort in immersing myself in other, more domestic aspects of life. On the flipside, of course, as much as home is a place of warmth and communication, it can also be quite a lonely place. And busying myself with cooking or mopping the floor became an avoidance reflex. It ate into time I could have been spending alone, thinking or writing in a room by myself. It wasn't until many years later that I realised I'd probably been suffering from a low-level depression throughout this period. It had settled in and made itself cosy; it became my normal. The experience on that fourth album cemented it. In retrospect, though, perhaps this time was also part of the creative process. Sometimes doing nothing is as good an inspiration as any.

•

After the unhappiness of our brief separation, Cam and I decided to leave that misery mews behind us. We moved to a bigger house, in Gloucester Crescent, Camden, and filled it with family and friends. Marlon came from Saint Vincent, where he was living with his mother, Vonnie, and little sister. Miquita lived with us for a while, and Andi was there a lot, by this point also with her man Garfield. All the kids seemed to have some friends or others coming in and out, staying for extended weekend sleepovers. This is how we are. If I'm feeding five people, I can just as easily feed five more. I will just make it work.

In spring 1997, Judy had gone to rehab to deal with his heroin addiction. He managed to kick his habit and, when he came out, he moved in with us. He had dabbled for many years. We were all partying pretty hard in those days, so who was I to judge? But heroin made me wary. It had cast a shade over most of my childhood and I knew far too much about how things were likely to go. As with any aspect of my life that brought up old feelings of fear, I coped by not engaging with it. The hedonistic days were beginning to catch up with too many of us, so when Judy got clean I felt like I could breathe again.

Then his beloved mother died, and that nearly wiped him out. He started drinking heavily. He would come downstairs in the morning, announce that he was off to buy some breakfast. He'd come back with four cans of Red Stripe, the papers, and some chocolate buttons for the kids. He had always been good at drinking but he was steadily graduating to a whole other level. It never stopped him from working, though, or being, at times, the biggest bitch and most glorious godmother. The kids were always up in his bedroom at the very top of the house. It doubled up as a small factory when Judy set them to helping him sew Kylie Minogue's stage accessories. Judy loved old black-and-white movies, but his favourite film was a bonkers late-fifties comedy starring Rosalind Russell. One rainy Sunday afternoon, he asked me, "Have you ever watched *Auntie Mame*?" I hadn't. "Well, darling, you haven't lived." He was right, of course. It is fabulous.

In short, Judy was of us, and we were of him. He featured heavily in our plans for living in Spain in old age, as both a neighbour and local stylist. I could just imagine him spotting me and Cam about to stagger out to grab a coffee in something unforgivably slouchy, and screeching, "You can't go out wearing that!" His dream for his own old age was to dress like a Spanish granny. But, sadly, it was not to be.

Judy died many years after we'd all moved on from Gloucester Crescent, on February 19, 2018. In the autumn of the previous year, his goddaughter Tyson had planned to go house-hunting with him in Madrid, but the trip was cancelled when he was diagnosed with cancer. On February 12, he celebrated his birthday with his siblings and his father. He was too ill to be alone at this point, so our dear friend Eddie Monsoon stayed the night at Judy's flat. At 4 a.m. on Valentine's Day, Eddie heard him moving around in the kitchen. He went to investigate, and watched as Judy made a cup of tea, lit a fag, and sat down in a chair. He was sewing something invisible, pulling thread for the last time.

As the news spread, people started arriving. His extended family of friends was vast. None of us had a plan, but there was an instinct, maybe rooted in something old and tribal. Judy was our queen and we all needed to be there. The inner circle stayed with him for another five days. The bugger just wouldn't die. There were three of us sleeping on his Frick and Frack coffee table. Another two sleeping head to toe on each couch. Philip Treacy was under a towel on the floor. Cam and I moved into the laundry cupboard, the only place with any privacy. The whole thing was complete heartbreak, but still it managed to provide funny moments bordering on the absurd. It is Judy we are talking about, after all.

After Judy died, Cam ended up living in that laundry cupboard for a month. He and Dave Baby, Judy's friend and collaborator from the House of Beauty and Culture days, had decided to watch Judy's entire DVD collection of cowboy movies, in what they described as "Judy's Posthumous Cowboy Movie Festival." After Judy stopped drinking, he had spent what would have been booze money every week on new DVDs. By the time he died he hadn't had a drink for eight years, so there were thousands of films stacked on the floor and in plastic crates. I visited nightly to join in the mourning process.

Judy had lived his whole life entirely indifferent to conventional success. It wasn't money that motivated him, or recognition by the mighty art establishment. They were just nice-to-haves. What he wanted was raw beauty. And he was granted it. He was an incredible cheerleader for creativity and for people who were making things and doing things. He was never threatened by others' achievements. He was too big for that. I miss him every day. He was and is my sister for all of eternity. Judy Blame was and is (by his own sharp tongue) a "LEG-END."

•

Our house was a whirl of perpetual motion: open door, pots on the stove, Cam calling me from the little studio we rented in Primrose Hill to ask if everyone he was working with could come for dinner. Mabel and Tyson having friends over after school. Naima and her crew holding teenage parties. I liked to have them all close. It is how I have known and shown love.

On March 28, 2003, my grandson Flynn was born. Nine months earlier, I was with Moki in Tågarp when Naima called to tell me she was pregnant and said she wanted me to be with her at the birth. It was beautiful. I was standing in exactly the same spot, and was the same age as my mother was when I had phoned to tell her about Naima.

She went into labour in Gloucester Crescent, and we got her into the big copper bath in our bedroom. When it was time, I went with Naima and her partner, Stevie, to the hospital. I was there to welcome Flynn, the sweetest small creature with a head of ginger hair.

I look back at this period now and can see that it happened as it needed to. I spent those years absorbing inspiration. I needed time to take in, as opposed to generating. I had always been on my way to something else. Those years of home life in London were not always blissfully harmonious, of course, but they were necessary for us. For me.

STOCKHOLM, MY LOVE

In April 2004, we moved to Stockholm, to a flat in Götgatan in the city centre. Next door to our apartment was the famous old drinking-hole and restaurant Pelikan, where they serve *husmanskost*, rustic Swedish home cooking. The lady who ran Pelikan became my friend and soon I was using the restaurant like my living room and office.

The transition of being back in Sweden, a Sweden that I had not lived in at all as an adult, was tough. Our family home in Skåne in the south is its own universe, but this was the *real* Sweden. The rest of the family seemed to adapt quicker than I did, and I am the one who is *Swedish*! I was born in Stockholm. But I had last lived there with Moki and Don in the little apartment in Gamla Stan when I was four years old. I felt both familiar and lost. I felt overdressed, underdressed, not clean enough, not fast enough, not fit enough. My Swedish had never left me, but my vocabulary did not have the depth that my English now had, so I felt stunted, that I couldn't communicate with ease. Most important, in Swedish my humour felt stilted. Old outsider feelings haunted me. I felt I was not Swedish enough to be accepted in Stockholm.

We had moved because the whole family needed a reset. Neither Mabel nor Tyson was happy at school, and though I had loved the Gloucester Crescent years in many ways, now I was yearning for peace. We wanted to leave London but could not face moving somewhere we knew nobody and didn't speak the language. *Sweden*, we thought. Great schools, progressive social policies, and old family and friends. Eagle-Eye was living in Stockholm, as was

Ahmadu, and my sister Titiyo and all the siblings on that side of the family. Decision made.

Crazily, we arrived at the start of winter. The city felt quiet, muted. The people felt distant. I'd open the front door in the morning to take the kids to school and stick my head out on Götgatan, looking up and down the street, wondering where we were. I was uneasy, stressed. At the same time, I wanted Sweden. I needed it. I began to walk around the city, wandering, and I always gravitated towards Gamla Stan. I felt a part of me still existed there. I'd roam the old cobbled streets and know where I was, but I also fought against that clingy desire to hold on to something past.

In the first few weeks, after dropping the kids at school, Cam and I were so anxious about them settling in that we would go home and smoke a whole pack of fags. In any gaps during the day, I'd gravitate towards my office, where a soothing glass of wine might take the edge off. Maybe it was here that the insatiable thirst began to creep into the sociable ritual I had always loved. But craving is a funny thing. Is it the root of addiction? I'm not hungry but I always want more from life. Something sweet, a fag, a grape in a glass to lift the mood, to just get a bit more. Craving sugar, craving love, craving drugs, attention, love, food, sex, love, food, craving.

Maybe the craving for wine and for company was a longing for intimacy—the click in the head—seeking a conversation that can open gateways—seeking a solution, no dilution, just effervescent joy. How did I belong here in this place, this country? The imprint of my Swedishness lay somewhere in my memory bank. I kept dissecting the different parts of myself—African-Swedish me—that just needed to merge. My intermingled cultural cells looking for home. Is my left or my right hand more Swedish? Where do I feel it? And where is Africa? In my thigh? Above my forehead?

A year or so after we moved, I was on the subway when I realised, *I'm the fucking problem. It's not anybody else. I am a self-conscious, awkward stranger in my own leftover life. Nobody cares what I look like and no one has put a gag on me—let it go.*

That was the beginning of a process of reconciliation with my Swedishness, and myself. Life is slower in Sweden than in the UK. Even though I had family and close friends in Stockholm, including three soul sisters, Annika, Marimba, and Deborah, the social whirl was more of a gentle swirl. That was a good thing. I needed to find ways back to the quieter parts of myself.

Eagle-Eye and I saw each other regularly. I needed to be near him. He had moved to Stockholm around the time Don was dying, when he was struggling with his grief and questioning what to do next in his career. Music was becoming the dominant force in his life. That weird, unsettled time enabled him to write his debut album, *Desireless*, and eventually took him to "Save Tonight." Released in 1997, it was his first big hit and a defining track.

I was very touched that he asked me to sing on a track called "Long Way Around" from his album *Living in the Present Future*. It was being recorded at the classic Electric Lady Studios in Greenwich Village and Rick Rubin was producing, which was an experience in itself. It felt very natural to record with Eagle-Eye, but it was interesting watching him in that setting. He's quite like Don: serious when in the music, a leader.

And, of course, being back in Sweden I was able to spend more time with Ahmadu. He always came carrying a pot of something—tender lamb and okra fearlessly seasoned in red sauce. We'd always pray for some of his Gbinti honey, homemade hot sauce—Pappa's Peppar. My siblings on his side were almost all living in Stockholm, and I became really close to my sister Amanda. She would come and stay with Mabel when I had to travel. My sister Titiyo and I have always needed each other in a very fundamental way, and we'd been growing that relationship since we were kids. Whenever we met up with my other siblings—Tiyoneh, Cherno, Mikailo, Senni, and Toomany—it was just as it is, love right there, right then.

One Saturday, Titiyo and I made a huge vat of Brazilian feijoada. Our flat was full of friends and family and, with the windows all steamed up, the love fell in and warmed us all. That led to Titiyo, Andi, and me starting a monthly Sunday feed communion at Pelikan, for which Andi would fly in. Very cosmopolitan-commuter chic, except that it was probably on a Ryanair flight. And slowly, slowly, in that beautiful city, I started to walk right into my quiet: as me, a mother, a woman, a wife, and a friend.

THIS IS WHERE MY LIFE WILL NEVER BE THE SAME

On *Midsommarafton* (Midsummer Eve) 2009, Moki went to a party, drank some wine and probably a few aquavits, and had a fall. I still remember answering the call. Eagle-Eye rang to tell me she had broken some ribs and was in the hospital.

A few weeks earlier, at the beginning of June, Moki had had an exhibition in a gallery in Stockholm, her first show in the city in forever. She was mostly showing collages—delicate, humorous, fierce, political. Considering her status as a Swedish-born artist, Moki hoped she would get some serious attention in the media. But there were only a few small notices, amounting to nothing. The disappointment was huge. I'd never seen her so empty. In the past, even when she was feeling deflated, her creative passion had usually pushed for even more reasons to express, to make, to carry on. Undoubtedly, she knew the value of her art—she was just bad at putting a price on it. Maybe that was part of her sadness. Now my normally indomitable mother seemed to feel that everything was pointless. She sounded exhausted.

The night before she had gone to the party, I tried to pep-talk her, but I just heard my voice grinding on, sounding as empty as she felt.

Moki said, "I don't want to go. *Jag hatar miss sommar!* I *hate* missed summer!" But she did go, she did have a good time, and she did have a fall. Afterwards, she was ill all summer with water on one of her lungs.

Eventually, she started to get better. A month or so later, I spent a weekend with her. It was just me and her in Tågarp. Normally there was endless stuff to do, tidying, but during those days we just lay in bed together. We listened to surreal late-night Swedish radio shows and did crosswords. And we laughed, so much.

•

Moki died in Tågarp on August 29, 2009. Two months earlier, when she came out of hospital after her fall, she had said, "Just so you know, when I die, I want to be buried." All my life she had been saying crazy things like "Just put me on the compost" or "I'm going to go out into the woods and lie down and let the worms eat me." I never wanted to listen. But that day, I heard what she said and felt what it meant. My mother's mortality was in the room.

Moki had been due to go back to New York in early September, so that last week in August, Tyson, Naima, and I went to help her close up the schoolhouse. Those were the last days we were together. Still tinged with her weariness and disappointment over the exhibition, she said she didn't want to go to the States.

The day after we got back, I couldn't get hold of her on the phone. It was my brother Mikailo's birthday, so Ahmadu and the clan were all coming to ours. Andi and I were cooking for the party, but I couldn't concentrate or sit still. Andi was at the kitchen table, chopping her way through a small mountain of onions, peeling sweet potatoes, seasoning the chickens. "Don't worry, honey. I got this. She's going to be all right."

I went to have a bath. Lying in the hot water, trying unsuccessfully to calm my stress, I thought, *This is where my life will never be the same*. It was as if something in me just knew what was coming.

I got out of the bath and called our Tågarp neighbours, Jack and Kerstin McNeil, and asked them to go check on Moki. Pacing around waiting for the phone to ring, I couldn't even get dressed.

When it did, Cam took the call. Kerstin told him that Jack had had to break into the schoolhouse. "Oh, my God, I'm so sorry," she said. "She's gone."

Still wrapped in my towel, I collapsed onto the floor. My mouth opened and nothing came out, but at the same time I could hear someone screaming. It sounded like an animal—it was me. I couldn't fathom that Moki was dead. My voice kept saying, "*Min mamma, min mamma.*" My skin, my body, of her, of me, my life, my breath, Mamma.

In the front garden of our house were a few large archipelago rocks. My grandson Flynn, Naima's little boy, had climbed up and sat himself on the top of one. As we were trying to understand the word "gone," he started singing right from his heart. From up there on the rock came a blues.

The police wanted to take Moki away, but Kerstin, who was a nurse, said, "No. Her children are driving down from Stockholm. Please leave her. They need to see her here in the house." Cam and Matt, Tyson's boyfriend, jumped on a train and were the first to arrive in Tågarp. We left Flynn with Andi while Jack and Kerstin's son Harry drove me, Eagle-Eye, and Tyson. Naima had gone back to England for a wedding, but when we got the news she booked the next available flight.

Moki had been sleeping upstairs in my childhood bedroom. She was never a deep sleeper. She'd sleep for three hours, wake up, read and listen to the radio. I think she must have come downstairs to the kitchen and made some porridge, which was still sitting there on the stove. Then she'd gone into the blue room on the ground floor and lay down on one of the day beds. I think she'd maybe had a smoke, because there was an ashtray next to the bed, along with a cup of coffee. When Jack and Kerstin found her, she was lying there, a big old atlas with a dark-blue cloth cover resting on her body, open on Greece and the Greek islands. She had travelled so much in her life, but she had never gone to Greece. Steve Roney said, "Maybe she was looking for the gods."

She died in her sleep. Her heart just stopped. She was only sixty-six, so young. But she had lived with such persistent force and worked so hard—all the time, seeking and creating beauty and art, battling for her space.

After she died, the phone started ringing with people eager to organise exhibitions and to publish a book celebrating Moki's life and work. That was wonderful, of course, but it also made me rage that, much too often, you have to die before anyone gives a shit. Why didn't she get that recognition when she was alive?

The police allowed Moki to stay with us for twenty-four hours. People kept coming to say goodbye to her and pay their respects. We were broken into many million scattered pieces, all of us in a total mess.

Finally, the undertaker took Moki's body away to the hospital morgue. We went to see her and placed a small pair of scissors and a bottle of red wine beside her, stuff she needed for this next step on her journey.

In the days after she died, the hours seemed to crawl by so that the days were never-ending. I kept asking what time it was. Every time I asked, only thirty minutes would have passed. Moki's confidantes—bound to her by sweat, tears, laughter, bleeding, and life—held me together, just about. Thank God Eagle-Eye and I had each other, both then and now.

A few days before the funeral, we thought we should put some of Don's ashes in the coffin with Moki. We couldn't find them. It's a big house. It wasn't just a question of checking a couple of cupboards—there are several attics and basements—but our friend Shanti Roney was determined to find Don. For two whole days, he searched. He looked inside the piano, prised open a locked chest. Don was nowhere to be seen. The location of Don's ashes was all we talked about. Could Moki have scattered them in the garden, ignoring the local law? Maybe she'd taken the odd spoonful and sprinkled it in the long grass, but she wouldn't have scattered all of Don and not fucking told us. It just wasn't possible. In the end we put some soil from the garden in a little purse and left it in the coffin with her.

We buried Moki in our local churchyard. That summer before she died, I remembered that she had said, "I don't want to leave. I don't want to go." At the time I hadn't understood. I thought she meant she didn't want to go to New York. But I now realised she was telling me that her roots were in Tågarp. Although Moki was utterly unconventional, she was also oddly traditional. I think she liked the idea of being in the ground in the churchyard, near the schoolhouse and her ancestors, with a stone with her name on it.

Every now and then over the next ten years, we'd start puzzling about the location of Don's ashes. I just knew he was there somewhere. Then, that day when I found the box with the letter that Moki had written to Ahmadu about me, Naima was poking around in the attic behind some of Moki's paintings from the late sixties. She found an old Japanese tea chest; inside, with some incense, was Don. We took him down, put him by the piano, and lit the incense.

BREAKDOWN AND REBUILDING

After Moki died, I completely lost myself. The loss took me and held me, bound and gagged, for almost two years. There had already been some other changes. Ahmadu had started to develop dementia. Naima had moved to Hackney with Flynn, and Tyson had left home to go to Goldsmiths, University of London. Being a mother subsumes many of us, and though I had always worked, always made music, my role as a mother shaped the work, the music, me. My idea of family was fundamental to my creativity. The music took me out into a place where I was visible in the world, then I came back in. Family is my centre. Now two of my daughters, people I'd brought into the world, were living their lives elsewhere and I struggled to understand who I was without them being near. You can tell yourself you'll finally have the time you've always needed for yourself, and an extra room or two to do something with—but what do you do with all the empty space? It's a huge reset.

In November 2009, we held a memorial for Moki at the loft. Ari came and I knew that she was ill. Tessa had told me that she had breast cancer and was refusing traditional treatment, but here she looked a picture of health, freckly and fresh, regal in gold leather shorts and her locks tied up in a crown. Ari had come to the memorial out of a deep sense of love and respect for Moki, and I was touched to feel her embrace.

The next day, she came back over. We went for a walk, talked about life. We'd been apart for so long, but all that time and distance melted away and we were just as we once were, those two teenagers off on a tangent together. Before she left, Ari pressed a dog-eared school notepad into my hand. Ari had always jotted down her observations, but here, in her familiar handwriting, was a collection of Moki's words, wisdom, and sometimes very funny remarks from conversations they had shared. I received the notebook as a blessing. It was pure love, weaving the three of us together despite the years.

You live, you die. We all know that, but nothing can prepare you for how fucking hard it is for the ones left behind. Moki's memorial allowed me to grieve and celebrate with others who had known her, but I was unravelling. The late-night phone call I had been dreading ever since I was a child had finally come. My whole life I had been terrified that someone I loved was going to be taken in an instant. It began when Don didn't come home for two days, and Moki was throwing up with anxiety. For years I thought we had dodged disaster, but my brain had been imprinted with fear, and it shaped my responses to every stress. I became anxious whenever I heard sirens, or if one of the kids still wasn't home when it got late, and always, always when the phone rang early in the morning or last thing.

Until the day Cam answered the phone and heard that Moki was dead, my terror had always dissipated. Now there was no consolation in telling myself that things would be all right. Moki's death pushed me into knowing that anything can and quite possibly will happen. It opened me up to new levels of feeling completely unprotected. And once you have children, the worst thing is so catastrophic that you fear you cannot survive its possibility.

Cam was spending more time in London, where his mother, Mumma Jean, was ill, so mostly it was just me and Mabel in the house in Stockholm. I began to drink differently. Looking for peace in a wine bottle, then a vodka bottle. I wanted to bypass the grief and numb my constant anxiety. Every day was a battle in my mind. I would make plans, have a few shots to calm my nerves, then end up getting too drunk to go out. I'd wake up in the morning and have a shot of vodka just to push away the anxiety, only for it to hit me harder when the alcohol wore off.

Mabel never knew which mother she was going to find when she came home from school, whether I would be functioning or a mess. She just wanted me to be OK and in charge, and often I was neither. We fell into a nightly rigmarole around what I was going to cook her for dinner. I needed so badly to prove to her and myself that I was fine, that of course I could do this simple essential thing: make right the disarray by cooking something delicious. Every evening I would ask her what she wanted. She would struggle to tell me. Eventually we would come up with something. I would shop and cook, and Mabel would eat. I would hover nervously. When I got it right, there were a few precious minutes of relief and balance, but they never lasted long.

Mabel is my child. I would take bullets, climb mountains, die to protect any of my children, but now I knew I was incapable of properly looking after her, or myself. Based on my own lived experience, I was acutely aware of how frightening that can be for children in the care of an adult. I could imagine what this was doing to Mabel, but I couldn't stop. I broke her heart, and her trust.

We spent the Christmas after Moki died at the schoolhouse. It is a season that can be a test at the best of times. Growing up, we always had a Swedish Christmas. Sometimes we would go to Mormor and Morfar's house, but often I'd find Moki in tears on Christmas Eve because she didn't have the money to make it how she wanted it to be, and she felt she had failed. So, from when I was about fifteen, I took over Christmas. I've been in a fight with the occasion ever since. I have visions of creating the perfect *Fanny and Alexander* scenario, with vats of melting chocolate, ten different types of pâté, and the entire house festooned with fairy lights and candles. Some years, it has tipped me over the edge. That year, Eagle-Eye and his wife, Sofia, brought joyous tidings: they were going to have a baby. Other than that, it was fucking horrendous. On New Year's Eve I was pissed, again. A family friend and I, already drunk, had ended up doing vodka shots in Moki's old closet when I started crying and told her I thought I was having a breakdown. "I can't do this," I said. "I don't think I'm OK and I can't deal with it on my own."

I was shocked by this new feeling of being unable to cope. I was coming undone, unable to function. I couldn't give or receive love. I guess I had to be drunk to say that I needed help.

The next day, Cam asked if I was OK, but no one else said anything. Everyone was worried about me, but if I was shocked by my inability to cope, so were they. My family had grown used to my keeping on, despite the worries that dogged me. They were not to know that this time it was different. But I thought they needed me to be OK. And so, despite how I might have felt inside, I kept up a front. The truth is that we were all close to breaking point.

In February, we celebrated Mabel's fourteenth birthday together in London. It was a disaster. We went to a restaurant in the East End. Cam looked up and saw me outside necking a bottle of red wine. Mabel said to him, "Over to you. I'm the fuck out of here," and went back to Sweden.

Driving to Mumma Jean's house the next day, overwhelmed with shame and despair, I tried to jump out of the car. By then, Cam knew I needed treatment. He called our longtime family GP, who arranged for an emergency psychiatrist to come and talk to me. Afterwards, the psychiatrist told Cam that although he didn't think I was at risk of harming myself, I needed medical care, and he arranged for me to be admitted to hospital. I didn't want to go, but I knew I had to. I needed help.

I went into the Cygnet in Harrow, a treatment centre not just for drugs or alcohol but all sorts of mental health crises. I stayed there for six weeks. No one forced you to go to group therapy. You didn't have to do anything if you didn't want to, but I went to everything they offered. Most of the other patients had depression. Just up the hall from me there was a woman who was suffering from psychosis, who thought people were trying to destroy her. When I first saw her, she was sitting with her body folded over, cowering, so no one could see who she was. It was as if she was covered in a shroud. A week or so before I left, we were in a group session and she was sitting upright with her head held high. She was beautiful. I'll never forget that. It was as if she didn't want anyone to see her until she was ready to be seen. Each of us there was separated from our normal life for a limited period of time, and so we bonded over the experience of being in this unfamiliar, institutional environment and formed oddly intense friendships.

I wish I could say that by the time I left the centre I was completely recovered, but it wasn't so simple. I had four subsequent episodes bordering on psychotic, all triggered by alcohol. I would go binge-drinking for three days, then break down, screaming and crying in uncontrollable grief.

And then, in October 2010, Ari died. As the cancer had progressed, she had allowed only Nora to be with her. Tessa and Hollie Cook, who'd re-formed the Slits with Ari, flew to LA to visit her, but she refused to see them. In the end, she wanted to face death on her own.

•

A few years later, there was a second Christmas when everything fell apart. Everyone was there—Eagle-Eye, Sofia, their daughter, Daisy, our girls, Marlon and Flynn—and I had a box of wine hidden in the attic. I was just fucking insane. We call it "the Crazy Christmas." I lost control, which was both painful and horribly shameful. I didn't know why it was happening, since I'd been in hospital and worked on my recovery. Why couldn't I stop myself? Those questions were just too difficult. I didn't want to confront what was going on.

I was living with the after-effects of trauma, the stress of which made it impossible to deal with my feelings. I wanted to check out, to numb myself by drinking. Then I would lose control, freak out, black out. I had been unable to face the pain and shame of all my feelings, but until I did, I couldn't heal.

Then began another, longer period of recovery. I tried to protect my kids as much as I could, but the pain and sadness was still oozing out of me. It has been difficult for my daughters. There is a limit to how far you can push the people who matter the most. It's a very fine line and I came close to the edge. At night I still sometimes wake up thinking, *Fucking hell, what the fuck? What have I done?* But those aspects of their life experience are also part of *my* life experience. We must find a way to work with them. I can't change the past, but I can take responsibility, even love the most challenging things and work towards a place where forgiveness can allow change. I decided to embrace hope and seek joy rather than allow the fear and pain to pull me under, and, fortunately, my family is my lifebelt. They are my reason to get up and go on every day.

BACK TO LIFE THROUGH MUSIC

In 2011, I made a record with The Thing, my first in sixteen years. It gave me my wings back. The Thing were an incredible free-jazz trio of Swedish and Norwegian musicians who formed in Stockholm in 2000. They took their name from a track on Don's *Where Is Brooklyn?* album. The guys are pretty much the same age as me, so we grew up listening to the same music. They're musical kin.

After hearing them play on a night out in Stockholm with my friend Conny Lindström, Cam said their raucous sound had reminded him of me. It was a head-to-head collision that needed to happen, he said, so he arranged an introduction and suggested that we make the album, *The Cherry Thing*. The record ended up being mostly covers of songs by the different artists who formed me—a revisitation of where I come from, who I am, and how I got here.

But by then I had started, ever so slowly, to write songs again, including "Cashback," which became the album's opener. That song was the first thing I'd written in the two years since Moki had died. They were tense and difficult years, but I had begun to learn new ways to co-exist with my sadness and anxiety.

It had taken time, but now I could feel Moki near me, telling me that I had to move on, that I needed to work, and that the work was going to set me free from the burden of trauma. *The Cherry Thing* was one definite step towards songwriting and live performance.

Just after the album was recorded, we played at the Moderna Museet in Stockholm, a launch event for a month-long anniversary celebration of the dome, during which the amazing creation stood re-erected in the gardens. My brother David came from Portland,

Oregon, to play with Christer Bothén and Bengt Berger, who had worked so much with Don and Moki. The lovely man in charge of the Museum of Architecture at the time realised that it was nuts not to also stage a show of Moki's art. Two of my mother's closest friends organised a small but beautifully curated exhibition. It was deeply moving to be back playing in the place where we spent those three months in 1970, and where my mother painted the mandala on the floor. When the exhibition closed, the museum bought one of her pieces for its permanent collection.

•

The Cherry Thing led me to *Blank Project*, my first solo album in seventeen years. Cam and I wrote the songs together, some on the same Casio synth we've been using for two decades. The seeds for many of them came to me as I was sitting on the bed in Stockholm. They came straight out of my grief for Moki, and in tribute to her. The lyrics were shaped by the years I had spent struggling with anxiety and perpetual sadness, even from before she died. I had started to wonder whether the black-dog state of misery that settles in and makes its home with you is weirdly addictive. Misery is habit-forming; so is alcohol, and the two feed off each other. I wanted to turn away from both, to embrace the music, which has been part of me far longer than either of them. I wrote the songs that ended up on *Blank Project* to find my way out.

We went into a studio in Woodstock, New York, with Kieran Hebden, aka Four Tet: DJ, producer, and electronic musician. It was the beginning of a very important musical relationship. Kieran had a really clear vision: it should be raw and unfiltered, as raw as I had felt when I was writing the songs. We recorded the album quickly: ten tracks in five days, not hundreds of takes. The music, led by RocketNumberNine, was heavy but liberating. I also, finally, got to perform with my dear friend Robyn. I loved it. Performance, for me, is where I talk, where I communicate most purely. I have had my deepest conversations inside sound and, yes, on the dance floor. Sometimes it's primal and futuristic, sacred and menacing; communications reverberating on a deeper level, revealing meaning in a language beyond words.

I have been blessed in that sense. When I get onstage, or when the notes to a song fall into place, it sometimes leads to magic. When I am there in front of an audience, I know that I have purged, faced demons, celebrated some deep things in the songs. Yet I know that I don't own my musical expression. It's an independent force, created with the people I am playing with. That's why performing still makes me nervous. I don't know if I am going to be visited by that Holy Ghost. But I can be sensitive to it and I can work to earn it. I never take it for granted. In performance, as in life: *Do it like you mean it*.

The title of the next album, also produced by Kieran Hebden, *Broken Politics*, came from a line in a song I wrote in late 2016 and 2017 called "Synchronised Devotion." I was thinking about nights on dance floors in my youth, and the resistance my peers and I crafted when the politics outside felt utterly broken. It was just after the Brexit referendum and Trump's election, the clamping down on rights to safe and legal abortion across Europe, and the drowning of refugee children in the Mediterranean. I wanted to respond not just to the injustice and anguish, but also to the hope. Polish women activists were resisting the new laws that stripped them of their right to a safe abortion. I found it so moving to read about the solidarity of Polish men, who stood with them on the streets.

Writing that album was a return to the ease and simplicity of my earlier songwriting. Cam and I wrote together, almost holding hands: just us and the old Casio keyboard. The process was very personal. I see now that it was part of my healing. There had been too many years when I was just not able to get out of that damn waiting room and go.

One summer during those stuck years, I had cried in Moki's arms when the time came to leave Tågarp and return to London. I'd not been able to find two seconds to sit down and write songs, as I'd been hoping I would. I could feel my words, but I couldn't catch them. I tried, struggled, didn't manage it. It was intensely frustrating. Sometimes I felt inadequate and sad. Other times I told myself that I would just keep going. I knew I needed to go through this period. I knew I would, and I did. From *The Cherry Thing* onwards, I was writing again, coming back to myself. With *Broken Politics*, it felt easy. Like coming home.

By the time we were doing the photos for the album cover in early 2018, tragedy had arrived in my London neighbourhood. Six months earlier, on June 14, 2017, fire ripped through Grenfell Tower, a residential block in North Kensington, five minutes from where I live. The tower was mostly social and council housing for people on low incomes. The cladding that had been used by contractors carrying out renovations for Kensington and Chelsea Borough Council was highly combustible, and when an electrical fault caused a fire on a lower floor, it engulfed the whole 24-storey block in flames. Seventy-two people died.

When I went out into the streets around Golborne Road, my local community, everyone was in shock. Many had friends or family living in the tower and didn't know where they were. One of Mabel's friends lost a niece, a little girl of twelve years old. Despite the shock, everyone was rushing to help in whatever way they could. We bumped into a young Black boy in a flash car full of boxes of trainers, bringing shoes to the people who'd had to run out of their burning flats in the middle of the night. Cam and I were volunteer drivers for the folk at Makkah, a Malaysian restaurant on Portobello Road, who were feeding 140 people every day.

We all did what we could and still it would never be enough. Andi, the girls, and I lent a hand in Acklam Village, under the Westway, helping to sort through the mountain of clothes donations. It was a community coming together. But in spite of all the spontaneous support from individuals and local organisations, neither central nor local government did a thing. They didn't set up an emergency centre. It was left to the community centre at the Methodist Church to coordinate the response. Andi and I went with another woman who was doing deliveries with us to pick something up from the Tabernacle. An Eritrean or Sudanese funeral was taking place in the main hall. Thirty people from that community were missing, presumed dead. Women were howling in grief. It was unthinkable.

Grenfell was a cruel awakening to social injustice. We had all known it, but to be confronted so directly with just how fucked up society is—with the reality of being Black, being Asian, being an immigrant, being a poor working-class person of any race . . . It was so painful. And this happened in one of the richest boroughs in London. It was the start of several summers and winters of awakening, of blunt realisation: George Floyd, Covid, and all the insights these events brought about. The world isn't what we'd like to think it is. We'd always known it deep down. My album may have been written before Grenfell, but the timing underlined to me that our system was broken before, during, and after.

GOING HOME

It was September 11, 2018, and Ahmadu was dying. I was in bed, holding on to the covers, feeling the undertow. I was convinced that I could sense that life was leaving his body and, as he went, the air was changing around me. Getting up, making a cup of tea, washing my body, looking at what I saw in the mirror, parts of me were changing. I want to say that they were going with him.

The phone rang. My sister Titiyo told me he was gone. I had felt this news coming. The clouds were moving, life was shifting again. I was being pushed out into a new existence. Even though I was thankful for my siblings, the loneliness was profound.

I went to the other room and told my sister Amanda. I held her in my arms. I didn't cry, even though I wanted to. Perhaps because I am her big sister—or was it that thing, again, of feeling different? I was so conscious of not having had the same everyday relationship with Ahmadu as Amanda and the other siblings. Our stories are different. Maybe that was also at the root of my loneliness.

I saw him for the last time only a week before he died. Titiyo and I went to the care home. I'd been playing a gig in Stockholm and was leaving later that evening. When we got there, the manager told us that Ahmadu had been taken to hospital the day before.

In the taxi on our way to see him, it was as if we were travelling in a void, knowing that nothing was ever going to be the same. We finally found our father lying on a bed in a hallway in the emergency department, waiting to be moved to a ward. I noticed how clean everything was. And the floor was blue. Very blue.

So there we were in this slick Stockholm public hospital and there was my father in his own Alzheimer's world. *He looks content*, I thought, and he looked me straight in the eye and seemed to recognise me. Then he was gone again, but we were holding hands and I knew we had exchanged something deeply familiar and intimate. I took in every second, every molecule around me, as I stood, my father's hands in mine. I felt how much I loved Titiyo and how much I valued our closeness.

The doctors came on their rounds and Ahmadu was laughing, trying to make a joke. I think they enjoyed seeing him. There was something very contagious about his life force. He really touched people. I felt that. My brother Cherno was on his way, but I had to get my flight.

Andi once said to me, "God, you're always saying goodbye." Her words struck a chord. I've never forgotten them. I said goodbye to my father. I held him, and I told him that I loved him. When I left the hospital, I knew I was not going to see him again.

•

After Ahmadu died, my eight siblings—Titiyo, Cherno, Mikailo, Salim, Amanda, Tiyoneh, Alusenni, Toomany—and I talked. We weighed up what we should do. As the days passed, it became clear that we needed to take our father back home to Gbinti, to bury him in the village where he was born. When you leave you migrate, but what do we call it when we carry someone back to the source?

He had always dreamed of returning to live in Sierra Leone, but like a lot of people that leave, he didn't go back. As his commitments changed and his children grew up, it might have been possible. Then, late in life, he had another family, his last little clan of kids—Alusenni, Toomany, and Tiyoneh. Maybe he also realised when he visited in his latter years that he could no longer live there.

A part of him had changed too much. He had always been saying goodbye, too.

It was to be a proper Muslim funeral. Cherno found a Gambian funeral director to carry out the rituals of washing and wrapping his body in cloth. We were allowed an extension and the date was set. We booked our flights.

Until then, we had never all been together in the same room. In fact, I met my brother Salim for the first time at the airport in Freetown. But somehow, without even really planning it, we all managed to get on the same flight from Paris. When I arrived at the gate and saw everyone, I was overwhelmed. Tyson was with me, thank God! I wish all my children had been able to come with me, but having one of them by my side meant I was able to look at my daughter and think, *Yes, this is the reason we carry on.*

Once we were in the air, Titiyo said, "Ahmadu is on the plane with us." We'd known his body would be on a flight that day, but not which one. She'd received a text from the funeral director just before take-off. We were carrying our father home. We landed at Lungi Airport and, the instant the doors opened, I recognised the scent.

It had been more than thirty years since I was last there, but I felt a familiarity straight away. The faces, the eyes, the smiles. That beautiful skin. Coming through arrivals, I embraced my brother Salim. There's a lot of Ahmadu in his face and his body language, as I would realise more and more.

Out in the parking lot, there was an eighties ambulance; inside was Ahmadu's coffin. With Salim, from eight brothers and sisters we had become nine. We spread ourselves out in five waiting jeeps. I wanted Tyson and Titiyo with me in the car. Led by the ambulance, we drove in a caravan out towards the bush. We carried Ahmadu home, like a warrior chief, to the village where he was born. It was the back end of the rainy season. Every now and then, the sky lit up electric for a second and, no shit, when it rumbles in the jungle, it roars.

"I am strong," she says. "I am the mother of nature, come to me."

As we went deeper and deeper through dark, tall reeds, the red dirt road becoming smaller and smaller, the rain-filled potholes bigger and bigger—big enough to maybe swallow us up—the immensity of my father's journey hit me. The fact that Ahmadu got out from this somewhere in the middle of nowhere—and in the goddamn fifties!—seemed incredible. I thought of him as a six-year-old boy, leaving his mother to live with his uncle so he could go to school in Port Loko. His story weighed in my heart with such love and respect, I lost my breath.

At 7 a.m. the following day, we went for prayers for my father at my grandmother's house. It was hot, already 29 degrees. We shook everybody's hand as they welcomed us. We didn't realise that we were supposed to have our heads covered for the morning prayers, so we had to take the white cotton doilies off the chairs. We looked like Spanish brides. Outside sat a crowd of people, because of course our father was a pioneer, the first child to leave his village. He had been greatly respected by all those who stayed behind in Gbinti. The village elders spoke in Temne about him. Then the women came in, all dressed in white, and sang.

Later, in the afternoon, the ceremony was held at the mosque. At the end, the men lifted Ahmadu's coffin and carried him to his final resting place, near to his mother in the burial ground at the edge of the village.

COMING FULL CIRCLE

After Moki died, we fought for years to keep the loft in New York as a creative space for people to stay and work in, but the landlord wasn't having it. It's still empty—no one has been inside it except our neighbour Ernie. Our net curtains are still in the windows.

Two years after her death, our whole family and Moki's closest friends peeled that multi-layered environment apart—an installation that recorded a life lived, collected, and made over thirty years. Moki's hair caught in a hairband, entangled in the bristles of a brush. The shape of her feet, moulded in her shoes. Scraps of works in progress, so much material; things found on the street and turned into art. Lids from the sardine tins that we put on a Christmas tree one year in lieu of decorations. Her touch, so near, had now gone.

After three weeks of packing, I was the last person to leave. Empty, the space looked as it did when we'd first moved in—we had come full circle. As I closed the door that last evening, there was the most sensational sunset. Manhattan was right across the river, the purple light flooding the floor that Moki had painted white. I was heartbroken, but the light was perfect. All was quiet. It was like the final scene of a very long play. As we had been packing up, memories had surfaced. In the mix, not everything was good. Moki struggling with Don, fighting to keep him alive. It was easy to remember it as an amazing place, but I also had to acknowledge that it was built on a lot of difficult and emotionally harrowing times. In a way, the process of packing and unpacking those emotions was healthy, like a purge.

Don had an addiction, for which neither I, Eagle-Eye, nor Moki ever blamed him. But I now can see that in my parents' relationship, a marriage of two artists, there was still a fundamental imbalance. The inner group of those who were playing the music were mostly male. As a man, Don could submerge himself in his work in a way that Moki, like many women artists, could never afford to do. They say that behind every great man is a woman. Why not beside, or with, or in front? Alice Coltrane didn't hide behind anyone; nor did the writer and poet Jayne Cortez, who married Ornette Coleman. Like many hundreds of other amazing women, they were the spines who made great things possible within these environments. They were leaders and keepers. My mother was a similar figure. For Don, Moki provided that crucial energy and structure. Even if my parents and their peers approached marriage and parenthood differently from their own parents before them, the lion's share of childcare and the running of the household was still the responsibility of the women. Don had the luxury to sit and make his music for hours, but Moki had to do eighty other things before she could do the twenty she really wanted to. When I talked to my daughter Tyson about this, she asked, "Is this how we continue to be shaped as women?"

Moki's revolutionary example continued through me: I needed to be a creative woman and a mother in an environment where often you had to choose one or the other. So much of her approach has come with me. I'm used to working in the middle of my extended tribe, their activity going on around. I can find my silence in a room full of noise; my creative comfort zone is the comings and goings of my kids and their friends, the generosity and togetherness of the different menageries of people that have always gathered around our kitchen table. "Multitasking" is a relatively new word that I don't really relate to, because in my case it's just life. The domestic tasks feed the artistic ones, and vice versa.

When I'm writing, I can get trapped on two lines of lyrics for days, and the physical action of doing something with my hands often dislodges a stuck idea.

I take great pleasure in being able to give as a woman, a mother, and a creative person within the home, but I know it is essential to allow myself to be all those things at once. In making a family and trying to do my own work, like Moki and countless other women artists, I have had to make some sacrifices with my creativity.

There have been sacrifices and struggles for our family, as well. When the kids were small, I took them with me on tour as much as I could, but sometimes I had to leave them behind. I always felt naked without them, and coming back could be awkward. After the joy of seeing each other again, the hugging and the sharing of little presents, I sensed a resentment, a small dissonance that was in fact huge. That pain had to heal every time I came back.

Constantly moving homes—often across continents—and readjusting to new places was also not easy. When Naima and I once counted how many different schools she'd been to, we almost ran out of fingers—seventeen! It makes my head spin and I want to cry into my tea as the question arises: Did we do right by our kids? Did our parents do right by us? No, probably not always. But we did our best and, wanting to bring up our families in the world as we lived it, we made our choices, feeling blessed to be able to choose.

I've not had to do any of this alone. Cam has always been at my side. Visiting my Sierra Leonean family had shown me that it really does take a village, and those threads from my own upbringing always ran deep. Above all, I have brought up my family and made my music in the spirit that Moki and Don showed me and Eagle-Eye.

That world where I grew up might look chaotic to some, but it required determination and resilience to maintain a creative practice and a family, on limited funds and at the margins of conventional society. If Don and Moki had been merely dreamers, they would not have realised their groundbreaking joint projects with organic music. Don would not have shaped the development of jazz. Moki would not have exhibited her artworks in galleries from Los Angeles to Stockholm, designed sets for the Apollo Theater in Harlem, or been recognised, belatedly but blessedly, as a solo artist of significance with a retrospective at London's Institute of Contemporary Art.

Often her life wasn't easy and, of course, she had damage and deep scars as a result. She gave so much of herself. It was *her* vision and her labour that made it possible to build the amazing work of art that was their life: the realm unto itself that is the schoolhouse, the creative space that they brought out into the world on their continuous journey. None of that could have been achieved without Moki's heart and soul at the helm. Don was an extraordinary human being. He was a leader and a learner. Moki used to say that he was a pied piper: a different kind of magician. But he wasn't any good at many of the workaday aspects of turning love and collaboration into a way of life. As pragmatic and practical as she was creative, Moki was also stubborn. If she did not know how to do something, she would learn. And all the while she was making her vibrant, intense, playful, committed, and timeless tapestries, sculptures, and collages. She grew tired towards the very end. A part of her was broken. She was frustrated and confused by the lack of recognition she received for all her work. I also think she was all too aware of the sacrifices she'd made in her career, ever since that day in Williamsburg when she ran from her sewing machine and pulled Don from his burning bed. But she had made a choice and she never stopped creating. Don used to say, "The time is now." And now I see Moki's drive vibrating through three generations of my family.

I was so dependent on Moki. She was my emotional barometer.

She was also my teacher and guide. She had so many interests and insights. She was inquisitive, deeply engaged with environmental issues and politics, and she kept us all clued up. When she wasn't up and making, creating, expanding, she loved to lie in bed, taking *in* inspiration and information. She was a great reader, always had several books on the go, ordered endless magazines, and read cookery books like novels. When I got into cooking in London, she introduced me to the work of Edna Lewis, the great African American food writer and historian, and gave me the Elizabeth David books, telling me, "It's not about the pictures, it's about how she writes about the food. So just read her and feel it." And she listened to the radio all the time. Especially after Don left, she would sometimes stay in bed for a day or two at a stretch. It was her place of respite and retreat, her cosy haven where she could be cocooned and take space, but it was never to just lie under the duvet. Well, maybe sometimes . . . She would read, listen to the radio, and eat loads of sweets. We used to have bed parties with my kids. We'd all get in and drink tea. When she said, "I'm a fiend for beauty," she would often add, "and we can make that with nothing. We don't need to be rich: I'm poor, but I'm rich." For Moki, everything was art, and she always said *we* were her finest creations. *Tack*, Mamma.

She liked a glass of red wine, or ten, and she never wanted to go to sleep, so when we were older and came to hang out, she would want to sit up all night. "We haven't seen each other. Let's talk!" Then, at about 4 a.m., you would hear her trilling away in an attempt at Mongolian throat singing.

Moki was funny, sharp as hell, mischievous. She loved the sweet things in life. She dressed with connection and style. She let herself be inspired by diversity and became herself—just as, for me, punk and Africa became my vessel. She was self-made and beautiful—she found herself and her freedom as she discovered the world.

I think constantly about the parallels between my and my

mother's life. Even now, every day, I feel my mother in me. In the way I see things and the way I do things. I used to hate that when I was younger, and sometimes everything she said or did would annoy me. I'm finally able to really acknowledge, value, and love how alike we are, but also how much Moki gave to all of us. And how that now is passed on in what I've tried to give to my children.

•

It was never a given, a requirement, or an expectation that my children would continue in my footsteps, but lo and behold, here we are, all of them making music and art. Even my grandson Flynn is studying fashion and design. His sewing machine hums through the night, as Moki's once did, in rhythm with a concentration so deep it filters through generations.

Our children are all musicians. Mabel, my youngest, sings and writes music that has taken her to the front row of the pop world. Marlon is a singer, writer, and producer, and frequent collaborator with Mabel. Tyson is a singer and songwriter making more left-field R&B. She runs an organisation and record label called Ladies Music Pub and they do some amazing work for women, non-binary, and trans people in the industry. Naima is a multidisciplinary artist and composer, making experimental music. She has a project called Exotic Sin, which is partially inspired by Don and Moki. She was a visual artist until one day she returned to the piano, not having played since she was a kid. Then she met Kenichi Iwasa, a Japanese experimental percussionist and musician, and they started making music together.

Mabel has always been sure about what she wants. When her career started taking off, and the tempo of life was so crazy, she took it in her stride, but no one can ever prepare fully for it. Having us as her parents, at least she's grown up in an environment where we've stood against some of the more superficial aspects of the industry. Also, being part of this family, the success is less likely to go to her head.

One of the things I try to pass on to all my children is that success is also about making mistakes—without them, you won't learn how to grow. This is a tough thing to do in public. Being in the public eye can be very empowering, but it also leaves you vulnerable. I find myself wanting to remind my children about what matters, and what I see in them: their gifts. We talk about how to nurture those gifts, so they can recover from the things that don't go so well and continue forward.

Is it better and easier for young women in music these days? Unfortunately, no. It's still a fucking battle, and an even harder battle for women of colour, who have never been respected, allowed their creative freedom, given their due as innovators and artists, or paid anywhere near what they have earned. I used to get very frustrated when I was asked by people in the industry to define my music by comparing myself to other singers. "Who are you?" they would ask. "Are you more Whitney Houston or Janet Jackson?" *I'm me*, I wanted to say. *Could you please just listen to the music?*

Now I offer an older woman's perspective in the conversations I have with my daughters, but I'm no wise guru. I'm their mother but wisdom travels both ways. I'm learning all the time from them: about music, life, art, politics.

Their generation is defiant and energetic, and even though they're disillusioned with conventional politics, they're convinced they can make a difference on the streets and online. Our children are standing up to demand necessary change. Their optimism makes me hopeful and inspires me to keep opening my mind and my heart.

•

I've been thinking a lot lately about the women who have been important to me: Moki, Moki's friends, Mormor and my other grandmothers, Mumma Jean, Donna, my auntie Barbara, Daisy and Nana in LA, Haja Neneh in Gbinti. The women in Africa who helped me to be aware of our power. My friends, my daughters. We stretch our arms beyond blood and flesh. I am a product of all of them. Their example has given me strength to feel that there is a way to be in this world as a woman, a wife, a mother, and an artist. I have become the person I am by growing up with people who lived by their philosophy of trying to make something good, new, and beautiful for the benefit of many. That has kept me sane and kept me motivated, and it makes the world—or at least my world—a better place.

I keep doing my best. I like to get it right, but I don't have to be right. Sometimes I wake up feeling my human limits: strained and pointless. Time against my clock. Now I try to listen to what I know—and I know a few things. Being in a family is natural to me as mine continues to grow. I have three wonderful children, a stepson, and three grandchildren. My body has done this. I am a collaborator in life and work. I am proud to be a woman. Womanhood is boundless.

The beauty of becoming an older woman is that you finally feel that you're enough. You recognise that the failures and the fights are part of life. You know the preciousness of time, how very delicate it is, so you try to find a bit of stillness in which to be thankful. You try to make a difference, and to resist the panic of being overwhelmed. In this next phase of my life, I aspire to be like the powerhouse older women I have known: fun, naughty, sexy, dancing at night as I smoke a cigar.

EPILOGUE
NAVIGATION NOTES

I pride myself on being able to move between the places that have been my home. What I left behind will be waiting for me on arrival. I know where I am, so I know where I'm coming from. I am good at making a home in transit: a piece of fabric in the suitcase; a few books; when the kids were small, their toys, crayons, paper, Polly Pocket dolls; creating *our* space wherever we are, so that we own it for the time we live there.

I can come, go, arrive, leave, reset, adjust, be in many places, of many places, but I am constantly playing catch-up with the present. Navigating planes, trains, automobiles, hotel rooms, lands, people, my colour, relationships, cities, forests—this has become my normality. It's like when I put things in my bra—keys, money, gum—so I always know where they are. When I get undressed, all kinds of shit falls out. How did it get there? How did I get here? I am finding change much harder as I get older: leaving is more painful, landing takes longer.

The other day I was heading for Tågarp, going through that drawn-out process of saying goodbye to everyone, and Mabel said, "You're always leaving." My heart stopped for a long second. *I am always leaving.*

"Mabel," I said. "I'll be back before you know it. Time will fly!" When Don went away, he always used to say, "See you in a minute."

This time, when the taxi drove me away, my heart was in my throat. I drank in the pulsing rhythm of my London neighbourhood:

the Moroccan food stalls; the Golborne Deli; the cash and carry, my favourite shop; the Moroccan butchers; the newsagent; Kokon To Zai; the junk shops; the antiques shops. It will all carry on without me. It matters when I'm there. It matters when I'm away. A pocket of community within a huge city; the local heartbeat of the people who live and work there every day with such grace. These gentle, long-standing universes within a universe are precious and feel fragile.

As the taxi crossed Ladbroke Grove, I saw the Tube station; Dub Vendor record shop used be there, under the bridge, spilling out reggae tunes in time with the trains. A few doors down, 145A, Viv Goldman's old house, where I spent a light-year of time. I thought about city life. How important it can make us feel. We pride ourselves on the notches in our belts; for surviving and sustaining grief, hardship, and pain. Walking out through concrete heights, sucking for air in a park, culture is *here*, we say. The city is everything. We grow here, dodge a bullet, duck fast, run, see a painting, hear a fight. Claiming our space, marking territory, being seen, making money, spending it, squeezed in tight, we live it out. Navigating the city, I used to advertise my street credentials. I know how to do it. In New York, crossing Sixth Avenue—alert, senses heightened, aware, capable, strong—feeding on city adrenaline, I have felt alive, felt cooler there than anywhere else.

Yet when I tread the streets of my cities, I know I'm not bulletproof. City life is loud and empowering, but its relentless whirl can also make you feel insignificant. To be somebody, you need this bag, those shoes, that car. Some days it drives over you like a truck. Sometimes I make it through only by acting bigger than I feel, my clothes another skin that holds me and tells who I am, sometimes loud, sometimes quiet. But when I step out of bed in the skin I was born in, I know I'm just naked. Ornette Coleman said, "My race is my face."

I fly to Copenhagen, my heartstrings still ringing with the pain of leaving those I love in London. I get on a train and as soon as I cross "the bridge" into Sweden, instantly it is quieter, in that very particular Swedish stillness. I call this land home, *hemma*: my homeland. I have withstood the exhaustion of sticking out because of my skin, my hair, me. "*Vilken tur du har som få vara här i Sverige där vi har det så bra?* Aren't you lucky to get to be here in Sweden, where we have it so good?" My resilience is an internal signal, a stubborn heat that refuses to succumb. I am from here and I am good enough.

I get off the train in Hässleholm, smell the air. I am complete. This funny, muted town is so quiet, my fight is no longer necessary. I leave, but when I come back, it's fundamental. I know it, it knows me. Naima is waiting in the car park. As a child, coming back from our travels, as we got nearer to the house with each turn in the road—through Gammalstorp and Farstorp, my school on the left not far after the sign, then on to the village ahead—I noted everything in its place: the sameness was a relief. The village: on the right, the little brick building of Farstorp's Sparbank. Then the church where Naima and Stevie got married and where we held Moki's funeral. At last, we are in Tågarp, pulling up at the schoolhouse. My inner sanctum, the source. The city has no sway here. My colour, my clothes, my shape, all fall away. The landscape puts me in my place.

Here in Tågarp, in the forest, is the realisation that you are alone. That can be powerful, or really frightening. You're there with only yourself, and there's a quiet to it, but also an intensity. That's what makes the silence loud.

Many people haven't experienced that sense of aloneness in the universe—what it feels like as a child to stare up at that vast sky in the middle of nowhere and suddenly be flooded by an almost overwhelming sense of wonder. It's both peaceful and alive.

Stepping on a branch over dried pine needles, the crackle is deafening. Above, the trees hum. I listen, I am in awe, I surrender. The smell of the forest alive—light, dark, deep pine—is so good I draw my breath in over and over again. Belonging, equalising, levelling—in this moment I am surrounded and held by the significance of nature. Respect—I feel respect. It is green; it's light, dark; it's wild, it's refined. My wellies sink into the moss, twigs crackle, moisture seeps into my skin. Micro-universes in every step I take.

After Moki died, for a long time none of us could face the task of sorting through her things. We didn't want to alter a single detail of her, or of our life here—so we just left everything exactly as it was. It was as if the whole house had gone to sleep.

One hot sunny day, Naima, our friend Hannah Pearl, and I threw everything that was festering in Moki's old closet out the window and straight on to the ground. I can't explain how good it felt: a blessed release to finally face this, to hurl the darkness—a twisted black whirlwind of trapped, grief-stricken material—out into the fresh light of day. In an old bag at the back of the wardrobe, we found a mouse nest with a remarkably orderly pile of stashed hazelnuts; a grimy black plastic bag full of ironing that had never been done; many of Moki's clothes. We kept some things, of course, including three pairs of shoes. I'm still not ready to have none of my mother's shoes.

We scrubbed the closet and purified it with white sage. No longer possessed by a black cloud, the space clearly also felt the gasping relief. The house thanked us for letting go. We moved the kitchen around. This shift was huge. We opened up the space with no need to take down any walls—just a piece of fabric divided the kitchen area from the hallway. We pushed the stove and a massive shelf unit out into what in olden days had been the schoolkids' coat room, making it a wonderful, new and improved space. Moki and Don would totally object to us not carrying on, not moving forward. We were taking them with us.

That evening, we went to the graveyard, to the place where we put Moki's body, facing the church, the open fields on the left. Standing by her gravestone, we watched birds rising as one from the pasture. I think we released a final bit of Mamma to fly away that day. And a final bit of us, too. We let go of something lodged very deep inside. As it lifted, the darkness spread its wings in good health.

•

I always come back to Tågarp. In this place, the memories surface through the spaces between the songs. I'm listening to music. Our record collection is like a living organism containing endless material that seems to secretly reproduce. All the time, I'm finding records that I have never seen or heard. The seasons in Sweden are changing: summers now too hot, the winters weirdly warm. Sometimes we have no snow in southern Sweden—just bleak, grey, wet weather like in London. But for two weeks at the end of 2020, we felt a *real* winter: crisp, cold, white. The light dropped so quickly on the snow-covered land and leafless trees, making for a uniformly black-and-white environment. Except for the odd red house, colour there is limited.

The schoolhouse is heated only by the wood-burning fires, and they were always hungry. The same routine every day: putting on the coffee, lighting the fire in the big room. Often, as I fed wood into the huge stove, I thought about how it must have been when the schoolchildren sat there, what the stoves have seen and how the same space is now full of us: my life, my parents' ideas, the children, vinyl from all corners of the planet. The resonance of all the music that has formed or been played there.

I go through old photos. I remember where they were taken and for a moment what we were doing. I see myself, trying to remember how I was back then. I looked pretty good, but did I feel that good in myself? Which leads me into the next room of feeling—too many, too much: the blue room makes me feel sad though not remorseful. Well, maybe a little. Time lost, or is it just gone? I look at pictures of my kids: their innocent, clear faces; chubby baby bodies relying on our arms to catch them and hold them tight—reassuring them with our hugs that we were there and that nothing would come in the way.

I put as much as I had into feeding our togetherness: making our space about family and unity, our table a gathering place where food and love are served as one. We did not get it all right, I know that. I love my children endlessly, compulsively, passionately. They were never the problem: it was me. I know that I could be absent. I didn't want to be, but I know it's true. The silence, many miles distant, was within me, waiting to catch up. Sometimes lost in my own translations, I was only able to go through the motions of providing.

Now it is summer. I sit on the steps of the schoolhouse in southern Sweden. Naima and Flynn are arriving later tonight, but for now I'm alone. It is the end of the day, the garden bathed in that light which makes everything look perfect and soft. The steps are warm; the air holds me in an embrace. I become aware of everything around me: the birdsong, the trees I have known since they were saplings wisely swaying in the twilight's groove. I realise that perhaps I needed to go away and live elsewhere to be able to celebrate the Swede that I am.

In this moment, I also understand my parents' investment in this creative space that provided us a free zone in which to grow up. They wanted us to be proud of who we were and where we came from. I have made home with love and family in many other spaces.

Today, London is home for all of us. But *here*, the schoolhouse in Tågarp, is the mothership.

So on this perfect evening, as everything crystallises, I give thanks to Don and Moki for their legacy, for everything: their warrior spirit, the devotion, the faith, the unpaid bills, the total commitment to life, generosity, love, creativity. I see how all the threads that have become my own story connect back to this place.

ACKNOWLEDGEMENTS

Those who know me will know that I often talk about the domino effect: one tips, the rest follow; one thing leads to another and becomes history. I came to a place in this life—so beautiful and hard—where I felt compelled to recognise my journey.

I'm kind of allergic to nostalgia but I needed to honour it, to figure out how I and we got here, how the cookie actually crumbled, and just to remember while I still could. Having said that, my words come from the pictures in my head—not every single thing might be the way someone else remembers it. Many of the threads, ideas, and inspirations were pulled through conversations, many in my kitchen with my kids and family. I've done my best to tell my version, but I never would have started writing this book on my own.

Hard fact: if Robin Pasricha (my dear friend and manager) and Cameron McVey (my dear friend and husband) hadn't pushed me out of my cosy headspace, I never would have started writing, so I thank you both.

Tyson, my daughter, has been in this with me the whole way as my spirit guide and support. She kickstarted the whole thing by translating a script I wrote for a classic Swedish radio show, *Summer Talk* (*Sommarprat*), which became the backbone of this book, and then fought on with me to the bitter end. I love you, T—couldn't have done it without you.

To Rose Davidson, my sometime shrink, problem solver, and absolute frontline soldier. I love you. To Claire Conrad, my agent, thank you for being there—thank you for everything! To Michal

Shavit, my editor, thank you for your insightful calm that's held me like a prolonged caress, and to Seán Hayes and everyone at Fern Press for being so damn patient with me!

To Ant and Steph, for the cover artwork and for thirty-five years of visual collaboration—I thank you for your honesty, razor-sharp eyeballs and true friendship.

To the other people who might not have been named in the book, know that your presence is very much deep within these pages and, of course, always in my heart: Warren and Libby Bradshaw; Garfield Hackett, sweet brother, thank you for midnight jumping dreadie sessions and for putting up with me and Andi all these years; Ben and Tom Page; Bafic; Akinola; my niece Amber and fam; Daryl, my cousin; the Copenhagen Cherry clan, Cassius Boom, Felicia, Mason, and Lärke; Femi Jah; Lucy Sjölen, now with the angels; Nora Kryst; Joakim Hauglund; Conny Lindström; Peder Wolfbrandt; Johnnie Sapong; Lyall Hakaraia; Kahil El'Zabar and Ethnic Heritage Ensemble; David Levi; Don and Marianna DeFina; Kimoney Roney; Ulrika and Tiffi Malmgren; DJ Jazzy Joyce; Tonie Roos; and Silvio Pacini, my longtime friend, DJ spar and younger brother from another mother.

Big love to all the family people who have passed through our house during Carnival. A note left on kitchen blackboard, which remained there for two years, sums it all up: "It was epic."

Tyson and Mabel have brought two magnificent men into the family, and the gift of theirs, Selassie and Preye. I love you with all my heart! On the subject of the family tree sprouting new branches: since starting these acknowledgements, I became a grandmother again! Tyson and Selassie had a baby girl. Welcome, you precious being—you have my heart.

To all the sisters who took part in the *Versions* project: bless you for this divine gift.

To Leon Thomas, Alice Coltrane, Thelonious Monk, Jayne Cortez, Chan Marshall, Sault, and Lil Wayne for keeping me sane and telling it like it is.

To anyone else I've missed out: you know who you are and that I love you.

CREDITS

Every effort has been made to trace copyright holders and to obtain their permission. The publisher apologizes for any errors or omissions and, if notified of any corrections, will make suitable acknowledgement in future reprints or editions of this book.

PICTURE CREDITS

Frontispiece
Courtesy of Neneh Cherry

Part One
My mother, Moki, and me, circa 1966: Carl Johan De Geer
The only photo I have of my mother and father together: Courtesy of Neneh Cherry
Moki, Don and me, and my doll Anita, in Gamla Stan, Stockholm: Peder Björkegren
Outside a café in Paris: Philippe Gras
Family time: Peder Björkegren
A lazy Sunday afternoon: Courtesy of the Estate of Moki Cherry
When Eagle-Eye left his seat to join Don on stage: Courtesy of the Estate of Moki Cherry
I loved being in New York: Rose Boyt

Part Two
With my siblings Titiyo and Cherno, Ahmadu, and my Gbinti Jah family: Courtesy of Neneh Cherry

My first braids in Sierra Leone: Courtesy of Neneh Cherry
Taking the subway with Ari, New York: Tonie Roos
The Rip Rig + Panic crew: David Corio
Eight months pregnant, eighteen years old: Courtesy of Neneh Cherry
Sean Oliver's send-off, the Tabernacle, West London: Courtesy of Neneh Cherry
One of the test shots that got me the Japan modeling trip with the Buffaloes: Clare Thom

Part Three

Last vacation with Marlon and Naima before Tyson!: Courtesy of Neneh Cherry
So many wonderful nights out together: Eddie Monsoon
With Queen Latifah: Courtesy of Neneh Cherry
On the cover of *Face*, 1989: Eddie Monsoon
The invitation designed by Judy, with Ant and Steph (Michael Nash): Courtesy of Neneh Cherry
With Tyson in Spain, 1993: Courtesy of Neneh Cherry
With Don in those last months in Spain, 1995: Courtesy of Neneh Cherry
Wearing a nice bit of Noki, with Mats Gustafsson playing to my left: Courtesy of Neneh Cherry

Epigraph credit: Excerpt from *A Burst of Light* by Audre Lorde. Copyright © 1988 by Audre Lorde. Reprinted by permission of Abner Stein Agency